FIRST

LAND OWNERS

Livingston County,

Michigan

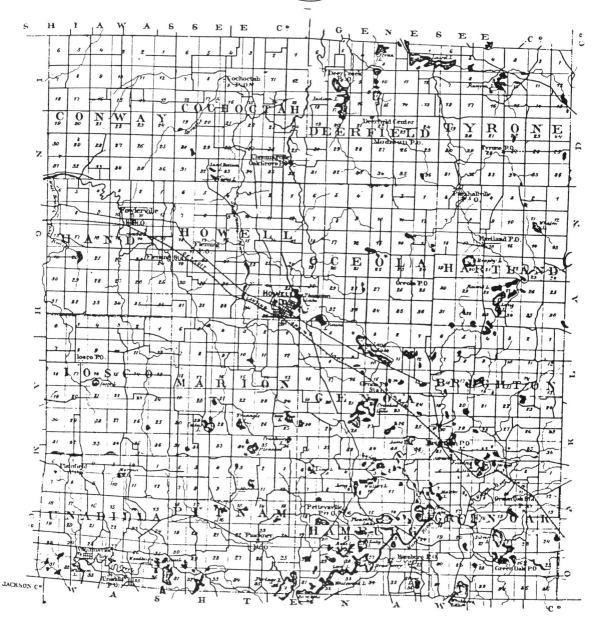

Early map of Livingston County. (1859)

FIRST

LAND OWNERS

Livingston County,

Michigan

from

U.S. Tract Records

Compiled by

MILTON CHARBONEAU

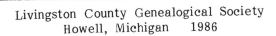

Livingston County Genealogical Society
Howell, Michigan   1986

Library of Congress Cataloging-in-Publication Data

Charboneau, Milton.
   First land owners, Livingston County, Michigan.

   Includes index.
   1. Livingston County (Mich.)--Genealogy. 2. Land
tenure--Michigan--Livingston County. I. Title.
F572.L8C48 1986   929'.377361   86-7239
ISBN 0-9616142-1-8

Manufactured in the United States of America

Published by LIVINGSTON COUNTY GENEALOGICAL SOCIETY
              P.O.Box 922, Brighton, MI 48116

CONTENTS

Introduction

First Land Owners of Livingston County

The records are taken from the United States Tract book found in the archives of the Register of Deeds office of Livingston County, Michigan.

The track book is a copy of the original purchases made at the land office in Detroit from the government of the United States.

It also includes later purchases made from the state of Michigan, such as the school sections, number 16 in each township.

The records have been checked against "Everts & Abbotts, Livingston County History" published in 1880. Variations of land owners names have been included in the index.

LOCATING ANCESTORS BY LAND RECORDS

This book contains the names of those persons who were the first purchasers of land from the government of the United States in what would be known as Livingston county. The first land taken up was bought in May of 1828 while Michigan was still a territory.

Not all those who bought land from the government came to Michigan, but a large majority did settle on the land, mostly people from New York state and the New England area.

To locate a person who purchased land, first check the index, which is arranged alphebetically by the last name. Also check any name which might be close to the name you seek. Check all townships and sections in which that person purchased land. Often one of these will give the county and state that the person migrated from. Where a person comes from another county in Michigan it will be necessary to seek the land records of that county for information on the person's migration from another state or country.

Land records give the name of the person who buys the land, the date of indenture or purchase, the address they used and the name of witness. When land is sold, the record will often contain the name of the spouse and the present location of the person for that time.

You may wish to write our society for help. Address the Livingston County Genealogical Society, P.O. Box 922, Brighton, Michigan 48116.

The townships of Livingston County are divided up into 36 square mile sections. There are 16 townships.

Because of irregularities in the original survey the north and west boundry sections will often be fractional sections. Some smaller, others larger than a square mile.

The map of a section will give you an idea of the descriptions used in land sales.

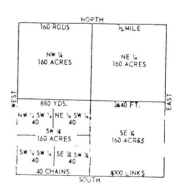

Livingston County is one of ten counties surveyed and set off after the War of 1812. All these counties were named after members of Andrew Jackson's administration. Edward Livingston was his Secretary of State.

Although Livingston county was set off March 21, 1833 it was not organised until March 24, 1836. Before that the north two tiers of townships were in Shiawassee county and the south two tiers of townships were in Washtenaw county. Until the county government was formed in 1836 all judicial proceedings and all vital records were held in Shiawassee and Washtenaw counties. (There is some exception, along the northeast border where some sections were part of Oakland county.)

The first townships organised in the county were in the southern tier. Green Oak was first, then Hamburg, Putnam and Unadilla. They were soon followed by Howell and Hartland in the north.

CONWAY	COHOCTAH	DEERFIELD	TYRONE	T 4 N
HANDY	HOWELL	OCEOLA	HARTLAND	T. 3 N.
IOSCO	MARION	GENOA	BRIGHTON	T 2 N
UNADILLA	PUTNAM	HAMBURG	GREEN OAK	T. 1 N.
R 3E	R 4E	R 5E.	R 6E.	

LIVINGSTON COUNTY TOWNSHIPS

Brighton (Bri.) T2N,R4E, set off April, 1838. Was first part of Green
        Oak township.

Cohoctah, (Coh.) T4N, R4E. Organized March 6,1838.

Conway, (Con.) T4N,R3E. Organized March 6,1838.

Deerfield, (De.) T4N,R5E. Set off from Howell township, spring of 1837
        and included Tyrone township.

Genoa, (Gen.) T2N,R5E. Set off from Hamburg township, March 11,1837.

Green Oak, (GR.) T1N,R6E. Organized March 17,1835 and included
        several other townships.

Hamburg, (Ham.) T1N,R5E. Organized March 26,1835. Named after the
        birthplace of the Grissom brothers of Germany.

Handy, (Hdy.) T3N,R3E. Set off March 6,1838 from Howell township.
        Named after Calvin Handy, its first settler.

Hartland, (Ht.) T3N,R6E. Organized March 23,1836.

Howell, (How.) T3N,R4E. Organized March 23,1836 and included six
        other townships. Contains the county seat.

Iosco, (Ios.) T2N,R3E. Set off from Unadilla township, March 6,1838.
        Iosco is a Chippewa Indian name.

Marion, (Mar.) T2N,R4E. Set off from Putnam township in 1837. Named
        by Hiram Wing of Marion, Wayne Co. N. Y.

Oceola, (Oc.) T3N,R5E. Set off from Howell township, March 1838.

Putnam, (Put.) T1N,R4E. Organized March 23,1836.

Tyrone, (Ty.) T4N,R6E. Set off from Deerfield township, March 6, 1838.
        Named after Tyrone, Schuler County, N. Y.

Unadilla, (Un.) T1N,R3E. Organized March 26,1835. Named after
        Unadilla, New York.

Brighton township

Section 17

Peter LANE	Wayne	MI	Dec. 14,1835	E½/SE & SW/SE	120
Nehemiah PAYNE	Washtenaw	MI	June 1,1836	SE/SW	40
Florus A HOUSE	Livingston	MI	June 24,1836	SW/SW	40
*John McKENZIE		NY	Aug. 2,1836	NE¼	160
*William TUNIS		NY	Aug. 2,1836	NW¼ & N½/SW & NW/SE	280

Section 18

Orman COE	Genessee	NY	May 20,1833	Wp/SWf	133
William WINCHELL	Wayne	MI	Sept. 6,1834	NE/NW	40
			Sept. 22,1835	SE/NW	40
Hugh GORDON	Washtenaw	MI	Nov. 26,1834	SW/NWf	66
			Feb. 5,1835	NW/NWf	66
William S CONELY	(New York city)		Sept. 7,1835	W½/NE	80
			July 5,1836	E½/NE	80
Abram PIETCH	(New York city)		Aug. 2,1826	W½/SE & E½/SW	160
George POST	Washtenaw	MI	July 1,1836	E½/SE	80

Section 19

Ephriam C ALLEN	Genessee	NY	May 20,1833	Wp/NWf	134
John CROUCH	Wayne	MI	Aug. 26,1835	SW/SWf	77
Erastus KELLOGG	Washtenaw	MI	Feb. 17,1836	Ep/SW	80
John MOORE	Oakland	MI	July 8,1836	NE/NE	40
John DEAN	Livingston	MI	Nov. 16,1836	E½/SE	80
Elias SPRAGUE	Livingston	MI	Nov. 26,1836	W½/NE	80
Oliver SPRAGUE	Livingston	MI	Nov. 26,1836	SE/NE	40
George MOON	Livingston	MI	Apr. 1,1837	NE/NW	40
Rastus H RANSOM	Madison	NY	Apr. 13,1837	SE/NW	40
Samuel H FOX	Oakland	MI	June 25,1838	NW/SWf	67
Lyman JUDSON	Livingston	MI	Nov. 1,1853	W½/SE	80

*(may be from New York city)

Brighton township

Section 20

B B KERCHIVAL	Wayne	MI	Nov. 26,1836	NW/NW	40
John Stephen WINKLER		NY	Aug. 2,1836	W½/SW	80
Joshua SHEFFIELD	Ontario	NY	June 1,1835	SE/NW	40
Abel PALMER	Ontario	NY	June 1,1835	SE/NE	40
William PALMER	Ontario	NY	June 1,1835	SW/NE	40
Orange BRUCE	Ontario	NY	Sept. 15,1835	NW/SE	40
Sarah KNOWLES	Ontario	NY	Sept. 17,1835	NE/SE	40
Samuel M CONELY	(New York city)		Sept. 20,1836	SW/SE	40
Elias SPRAGUE	Livingston	MI	Jan. 15,1836	SW/NW	40
Simeon CARPENTER	Cattaraugus	NY	June 1,1836	NE/NW	40
John POWELL	Oakland	MI	July 13,1836	E½/SW	80
Saloma PORTER		NY	Aug. 2,1836	SE/SE	40
William PAUL		NY	Aug. 2,1836	N½/NE	80

Section 21

Benjamin W CONKLIN	(New York city)	Sept. 29,1834	E½/SE	80
Robert L LANE	(New York city)	Sept. 29,1834	W½/SE	80
Peter WEMMELL	(New York city)	Sept. 29,1834	E½/SW	80
		Aug. 1,1835	NW/SW	40
George RUCKLE	(New York city)	Mar. 3,1835	SW/SW	40
John S JOHNSON	Livingston MI	April 2,1835	NE¼	160
Isaac L PLATT	(New York city)	June 1,1835	NW¼	160

Section 22

Samuel D TUTHILL	Genessee	NY	Aug. 29,1833	SW/SE	40
Aaron BEACH	Ontario	NY	Oct. 1,1833	E½/SE	80
Smith BEACH	Ontario	NY	Oct. 1,1833	NE¼	160
Richard LYONS	(New York city)		Sept. 29,1834	SW¼	160
			Sept. 7,1835	NW/SE	40
William VALENTINE	(New York city)		June 1,1835	NW¼	160

Section 23

Abram J ANDREWS	Monroe	NY	June 10,1834	E½/SW	80
Harvey C ANDREWS	Oakland	MI	May 25,1835	SW/SW	40
Otis DURFEE	Montgomery	NY	July 20,1835	W½/SE	80
Hiram JOHNSON	Livingston	MI	Nov. 5,1835	NW/SW	40
Robert C LANE	(New York city)		July 14,1836	W½/NW	80
Jacob BENDERNAGLE	(New York city)		Aug. 2,1836	NE¼ & E½/SE	240
Andrew WOLFRAKE	(New York city)		Sept. 24,1836	E½/NW	80

Brighton township

Section 24

Name	County	State	Date	Description	Acres
Hiram JOHNSON	Oakland	MI	Nov. 17,1835	SW/SE	40
George BAILEY	Livingston	MI	Nov. 17,1835	SW/SE	40
Jacob BENDERNAGLE		NY	Aug. 2,1836	NW¼ & SW¼ & W½/NE	400
			Feb. 7,1837	E½/NE	80
Andrew WOLFRAKE		NY	Feb. 7,1837	NE/SE	40
Henry THURSTON		NY	Sept. 24,1836	NW/SE	40

Section 25

Name	County	State	Date	Description	Acres
William STERLING	(New York city)		May 11,1835	NW¼	160
Philip T JOHNSON	Allegeny	NY	June 24,1835	N½/NE	80
Elijah JOHNSON	Allegeny	NY	Sept. 30,1835	W½/SW	80
John ARNOLD	Ontario	NY	June 15,1835	E½/SE	80
Caleb CARR Jr.	Oakland	MI	Oct. 1,1835	SE/NE	40
William T & Alfred W, John W & Lucius WARD	Lenewee	MI	Apr. 26,1836	E½/SW	80
Garret MARTIN	Yates	NY	May 21,1836	SW/NE & W½/SE	120

Section 26

Name	County	State	Date	Description	Acres
John McCONNELL	Monroe	NY	May 11,1833	NE¼	160
Daniel DURFEE	Montgomery	NY	July 21,1834	E½/NW	80
Robert EDGAR	Livingston	NY	Nov. 11,1834	NE/SE	40
	Livingston	MI	Aug. 28,1835	NW/SE	40
Henry C ANDREWS	Oakland	Mi.	Feb. 23,1836	NW/NW	40
Obed J NORTON	Livingston	MI	Feb. 29,1836	E½/SW	80
Joseph FLANDERS & Samuel S KETCHUM	(New York city)		July 14,1836	W½/SW	80
Robert L LANE	(New York city)		July 15,1836	SW/NW	40
Isaac L PLATT	(New York city)		Aug. 3,1836	S½/SE	80

Section 27

Name	County	State	Date	Description	Acres
Hannah Hickok & Rueben HICKOK	Wayne	MI	Sept. 23,1833	W½/NE	80
Richard LYONS	(New York city)		Sept. 29,1834	NE/SW	40
			Mar. 3,1835	W½/SE	80
Francis T LECOUNT	(New York city)		Sept. 29,1834	NW¼	160
William S CONELY	(New York city)		Oct. 16,1834	W½/SW	80
Moses LYON	(New York city)		Mar. 3,1835	NE/SW	40
Isaac L PLATT	(New York city)		June 1,1835	E½/NE	80
Joseph N FLANDERS & Samuel S KETCHUM	(New York city)		July 14,1836	E½/SE	80

7

Brighton township

Section 28

Name	Location		Date	Parcel	Acres
Evander D FISHER	(New York city)		Sept. 29,1834	W½/NE	80
Moses LYON	(New York city)		Sept. 29,1834	E½/NE	80
			Mar. 3,1834	W½/SE	80
William T TUNIS	(New York city)		Sept. 29,1834	W½/SE	80
William S CONELY	(New York city		Oct. 16,1834	E½/SE	80
Mark HEALY &					
*BB KERCHIVAL	(U.S.)		May 28,1836	SW¼	160

Section 29

Name	Location		Date	Parcel	Acres
Elihu BANCROFT	Monroe	NY	Nov. 24,1835	S½/SW	80
Benjamin FLANDERS &					
Robert H BOWNE	(New York city)		July 7,1836	NE¼	160
Joseph WILLIAMS	Oakland	MI	Sept. 20,1836	NE/SW	40
Daniel DEAN	Livingston	MI	Mar. 24,1837	NW¼	160
Charles ROSS	Livingston	MI	Aug. 19,1837	NW/SW	40
Abraham N FOX	Livingston	MI	Feb. 6,1838	SW/SE	40
John G SPENCER	Livingston	MI	Sept. 21,1838	NW/SE	40
Robert THOMSON	Livingston	MI	Dec. 6,1843	NE/SE	40
Grace LITTLE	Livingston	MI	Sept. 21,1844	SE/SE	40

Section 30

Name	Location		Date	Parcel	Acres
Exra ROOD	Wayne	MI	Sept. 20,1836	NE/SE	40
Horace H COMSTOCK	Kalamazoo	MI	Mar. 25,1833	Ep/SE	40
Robert WARDEN &					
Kingsley L BINGHAM	Onondaga	NY	May 20,1833	Ep/NWf & SW/NWf	147
Ezra ROOD &					
Sophia ANDREWS	Wayne	MI	Sept. 20,1836	E½/NE	80
Eli M FARGO	Genessee	NY	Sept. 15,1834	NW/NWf	67
Elizabeth CUSHING	Wayne	MI	May 9,1835	Wp/SWf	135
William NOBLE	Hartford	CN	July 30,1835	NW/SE	40
	Livingston	MI	June 24,1836	NW/NE	40
Samuel R DAKINS	Wayne	MI	Jan. 1,1836	SW/SE	40
Anthony GALE	Livingston	MI	Jan. 22,1836	SE/SE	40
Josiah LEONARD	Livingston	MI	Mar. 4,1836	SW/NE	40

*(A judge, of Detroit; a land speculator)

Brighton township

Section 31

Name	County	State	Date	Description	Acres
Phillip STEWART	Wayne	MI	Oct. 28,1835	Ep/SW & SW/SE	120
			June 1,1835	NW/SE	40
Maynard MATTLEY	Washtenaw	MI	Aug. 28,1832	SW/NWf	65
John M COE	Oakland	MI	June 27,1834	W½/NE	80
Anthony GALE	Hartford	CN	Sept. 23,1834	Ep/NW	80
	Livingston	MI	Oct. 28,1835	NE/NE	40
Josiah LEONARD	Niagara	NY	May 21,1835	SE/NE	40
Trumen B WORDEN	Wayne	MI	June 1,1835	E½/SE	80
Elijah FITCH	Washtenaw	MI	July 29,1835	NW/NWf	65
Jonathan EDDY &					
James J HICKEY	Wayne	MI	Oct. 3,1835	Wp/SWf	123

Section 32

Name	County	State	Date	Description	Acres
John C MUNDY	Washtenaw	MI	Dec. 7,1832	W½/SE & NE/SE	120
Mary FULLER	Onieda	NY	June 29,1835	E½/NW & W½/SW	160
Orlando A FULLER	Oneida	NY	June 29,1835	SW/NW	40
Jacob LEROY	Genessee	NY	Aug. 11,1835	E½/SW	80
John HENRY	Livingston	MI	Feb. 16,1836	W½/NE	80
Edward MUNDY	Washtenaw	MI	May 6,1836	SE/SE	40
Prentice C BARTLET	Monroe	NY	June 1,1836	E½/NE	80

Section 33

Name	County	State	Date	Description	Acres
Lewis B FONDA	Washtenaw	MI	Oct. 9,1832	W½/SW	80
Stephen BONELL	Washtenaw	MI	May 23,1833	SE/SW	40
John HENRY	Livingston	NY	Oct. 11,1833	SE/SE	40
George McCRACKEN	Orleans	NY	Sept. 15,1834	NE/SW	40
Moses LYON	(New York city)		Oct. 5,1835	W½/SE	80
Mark HEALY &					
B B KIRCHIVAL	(U.S.)		May 28,1836	NE¼ & NW¼	320
Joseph L BRIGGS	Livingston	MI	Aug. 2,1836	NE/SE	40

Brighton township

Section 34

Elbert WOODRUFF	Oakland	MI	Mar. 21,1833	NW/NW	40
			Apr. 9,1833	E½/SW & SE/NW	120
George W GLOVER	Allegeny	NY	May 27,1833	W½/SE & SE/SE	120
Hugh ALEXANDER	Washtenaw	MI	Dec. 10,1833	NE/NE & SW/NE	80
Smith PARKS Jr.	Oakland	MI	Jam. 14,1834	NE/NW	40
Richard TONCRAY	Livingston	MM	May 27,1835	SE/NE	40
Joseph L BRIGGS	Livingston	MI	Oct. 8,1835	SW/SW	40
Daniel MARLAT	Washtenaw	MI	Mar. 26,1836	NW/NE	40
John DAVIS	Worchester	MA	Apr. 22,1836	SW/NW & NW/SW	80
Horace TONCRAY	Livingston	MI	July 5,1836	NE/NE	40

Section 35

Luther PARSHALL	Oakland	MI	May 16,1833	E½/SE	80
	Livingston	MI	Dec. 12,1835	SE/NE	40
Richard TONCRAY	Oswego	NY	May 24,1833	W½/SE	80
John W PEAVY	Allegeny	NY	May 27,1833	E½/SW & SW/SW	120
James COVEY	Livingston	MI	May 27,1835	SW/NE	40
Horace TONCRAY	Livingston	MI	May 27,1835	SW/NW & NW/SW	80
Joseph WATKINS		NY	Aug. 1,1836	NW/NW	40
Orlando ROGERS	Dutchess	NY	June 3,1836	E½/NW	80
Isaac L PLATT	(New York city)		Aug. 3,1836	N½/NE	80

Section 36

Thomas CURTISS	Oakland	MI	June 7,1834	SW/SE	40
			Dec. 22,1835	SW/NE	40
			Oct. 15,1835	NW/SE	40
George W GLOVER	Allegeny	NY	May 27,1833	W½/SW & SE/SW	120
Luther PARSHALL	Livingston	MI	Nov. 15,1833	W½/NW	80
Joseph WOOD	Washtenaw	MI	Apr. 12,1834	E½/SE & NE/NE	120
			June 27,1834	SW/NE	40
John S BEACH	Washtenaw	MI	June 7,1834	SE/NE	40
Emma PARSHALL	Livingston	MI	July 7,1834	NE/SW	40
Gary GRISWOLD	Tioga	NY	June 10,1835	E½/NW	80

COHOCTAH township-FIRST Land Owners

NAME	COUNTY & STATE		DATE	LAND	ACRES
Section 1					
James McGREGOR &					
John A McGRAW	(Boston,MA.)		June 4,1836	Np/NEf	214
Philander BIRD	Wayne	MI	June 18,1836	W½/SW	80
Thomas BUSSEY	Washtenaw	MI	June 28,1836	E½/SW	80
Ezra SANFORD	Livingston	MI	Nov. 15,1836	NWf¼	291
Amos HUFF	Livingston	MI	Nov. 15,1836	E½/SE	80
Orrin COLE	Oakland	MI	Dec. 5,1836	W½/SE	80
William H JOHNSON	Washtenaw	MI	Dec. 24,1836	Sp/NE	80
Section 2					
*Flavius J B CRANE	Livingston	MI	July 5,1836	SW¼ & W½/SE	240
Ezra SANFORD	Livingston	MI	Nov. 15,1836	NE/SE	40
Alva PRESTON	Washtenaw	MI	Dec. 13,1836	E½/NEf	144
Elias LITCHFIELD	Hartford	CT	Dec. 13,1836	W½/NEf	144
B B KERCHIVAL	Wayne	MI	Dec. 15,1836	SE/SE	40
Isaac DUNN	Washtenaw	MI	Jan. 19,1837	Sp/NW	80
George WALLEN	Washtenaw	MI	May 10,1837	Np/NWf	209
Section 3					
James WALDRON	Yates	NY	May 20,1836	SW¼	160
Elisha CROSS	Wayne	MI	June 4,1836	NEf¼	289
			Nov. 18,1836	Wp/Np/NWf	104
George BISBEE	Ottowa	MI	June 6,1836	W½/SE	80
Flavius J B CRANE	Livingston	MI	July 5,1836	Sp/NW & E½/SE	160
Nelson COSTON	Oakland	MI	Nov. 18,1836	Ep/Wp/NWf	104
Section 4					
Thomas P BRIGGS	Yates	NY	May 20,1836	SE¼	160
John F MAXSON	Genessee	NY	May 25,1836	SW¼ & Sp/NE	240
Elisha CROSS	Wayne	MI	June 4,1836	NWf¼	288
John KEMP &					
Levi BAYLEY &					
Charles GEORGE	Genessee	NY	June 27,1836	Np/NEf	209

*   early real estate dealer

11

Cohoctah township

Section 5

Dean RATHBUN	Washtenaw	MI	Oct. 29,1835	Np/NEf	208
Seth DUNBAR	Onondaga	NY	June 8,1836	NWf¼	289
Elisha CROSS	Wayne	MI	Nov. 18,1836	Sp/NE	80
Simeon ANDREWS	Wayne	MI	Jan. 17,1837	W½/SW	80
Michael THATCHER	Livingston	MI	July 27,1837	SE¼	160
David SANFORD	Livingston	MI	Jan. 8,1838	NE/SW	80
Michael DOWNEY	Livingston	MI	Nov. 29,1854	SE/SW	40

Section 6

John EDMONDS	Genessee	NY	June 14,1836	SE/NEf	101
Nehemiah M ALLEN	Livingston	MI	June 14,1836	Sp/NE	80
Jedediah D COMMINS	Portage	OH	June 15,1836	Np/NWf	198
Levi MOSHER	Monroe	NY	June 15,1836	W½/Np/NEf	101
Mortimer B MARTIN	Wayne	MI	Aug. 2,1836	SWf¼	153
Adolphus COBURN	Albany	NY	Aug. 6,1836	SE¼	160
George P TYSON	Oakland	MI	Feb. 11,1837	Sp/NW	75

Section 7

James B COOLEY	Monroe	NY	July 5,1836	NE¼	160
Levi COOLEY	Monroe	NY	July 5,1836	NWf¼	153
Henry HAWKINS &					
Van Renseller HAWKINS	Genessee	NY	July 5,1836	SE¼ & SWf¼	312

Section 8

John G KANOUSE	Washtenaw	MI	May 10,1836	E½/SE & SE/NE	120
Isreal N HARRIS	Wayne	MI	Oct. 26,1836	SW¼ & W½/SE	240
William WHITE	Wayne	MI	Jan. 20,1837	NW¼	160
			Jan. 26,1837	W½/NE	80
Daniel SCULLEY	Livingston	MI	Sept. 12,1837	NE/NE	40

Section 9

John G KANOUSE	Washtenaw	MI	May 10,1836	W½/SW & SW/NW	120
Aretus G SMITH	Onondaga	NY	May 20,1836	S½/NE	80
Thomas P BRIGGS	Yates	NY	May 20,1836	NE/NE	40
Elam MOE	Washtenaw	MI	June 14,1836	N½/NW	80
Joseph H STEELE	Wayne	MI	July 5,1836	E½/SE	80
James WALDRON	Yates	NY	Sept. 20,1836	NW/NE	40
David GUILE	Oakland	Mi	Oct. 26,1836	E½/SW & N½/SE	160
	Livingston	MI	July 6,1839	SE/NW	40

12

Cohoctah township

Section 10

James WALDRON	Yates	NY	May 20,1836	NW¼	160
Aretus G SMITH	Onondaga	NY	May 20,1836	SW¼	160
George BISBEE	Ottowa	Mi	June 6,1836	W½/NE & SE/NE	120
Abram KANOUSE	Washtenaw	MI	June 25,1836	SW/SE	40
Josiah BATES	Yates	NY	Sept. 20,1836	E½/SE & NW/SE	120
George W ALBEE	Livingston	MI	May 13,1837	NE/NE	40

Section 11

Hosea ROOT	Livingston	MI	June 28,1836	E½/SE	80
Flavius J B CRANE	Livingston	MI	July 5,1836	W½/NE	80
Thomas M HOWELL	Ontario	NY	July 5,1836	NW¼	160
B B KERCHIVAL	Wayne	MI	Nov. 18,1836	E½/NE	80
Alva PRESTON	Washtenaw	MI	Dec. 13,1836	W½/SE	80
Sarah STODARD	Washtenaw	MI	Aug. 1,1838	NE/SW	40
Nathaniel H BRAYTON	Livingston	MI	Sept. 7,1855	SE/SW & W½/SW	120

Section 12

Isaac PRATT	Washtenaw	MI	June 14,1836	NW¼ & SW¼	320
B B KERCHIVAL	Wayne	MI	Dec. 6,1836	W½/NE	80
			Feb. 16,1837	E½/NE	80
Leavens T HUCHINS	Madison	NY	Jan. 16,1837	SE¼	160

Section 13

Isaac PRATT	Washtenaw	MI	June 14,1836	NW/NW	40
William COOPER		NY	Aug. 2,1836	SW¼	160
Miles P LAMSON	Genessee	NY	Oct. 25,1836	NE¼ & SE¼	320
Harris HICKOK	Madison	NY	Mar. 3,1837	E½/NW & SW/NW	120

Section 14

Harrison COX	Livingston	NY	June 10,1836	SE¼	160
William COOPER		NY	Aug. 2,1836	SW¼	160
Miles P LAMSON	Genessee	NY	Oct. 25,1836	NE¼	160
Simeon ANDREWS	Wayne	MI	Jan. 18,1837	W½/NW	80
Patrick GALLAGAN	Livingston	MI	Apr. 8,1837	E½/NW	80

Section 15

Josiah BEERS & Stephen D BEERS	Tomkins	NY	May 27,1836	SE¼ & E½/SW & W½/NE & E½/NW	400
Miles P LAMSON	Genessee	NY	Oct. 25,1836	E½/NE & W½/NW	160
Mathew GOODING	Wayne	MI	Jan. 16,1837	W½/SW	80

13

Cohoctah township

Section 16 (school section)

Elias SPRAGUE			May 3,1850	NW/NE	40
			Mar. 11,1853	NE/NW	40
R GRANT			Sept. 12,1853	NW/SW	40
J RAMER			May 21,1855	SE/NW & NE/SW	80
George PALMER			May 29,1855	W½/SE & SE/SW	120
S CARPENTER			July 7,1855	SW/SW	40
Peter DEAN &					
William DEAN			Mar. 28,1856	SW/NW	40
E L SPRAGUE			May 13,1857	NE/NE	40
John RAMER			Apr. 12,1860	NW/NW	40
Edwin ALGER &					
Delos ALGER			Oct. 1,1869	SE/NE	40
Henry THOMAS			Jan. 5,1870	SW/NE	40

Section 17

Isaac GREEN	Wayne	MI	July 5,1836	NW¼	160
Gains DAYTON	Wayne	MI	Nov. 1,1836	NE¼ & SW¼	320
Mathew GOODING	Wayne	MI	Dec. 17,1836	SE¼	160

Section 18

Isaac S KIDDER	Stueben	NY	June 27,1836	SE¼	160
B B KERCHIVAL	Wayne	MI	Nov. 18,1836	E½/NE	80
Conrad HAYNER	Oakland	Mi	Dec. 29,1836	Ep/NW & Ep/SW	160
James GRANT	Oakland	MI	June 21,1836	Wp/NW & Wp/SW	149
George C HAYNER	Livingston	MI	June 2,1851	W½/NE	80

Section 19

Alvah EWERS	Wayne	MI	May 30,1836	NE¼	160
Gottlieb NIEMAN	(New York city)		Aug. 2,1836	SWf¼ & SE¼	318
Frederick RING	(New York city)		Aug. 2,1836	NWf¼	158

Section 20

Alvah EWERS	Wayne	MI	May 30,1836	NW¼ & W½/NE	240
Joseph HINES	Lenewee	MI	June 15,1836	W½/SE	80
Gottlieb NIEMAN	(New York city)		Aug. 2,1836	E½/SE	80
Frederick RING	(New York city)		Aug. 2,1836	SW¼	160
Joseph HYNES	Livingston	MI	May 16,1837	E½/NE	80

Cohoctah township

Section 21

Mary SANFORD	Oakland	MI	May 27,1835	SW/SE	40
			June 18,1836	SE/SE	40
Cornelius NEISSE	Orange	NY	June 20,1836	NE¼ & NW¼	
				SW¼ & N½/SE	560

Section 22

Gilbert W PRENTISS	Shiawassee	MI	Apr. 9,1833	SW/NE	40
			Apr. 15,1833	E½/NE	80
Ezra SANFORD	Oakland	MI	July 4,1835	W½/SE & E½/SW	160
Nathaniel PROUTY	Wayne	MI	Mar. 23,1836	E½/NW & NW/NE	120
Ira WALKER	Livingston	MI	June 18,1836	SW/SW	40
Horace R HUDSON	(New York city)		Sept. 24,1836	W½/NW	80
Miles P LAMSON	Genessee	NY	Oct. 25,1836	NW/SW	40

Section 23

William RICKER	Stueben	NY	Oct. 6,1835	NW¼ & N½/SW	240
Ephriam CRAWFORD	Stueben	NY	Oct. 6,1835	SW/NE & NW/SE	80
David THOMPSON	Wayne	MI	Feb. 3,1836	E½/NE & SW/NE	120
Leah PACHARD	Wayne	MI	May 10,1836	E½/SE	80
William PACHARD	Wayne	MI	May 23,1836	SW/SE	40
William STROUD	Livingston	MI	Sept. 23,1836	SE/SW	40
			Nov. 1,1836	SW/SW	40

Section 24

William PACHARD	Wayne	MI	May 10,1836	W½/SW	80
			May 12,1836	E½/NW & E½/SW	160
			May 16,1836	W½/NW	80
Ephriam WHITNEY	Oakland	MI	June 15,1836	NE/NE	40
Daniel BOUTELL	Onondaga	NY	Nov. 5,1836	SE/SE	40
	Livingston	MI	Mar. 1,1837	NE/SE	40
			Apr. 26,1837	W½/SE	80
Calvin W HART	Livingston	MI	June 14,1837	W½/NE	80
Lorenzo BOUTELL	Livingston	MI	June 14,1837	SE/NE	40

Cohoctah township

Section 25

William PACHARD	Wayne	MI	May 12,1836	W½/NW	80
Chancey D FISHER	Washtenaw	MI	May 30,1836	W½/SW	80
Joseph HOSLEY	Livingston	MI	Sept. 23,1836	E½/SW	80
			Dec. 29,1836	E½/SE	80
Samuel C KLUMP	Wayne	MI	Oct. 26,1836	W½/NE	80
Daniel BOUTELL	Onondaga	NY	Nov. 5,1836	E½/NE	80
	Livingston	MI	Mar. 1,1837	NW/SE	40
			Jan. 10,1839	SE/NW	40
William HOSLEY	Livingston	MI	Dec. 29,1836	SW/SE	40
John JONES	Livingston	MI	Oct. 26,1839	NE/NW	40

Section 26

William PACHARD	Wayne	MI	May 12,1836	E½/NE	80
			May 23,1836	W½/NE	80
Thomas GOLDSMITH	Monroe	NY	May 13,1836	W½/NW & NE/NW	120
Ambrose MOSHER	Monroe	NY	May 27,1836	SW¼	160
Joseph NEELY	Monroe	NY	May 27,1836	SE¼	160
Levi & Ambrose MOSHER	Monroe	NY	June 10,1836	SE/NW	40

Section 27

Benjamin CRAWFORD	Macomb	MI	June 13,1834	W½ of Sec.	320
John SANFORD	Oakland	MI	July 8,1834	W½/SE	80
			May 27,1835	E½/SE	80
Ezra SANFORD	Oakland	MI	July 4,1835	W½/NE	80
Thomas GOLDSMITH	Monroe	NY	May 13,1836	E½/NE	80

Section 28

Antony CLARK	Oakland	MI	Aug. 4,1834	E½/SE	80
	Livingston	MI	Jan. 1,1836	SE/NE	40
David W SHELDON	Ontario	NY	May 12,1836	NW/SW	40
Isaac T SHELDON	Ontario	NY	May 12,1836	W½/SE & E½/SW	
				SW/SW & SW/NE	240
Isaac VANDEBOGART	Tompkins	NY	June 18,1836	W½/NW	80
Abraham RIKER	Livingston	NY	Nov. 14,1836	E½/NW	80
Tobias C HOWLAND	Livingston	NY	July 9,1841	NW/NE	40

Cohoctah township

Section 29

David W SHELDON	Ontario	NY	May 12,1836	E½/SE & SE/NE	120
Hugh GILSHENAN	Washtenaw	MI	June 14,1836	W½/NE & W½/SE	160
John VANDERBOGART	Tompkins	NY	June 18,1836	NE/NE	40
Isaac S KIDDER	Stueben	NY	June 27,1836	W½/NW	80
Nelson PETTIBONE	Genessee	NY	July 1,1836	E½/NW	80
Roger GLINAN	Washtenaw	MI	Nov. 14,1836	SW¼	160

Section 30

Lott PRATT	Genessee	NY	May 10,1836	SWf¼	159
Sylvanus WEST		NY	May 10,1836	W½/SE	80
Isaac S KIDDER	Stueben	NY	June 27,1836	NE¼	160
Charles L HARRISON	Washtenaw	MI	Sept. 23,1836	S½/NWf	79
B B KERCHIVAL	Wayne	MI	Feb. 15,1837	E½/SE	80
James HOOPER	Washtenaw	MI	Mar. 2,1837	N½/NWf	79

Section 31

Justus BOYD	Livingston	NY	May 5,1836	SE¼	160
Warner LAKE	Livingston	NY	May 5,1836	SWf¼	158
John COUGHRAN	Genessee	NY	May 10,1836	NE¼ & NWf¼	319

Section 32

Nathan CHIDESTER	Genessee	NY	May 4,1836	SE¼ & E½/SW	240
William SLATER	Livingston	NY	May 5,1836	W½/SW	80
Simon WESTFALL	Cayuga	NY	May 5,1836	Ne¼ & E½/NW	240
William HORTON	(New York city)		June 15,1836	NE¼ & E½/NW	240

Section 33

Purdy WILLIAMS	(New York city)		June 15,1836	SW¼	160
Charles POPE	(New York city)		June 15,1836	NW¼	160
John DUNLAP	Oakland	MI	July 11,1836	NE/NE	40
Simeon ANDREWS	Wayne	MI	Jan. 18,1837	W½/NE	80
Rees LEWIS	Washtenaw	MI	Mar. 21,1839	SE/NE & SW/SE	80
William P CONE	Livingston	MI	May 30,1855	N½/SE	80
William McPHERSON	Livingston	MI	Mar. 2,1867	SE/SE	40

17

Cohoctah township

Section 34

Name	County	State	Date	Description	Acres
Lyman BOUGHTON	Oakland	MI	Apr. 6,1833	NW/NE & NE/NW	80
John SANFORD	Oakland	MI	July 8,1834	SW¼ & W½/NW	
				& E½/NE	320
			May 27,1835	W½/SE	80
James SANFORD	Oakland	MI	July 8,1834	SE/NW & SW/NE	80
Edward McMAKEN	Wayne	MI	Sept. 21,1836	E½/SE	80

Section 35

Name	County	State	Date	Description	Acres
William W SHUTES	Oakland	MI	July 8,1835	SW/SW	40
Ezra FRISBEE	Montgomery	NY	Oct. 19,1835	SE/SW	40
James GRANT	Oakland	MI	May 23,1836	E½/SE	80
Adam FISHER	Cayuga	NY	May 30,1836	N½/NE	80
Chancey D FISHER	Washtenaw	MI	May 30,1836	S½/NE	80
Horace HEATH &					
Appollos SMITH	(U.S.)		June 10,1836	N½/SW¼ &	
				W½/SE¼	320

Section 36

Name	County	State	Date	Description	Acres
Chancey D FISHER	Washtenaw	MI	May 30,1836	NW/NW	40
William NORTHRUP	Wayne	MI	June 6,1836	SE/NE	40
Joseph HOSLEY	Wayne	MI	June 6,1836	SW/NE	40
			June 9,1836	N½/NE	80
Levi MOSHER &					
Ambrose MOSHER	Monroe	NY	June 10,1836	E½/NW & SW/NW	120
Horace HEATH &					
Appollos SMITH	(U.S.)		June 10,1836	W½/SW	80
John W FARRAND	Tompkins	NY	Apr. 25,1837	SE¼ & E½/SW	240

CONWAY township—FIRST Land Owners

NAME	COUNTY & STATE		DATE	LAND	ACRES
Section 1					
Benjamin P SHERMAN	Washtenaw	MI	May 31,1836	Np/NE	211
Francis MITTLEBERGER	Oakland	MI	June 11,1836	SE¼	160
James HADDAN	Washtenaw	MI	July 8,1836	SW/NW	40
Alvin D SHAW	Washtenaw	MI	Nov. 3,1836	E½/SW & SE/NW	120
B B KERCHIVAL	Wayne	MI	Feb. 15,1837	Sp/NE	80
Gains FULLER	Washtenaw	MI	May 16,1836	Np/NWf	207
C(Christian) UMBIHAM	Livingston	MI	Jan. 24,1855	NW/SW	40
C W BUTLER	Ingham	MI	June 1,1854	SW/SW	40
Section 2					
Francis MITTLEBERGER	Oakland	MI	June 11,1836	SW¼	160
Samuel STREETER	Wayne	MI	July 9,1836	Sp/NW & SW/NE	120
			July 8,1836	SE/NE	40
James HADDAN	Washtenaw	MI	July 9,1836	NE/NWf	97
Mortimer B MARTIN	Wayne	MI	Aug. 2,1836	NW/NWf	97
Benjamin P SHERMAN	Washtenaw	MI	June 1,1837	SE/SE	40
	Livingston	MI	Aug. 25,1854	NE/SE	40
Gains FULLER	Washtenaw	MI	May 16,1836	Np/NEf	199
C W BUTLER	Ingham	MI	Dec. 23,1853	W½/SE	80
Section 3					
Mortimer B MARTIN	Wayne	MI	Aug. 2,1836	NEf¼	271
William RICHARD	(New York city)		Sept. 21,1836	SW¼	160
William A CLARK	(New York city)		Sept. 21,1836	Np/NWf	188
Cato ALEXANDER	(New York city)		Sept. 24,1836	SE¼	160
Jeramiah KENEDY	Washtenaw	MI	Sept. 17,1838	Sp/NWf	80
Section 4					
Miles A HINMAN	Genessee	NY	July 1,1836	Np/NWf	180
William GRAHAM	Wayne	MI	Aug. 2,1836	W½/SE & E½/SW	160
Nancy A BENJEAN	(New York city)		Sept. 21,1836	Sp/NW & W½/SW	160
William A CLARK	(New York city)		Sept. 21,1836	Np/NEf	184
			Sept. 24,1836	E½/SE	80
Thomas DAILEY	Genessee	NY	May 30,1838	Sp/NE	80

Conway township

Section 5

Miles A HINMAN	Genessee	NY	July 2,1836	Np/NEf	179
Ralph LESTER	Ontario	NY	July 5,1836	NE/NWf	89
Robert COLBORN	Wayne	MI	July 5,1836	NW/NWf	89
Samuel COLLISTER	Madison	NY	Aug. 2,1836	SE¼ & SW¼	320
Nancy BENJEAN	(New York city)		Sept. 21,1836	Sp/NE	80
Isaac N BARKER	Oakland	MI	Dec. 29,1836	Sp/NW	80

Section 6

Rueben ROBIE	Stueben	NY	Aug. 2,1836	SWf¼	142
Seman GIBBS & Thomas BLACKNER	Livingston	NY	Sept. 21,1836	NEf¼	256
William GRISWOLD	Chenango	NY	Sept. 21,1836	SE¼	160
Dennis CAHILL	Washtenaw	MI	Sept. 11,1838	Sp/NWf	73
Edward N BISHOP	Livingston	MI	Nov. 15,1854	Np/NWf	172

Section 7

Rueben ROBIE	Stueben	NY	Aug. 2,1836	NE¼	160
Thomas DUDLEY	Yates	NY	Aug. 2,1836	NWf¼	136
Andrew N DEWITT	Genessee	NY	Sept. 21,1836	SWf¼	127
			Oct. 22,1841	part of SWf	4
John MARTIN	Monroe	MI	Sept. 22,1836	NW/SE & E½/SE	120
Thomas MARTIN	Monroe	MI	Sept. 22,1836	SW/SE	40

Section 8

Samuel JESSUP	(New York city)		Sept. 21,1836	NW¼	160
Shellick WATERBURY	(New York city)		Sept. 21,1836	NE¼	160
John BISHOP	Livingston	MI	Nov. 15,1854	NE/SE	40
A P COOK	Jackson	MI	Feb. 10,1855	SW¼	160
				W½/SE & SE/SE	120

Section 9

William A CLARK	(New York city)		Sept. 21,1836	NW¼	160
Harriet NETTLEDON	(New York city)		Sept. 24,1836	SE¼	160
Charles ELLIOT	Onondaga	NY	Sept. 24,1836	W½/SW	80
Michael HARRIS	Washtenaw	MI	Aug. 20,1838	W½/NE	80
John BRENAN	Washtenaw	MI	Oct. 27,1838	E½/SW	80
John HALPIN	Wayne	MI	Nov. 14,1838	E½/NE	80

Conway township

Section 10

Robert KNIGHT		NY	Sept. 24,1836	SE¼ & NE¼	320
Horace A NOYES	Wayne	MI	Jan. 9,1837	SW¼ & W½/SE	240
Rice TYLER	Livingston	MI	Feb. 15,1839	SE/SE	40
C W BUTLER	Ingham	MI	Apr. 18,1854	NE/SE	40

Section 11

Julius F PARSONS	Franklin	MA	June 20,1836	SW/SE	40
Dan BARNES	Monroe	NY	June 22,1836	SW¼ & E½/SE	240
Lathrop G B GRANT	Orleans	NY	June 3,1852	NW/SE	40
C W BUTLER	Ingham	MI	Dec. 15,1855	N½ of Sec.	320

Section 12

Ruth WINTERTON	(New York city)		Sept. 21,1836	SE¼	160
B B KERCHIVAL	Wayne	MI	Feb. 15,1837	NE¼	160
Edgar PURDY	Livingston	MI	Dec. 27,1853	W½ of Sec.	320

Section 13

Cecil D PARSONS	Washtenaw	MI	June 20,1836	SW¼	160
Ruth M FAY	Franklin	NY	June 20,1836	W½/NW	80
Timothy WAIT	Hampshire		June 20,1836	E½/NW	80
William BALL	(New York city)		Sept. 21,1836	W½/NE	80
Joseph COTTRELL	Wayne	MI	Sept. 20,1836	W½/SE	80
James GRANT	Oakland	MI	June 21,1836	E½/NE & E½/SE	160

Section 14

Lorens K STRONG	Hampshire	MA	June 20,1836	SE¼	160
Frederick B PARSONS	Washtenaw	MI	June 20,1836	NW¼	160
Julius F PARSONS	Franklin	MA	June 20.1836	NE¼	160
Dan BARNES	Monroe	NY	June 23,1836	SW¼	160

Section 15

Samuel H DODGE	Seneca	NY	Nov. 16,1836	NW¼	160
William MERRILL	Wayne	MI	Nov. 16,1836	SW¼	160
George PARKILL	Washtenaw	MI	Nov. 26,1836	SE¼	160
William H JOHNSON	Washtenaw	MI	Mar. 11,1837	E½/NE	80
John WARBURTON	Washtenaw	MI	Apr. 10,1837	W½/NE	80

Conway township

Section 16 (school section)

Benjamin HODGE		Mar. 7,1870	NE/NE	40	
Henry RAMER		Mar. 7,1870	NW/NE	40	
Thomas STANFIELD		Mar. 21,1854	SE/SE	40	
BALCH & SPRINKS		Nov. 26,1853	SW/NE	40	
George HARGER		Aug. 12,1854	N½/NW	80	
G DALY		Jan. 19,1854	SE/NW & SW/NW		
			NE/SW & NW/SW	160	
George MORSE		Feb. 8,1861	NE/SE	40	
Jacob SHERMAN		Nov. 22,1853	NW/SE	40	
		Apr. 15,1854	SE/SW	40	
Frederick WELTZ		Oct. 8,1856	SE/SE	40	
E B BARKER		Mar. 9,1854	SW/SE	40	
John MILLER		Sept. 13,1854	SW/SW	40	

Section 17

Thomas HENSETT	(New York city)	Sept. 21,1836	SE¼ & E½/SW	240
William IRWIN	(New York city)	Feb. 14,1837	NE¼ & NW¼	
			& W½/SW	400

Section 18

Thomas MARTIN	Monroe	MI	Sept. 22,1836	Ep/NW	80
Thomas KIRK	Monroe	NY	Sept. 22,1836	NE¼	160
John LAFFIN &					
Patrick McKAIG	Washtenaw	MI	Nov. 22,1837	Wp/NW & SWf¼	176
Chancey GAYLORD	Onondaga	NY	June 21,1838	SE¼	160

Section 19

Samuel WINTERTON	(New York city)		Sept. 21,1836	E½/NE	80
John McQUILLAN	Monroe	NY	Sept. 21,1836	W½/SE	80
John KELLY	Monroe	NY	Sept. 21,1836	Ep/NW	80
Patrick McQUILLAN	Monroe	NY	SEpt. 21,1836	E½/SE	80
John TAFFE	Monroe	NY	Sept. 21,1836	Ep/SW	80
Patrick KIRK	Monroe	NY	Sept. 21,1836	W½/NE	80
Patrick McKAIG	Washtenaw	MI	Nov. 22,1837	Wp/NWf	44
John CLARK	Ontario	NY	Feb. 27,1838	Wp/SWf	40

Section 20

William A CLARK	(New York city)	Sept. 21,1836	Section	640

Conway township

Section 21

Name	County	State	Date	Description	Acres
George HOWLETT	(New York city)		Sept. 21,1836	NW$\frac{1}{4}$ & SW$\frac{1}{4}$	320
Justus BOYD	Livingston	MI	Feb. 22,1838	SE/NE	40
Augustus D DORRANCE	Livingston	MI	Dec. 16,1851	NE/NE	40
Henry SNIDER	Niagara	NY	Dec. 23,1851	NE/SE	40
Charles P BUSH	Ingram	MI	June 27,1854	NW/NE	40
			Nov. 17,1854	SW/NE	40
A P CLARK	Jackson	MI	Feb. 12,1855	SE/SE	40
John BUSH				W$\frac{1}{2}$/SE	80

Section 22

Name	County	State	Date	Description	Acres
Isaac L OSTRUM	Orleans	NY	May 25,1836	E$\frac{1}{2}$/SE	80
Moses D SHAW	Livingston	NY	May 26,1836	W$\frac{1}{2}$/SE	80
Eph TICKNOR	Tompkins	NY	May 26,1836	SW$\frac{1}{4}$	160
Norman GOODALE	Ontario	NY	Nov. 25,1836	E$\frac{1}{2}$/NE	80
Phebe BURNETT	Ontario	NY	Feb. 22,1838	NW$\frac{1}{4}$	160
Justus BOYD	Livingston	MI	Feb. 22,1838	NW$\frac{1}{4}$	160

Section 23

Name	County	State	Date	Description	Acres
Philip ECKLER	Livingston	NY	May 20,1836	W$\frac{1}{2}$/SW	80
Delsey BENJAMIN	Oakland	MI	May 26,1836	E$\frac{1}{2}$/SW	80
Justus N POND	Wayne	NY	June 1,1836	SE$\frac{1}{4}$ & NE$\frac{1}{4}$	320
Henry M MOORE	Genessee	NY	Aug. 6,1836	NW$\frac{1}{4}$	160

Section 24

Name	County	State	Date	Description	Acres
Morris TUCKER	Wayne	NY	June 1,1836	W$\frac{1}{2}$/SW	80
Betsey TUCKER	Wayne	NY	June 1,1836	E$\frac{1}{2}$/SW	80
Ruth POND	Wayne	NY	June 1,1836	E$\frac{1}{2}$/SE	80
William B COGSHILL	Wayne	NY	June 1,1836	W$\frac{1}{2}$/SE	80
B B KERCHIVAL	Wayne	MI	Nov. 18,1836	NE$\frac{1}{4}$	160

Section 25

Name	County	State	Date	Description	Acres
John COUGHRAN	Genessee	NY	May	SE$\frac{1}{4}$	160
Justin N POND	Wayne	NY	June	NE$\frac{1}{4}$	160
Jason SWIFT	Wayne	MI	July	NW$\frac{1}{4}$	160
Alvin WHEDEN	Onondaga	NY		SW$\frac{1}{4}$	160

Conway township

Section 26
Isaac L OSTRUM	Orleans	NY	May 25,1838	W½/NE	80
Henry NELSON	Wayne	NY	May 25,1836	E½/NE	80
William FARLEY	Orleans	NY	May 25,1836	NW¼	160
Augustus M SHERWOOD	Tompkins	NY	May 26,1836	W½/SE & E½/SW	160
Henry SHERWOOD	Tompkins	NY	May 26,1836	W½/SW	80
John OWEN &					
Marshall CHAPIN	Wayne	MI	July 14,183_	E½/SE	80

Section 27
Martin W RASDALE	Livingston	NY	Apr. 18,1836	W½/SW	80
John WESTFALL Jr.	Cayuga	NY	May 11,1836	W½/SE & SE/SW	120
Smith N NELSON	Orleans	NY	May 25,1836	NE¼	160
Enoch VANKIRK	Tompkins	NY	May 26,1836	NW¼	160
Henry SHERWOOD	Tompkins	NY	May 26,1836	E½/SE	80
Delsey BENJAMIN	Livingston	MI	May 1,1850	NE/SW	40

Section 28
John R WINTERTON	(New York city)		Sept. 21,1836	SE¼	160
Charles A WILLIAMSON	Ontario	NY	Nov. 2,1836	NW¼	160
William MERRILL	Wayne	MI	Jan. 12,1837	E½/NE & W½/SW	160
Andrew J WRIGHT	Livingston	MI	Nov. 15,1854	SE/SW	40
C P BUSH	Ingham	MI	July 6,1854	W½/NE	80
A P COOK	Jackson	MI	Feb. 6,1855	NE/SW	40

Section 29
William CLARK	(New Tork city)		Sept. 21,1836	Section	640

Section 30
Samuel WINTERTON	(New York city)		Sept. 21,1836	NE¼ & SE¼	320
Patrick TAFFE	Monroe	NY	Sept. 22,1836	Ep/NW	80
Conrad WOOL	Wayne	MI	May 25,1837	NE/SW	40
Rueben B WOOD	Livingston	MI	May 25,1837	SE/SW	40
Trumen JOHNSON	Genessee	NY	Oct. 27,1837	Wp/SWf	34
Benjamin D LEFEVRE	Washtenaw	MI	Feb. 4,1839	Wp/NWf	36

Section 31
Charles BUTLER	(New York city)		Apr. 2,1836	Frac. Section	540

Conway township

Section 32
Charles BUTLER   (New York city) Apr. 2,1836   Section   640

Section 33
John B FOWLER   Livingston NY Apr. 18,1836   NE¼ & SE¼ &
                                                         SW¼ & E½/NW   560
Phillip COON   Wayne   MI July 7,1837   W½/NW   80

Section 34
Homer T SMITH   Huron   OH May 26,1836   NW¼   160
Lorenzo CLARK   Wayne   NY June 1,1836   W½/SW   80
Olive REED   Wayne   NY June 1,1836   E½/SW   80
Hiram ADAMS   Livingston NY June 4,1836   E½/SE   80
Samuel BEBINS   Wayne   MI July 14,1836   W½/SE   80
Henry ELSWORTH   (New York city) Sept. 21,1836   NE¼   160

Section 35
Alvin HAMMER   Wayne   MI May 20,1836   E½/SE   80
Homer T SMITH   Huron   OH May 26,1836   N½/NW   80
Benjamin M ALLIGER   Ulster   NY June 7,1836   W½/SE   80
John BUSH   Tompkins   NY June 9,1836   SW¼   160
Henry ELSWORTH   (New York city) Sept. 21,1836   NE¼ & S½/NW   240

Section 36
James JONES   Livingston NY May 1,1836   SE¼   160
Elijah CLOUGH   Onondaga   NY May 1,1836   E½/SW   80
Legard S ADAMS   Genessee   NY May 10,1836   NE¼ & NW¼   320
Alvin HAMMER   Wayne   MI May 20,1836   SW/SW   40
Richard P BUSH   Tompkins   NY June 9,1836   NW/SW   40

25

DEERFIELD township–FIRST Land Owners

NAME	COUNTY & STATE		DATE	LAND	ACRES
Section 1					
Elijah CRANE	Wayne	MI	June 7,1836	Np/NEf	127
Hugh GORDON	Washtenaw	MI	July 16,1836	Sp/NEf &	
				Ep/NWf	187
Joseph WEISS	Oakland	MI	Aug. 2,1836	NW/NWf	67
	Livingston	Mi	Mar. 1855	SW/NW	40
Aleiram BLACKBURN	Washtenaw	MI	Oct. 21,1836	SE/SE & SE/SW	80
Jefferson EDDY	Genessee	MI	Mar. 9,1837	NE/SE	40
Ebenezer STERNS	Yates	NY	Mar. 28,1837	SW/SE	40
David S TOMLINSON	Allegeny	NY	June 26,1837	W½/SW	80
Section 2					
William BENNET	Washtenaw	MI	Nov. 6,1835	E½/NWf &	
				NW/NEf	188
Ara SPRAGUE	Wayne	MI	May 4,1836	SW/NW	40
James PRATT	Washtenaw	MI	June 9,1836	SW¼ & NW/NWf	236
Benjamin L KING	Wayne	MI	Aug. 1,1836	SW/NE	40
Joseph WEISS	Oakland	MI	Aug. 2,1836	NE/NEf	71
Hiram T BLACKBURN	Washtenaw	MI	Aug. 2,1836	SE/SE	40
Julius K BLACKBURN	Washtenaw	MI	Aug. 2,1836	W½/SE	80
John RISE	Livingston	MI	Dec. 6,1836	NE/SE	40
Section 3					
Caleb WOOD	Washtenaw	MI	Dec. 1,1835	SE¼ & E½/SW	240
James PRATT	Washtenaw	MI	June 9,1836	SE/NW	40
Isaac PRATT	Washtenaw	MI	June 9,1836	Sp/NE	80
Elias DAVENPORT	Wayne	MI	Aug. 1,1836	NE/NEf	80
Josiah DORT	Wayne	MI	Aug. 3,1836	NW/NEf	80
Russel M ORMSBEE	Wayne	MI	Nov. 4,1836	Np/NWf	170
Rebecca CRAMER	Washtenaw	MI	Aug. 15,1838	W½/SW & SW/NW	120
Section 4					
Ebenezer J PENNIMAN	Wayne	MI	Mar. 4,1836	SE¼	160
			Mar. 18,1836	E½/SW	80
			Apr. 20,1836	W½/SW	80
			Nov. 18,1836	Sp/NE	80
Clemens SHAW	Saratoga	NY	May 21,1836	Np/NEf	178
Clark C BOUTWELL	(Hillsborough,NY)		May 25,1836	NWf¼	267

Deerfield township

Section 5

Name	Location		Date	Description	Acres
William PEEL	(Westchester,NY)		June 7,1834	W½/SW	80
Bishop W SHEARWOOD	(Westchester,NY)		Oct. 1,1835	W½/SE & E½/SW	
				SW/NE & SE/NW	240
Ebenezer J PENNIMAN	Wayne	MI	Apr. 20,1836	E½/SE	80
			May 9,1836	SE/NE	40
Jonathan HOW	Livingston	MI	May 13,1836	SW/NWf &	
				Wp/Np/NWf	90
				Ep/Np/NWf	100
Sidney M HAWLEY	Livingston	MI	Mar. 11,1841	NW/NEf	97
George FAIRBANKS	Genessee	MI	Feb. 25,1852	S½/NE/NEf	48
Levi WARNER	Genessee	Mi	Mar. 17,1852	Nw/Np/NWf	50
Peter CROSBY	Livingston	MI	Mar. 1,1853	N½/NE/NEf	48

Section 6

Name	Location		Date	Description	Acres
John HOW	(Westchester,NY)		June 7,1834	SE¼	160
Rueben MOORE &					
Clark C BOUTWELL	(U.S.)		May 25,1836	NWf¼ & SW¼ &	
				Sp/NE & NW/NE	558
John MYERS	Cayuga	NY	Jan. 23,1839	NE/NEf	102

Section 7

Name	Location		Date	Description	Acres
John HOW	(Westchester,NY)		Sept. 27,1833	NE¼ & SE¼ &	
				E½/NW & Ep/SW	480
Vesparian ADAMS	Madison	NY	Jan. 12,1837	Wp/SWf	56
Daniel BOUTELL Jr.	Livingston	MI	Mar. 1,1837	Wp/NWf	56

Section 8

Name	Location		Date	Description	Acres
John HOW	(Westchester,NY)		Sept. 27,1833	W½/NW & W½/SW	160
Joseph COON	Wayne	NY	Aug. 1,1836	W½/NE & NE/NE	120
Lawrence JONES	Wayne	NY	Aug. 3,1836	E½/NW	80
Edmund FLOOD	Wayne	MI	Dec. 2,1836	SE/NE	40
William BAIN	Wayne	MI	Jan. 21,1848	NE/SE	40
	Livingston	MI	Apr. 18,1854	SW/SE	40
			Aug. 8,1855	SE/SW	40
John THOMPSON	Livingston	MI	July 13,1854	NW/SE	40
Eli HOWARD	Livingston	MI	Oct. 27,1855	SE/SE	40

Deerfield township

Section 9

Esick PRAY	Washtenaw	MI	June 21,1836	NE¼ & E½/NW	
				& W½/SE	320
Joseph COON	Wayne	NY	Aug. 1,1836	NW/NW	40
Edmund FLOOD	Wayne	MI	Dec. 2,1836	SW/NW	40
Terence HENNCOCK	Wayne	MI	Dec. 2,1836	W½/SW	80
Ira LAMB	Livingston	MI	Sept. 7,1847	SE/SE	40
Jacob L DEBAR	Livingston	MI	Aug. 27,1851	NE/SE	40
Bartimus PACHARD	Livingston	MI	June 5,1836	E½/SW	80

Section 10

Benjamin BENNETT	Washtenaw	MI	Jan. 19,1836	SE/NE	40
Philo STRICKLAND	Erie	NY	Apr. 14,1836	E½/SE	80
Lothrup BRIGGS	Lenewee	MI	May 7,1836	N½/NE	80
James VAN BENSCHOTEN	Cayuga	NY	June 3,1836	W½/SE & E½/SW	160
Nathan COLE	Livingston	MI	Dec. 2,1836	SW/NE & SE/NW	80
Joseph COLE	Livingston	MI	Dec. 9,1836	NE/NW	40
Samuel B BRADLEY	Livingston	MI	Nov. 11,1853	NW/SW	40
Franklin BRADLEY	Livingston	MI	July 3,1855	NW/NW	40
Silas LINDSEY	Livingston	MI	Mar. 10,1854	SW/SW	40

Section 11

Benjamin BENNETT	Washtenaw	MI	Dec. 10,1835	NE¼ & NW¼	320
Samuel HOGG	Washtenaw	MI	Mar. 18,1836	E½/SE	80
Lyman PURDY	Orleans	NY	Apr. 19,1836	W½/SW	80
John S DELANO	Washtenaw	MI	May 16,1836	NW/SE & NE/SW	80
Daniel D SMITH	Washtenaw	MI	June 2,1836	SW/SE	40
Dwight KELLOGG	Washtenaw	MI	July 16,1836	SE/SW	40

Section 12

Horace H NOTINGHAM	Washtenaw	MI	Nov. 23,1835	W½/SW	80
William HATT sr.	Washtenaw	MI	Nov. 24,1835	W½/SE	80
			May 27,1836	NE/SE	40
William HATT Jr.	Washtenaw	MI	Nov. 24,1835	E½/SW	80
Washington D MORTON	Washtenaw	MI	May 17,1836	SE/NE	40
Eliphalet S TOOKER	Washtenaw	MI	June 2,1836	W½/NW	80
Charles D TOPPING	Washtenaw	MI	June 20,1836	SW/NE	40
			July 7,1836	SE/NW	40
Joseph WELCH	Washtenaw	MI	July 12,1836	SE/SE	40
George GREEN &					
Julius K BLACKBURN	Washtenaw	MI	July 2,1836	N½/NE & NE/NW	120

Deerfield township

Section 13

Horace H NOTINGHAM	Washtenaw	MI	Nov. 23,1835	W½/NW	80
William HATT Sr.	Washtenaw	MI	Nov. 24,1835	W½/NE & E½/NW	160
Anson PETTIBONE	Genessee	NY	May 12,1836	SE¼ & E½/SW	240
Abram SPEERS	Washtenaw	MI	May 18,1836	E½/NE	80
Eliphalet S TOOKER	Washtenaw	MI	June 3,1836	NW/SW	40
Isaac L PLATT	(New York city)		Aug. 3,1836	SW/SW	40

Section 14

Horace H NOTINGHAM	Washtenaw	MI	Nov. 23,1835	E½/NE	80
Samuel LEONARD	Monroe	NY	Apr. 14,1836	NW¼	160
Jabez LINDLEY	Washtenaw	MI	May 20,1836	NW/NE	40
			Sept. 19,1836	SW/NE	40
Urbane PEASE	Cayuga	NY	June 27,1836	E½/SE	80
Jeriah G RHODES	Cayuga	NY	June 27,1836	W½/SW	80
Daniel R RHODES	Cayuga	NY	June 27,1836	W½/SE & E½/SW	160

Section 15

Samuel LEONARD	Monroe	NY	Apr. 14,1836	E½/NE	80
Darius LEWIS	Erie	NY	May 2,1836	W½/SE & E½/SW	160
	Oakland	MI	Aug. 8,1849	SW/NW	40
Elijah CRANE	Wayne	MI	June 7,1836	E½/SE	80
Leonard LOCKWOOD	Stueben	NY	July 5,1836	W½/SW	80
John B McCRARY &					
Phineas McCRARY	Stueben	NY	Aug. 3,1836	W½/NE & E½/NW	160

Section 16 (school section)

C W LEONARD	June 16,1842	SE/SE	40
T McKINLEY	June 11,1847	SW/SW	40
R CRAMER	June 11,1847	NE/NE	40
Ira LAMB	Mar. 4,1848	NW/NE	40
R T YOUNG	June 13,1848	W½/SE	80
Eli WARD	Oct. 11,1848	NE/NW	40
J CAMERON	Nov. 25,1848	SE/NW	40
	Mar. 30,1849	SW/NW	40
H ANDERSON	Mar. 21,1849	NW/SW	40
L LAMPSON	Aug. 25,1849	NW/NW	40
M CASKNER	Oct. 15,1839	SE/NE	40
Hugh ANDERSON	July 1,1861	N½/NE/SW	20
		S½/NE/SW &	
		SE/SW	60
James H PAGE	Apr. 16,1860	S½/NE/SE	20
A D ROYCE	Apr. 16,1860	N½/NE/SE &	
		Sw/NE	60

Deerfield township

Section 17

Name	County	State	Date	Description	Acres
William B HOPKINS	Monroe	NY	June 3,1836	W½/SW	80
Abram COOK	Wayne	NY	Nov. 26,1836	W½/NW	80
Flavius J B CRANE	Livingston	MI	June 13,1837	E½/NE	80
Joseph SIBLEY	Cayuga	NY	Sept. 1,1838	NE/SE	40
Sands SIBLEY	Livingston	MI	May 1,1850	SE/SE	40
Henry ROBB	Livingston	MI	Aug. 1,1854	SW/NE	40
*(H CRAMER)			(Dec. 2,1848)	E½/SW & E½/NW	160
*(Thomas POWERS heirs)			(Nov. 10,1879)	NW/NE	40
*(Charles WRIGHT)			(Aug. 17,1901)	W½/SE	80

Section 18

Name	County	State	Date	Description	Acres
John HOW	Livingston	Mi	Oct. 30,1835	NW/NWf	28
Lyman MORELL	Washtenaw	MI	Aug. 2,1836	E½/SE	80
Edwin P SPENCER	Washtenaw	MI	Aug. 2,1836	W½/SE	80
B B KERCHIVAL	Wayne	MI	Oct. 29,1836	Ep/SW	80
Daniel MILLER	Washtenaw	MI	Oct. 28,1836	NE/NE	40
Abram COOK	Wayne	NY	Nov. 26,1836	W½/NE	80
Charles S HUTCHINS	Madison	NY	Jan. 10,1837	Ep/NW	80
Vesparian ADAMS	Madison	NY	Jan.12,1837	Wp/SWf &	
				SW/NWf	85
Robert CRAIG	Washtenaw	MI	Apr. 4,1838	SE/NE	40

Section 19

Name	County	State	Date	Description	Acres
Myron H WARNER	Washtenaw	MI	June 3,1836	E½/SE	80
Joseph WILLIS	Oakland	MI	June 3,1836	E½/NE	80
Lucius WILLIS	Oneida	NY	June 3,1836	W½/NE	80
Aaron ABNER	Washtenaw	MI	June 18,1836	W½/SE	80
Lorenzo BANNISTER	Ontario	NY	July 1,1836	Ep/SW	80
Maria M WORDEN	Wayne	MI	Oct. 26,1836	Ep/NW	80
DAniel BOUTELL	Onondaga	NY	Nov. 5,1836	Wp/SWf	59

Section 20

Name	County	State	Date	Description	Acres
Freeborn LUCE	Oakland	MI	Feb. 26,1836	SE/NW	40
			Apr. 14,1836	E½/SE	80
Dean PHILLIPS	Montgomery	NY	May 9,1836	E½/SW	80
Robert CHAMBERS	Monroe	NY	May 21,1836	W½/SE	80
Luther HOUGHTON	Livingston	MI	July 8,1836	W½/NW	80
Ezra SANDFORD	Livingston	MI	July 8,1836	W½/SW	80
Isaac N HEDDEN	Livingston	MI	SEpt. 24,1836	NE/NW	40
Abram COOK	Wayne	NY	Nov. 26,1836	S½/NE	80
Hannah BLOOD	Monroe	NY	May 16,1839	NE/NE	40
John J SANFORD	Livingston	MI	Sept. 20,1841	NW/NE	40

Deerfield township

Section 21

Mathew SHANNON	Stueben	NY	May 12,1836	SW$\frac{1}{4}$	160
Thomas SHARP	Seneca	NY	May 12,1836	SE$\frac{1}{4}$	160
Robert McKINLEY	Stueben	NY	May 12,1836	NW$\frac{1}{4}$	160
Jacob COLE	Wayne	MI	June 20,1836	E$\frac{1}{2}$/NE	80
Job SLATFORD	Washtenaw	MI	July 13,1836	W$\frac{1}{2}$/NE	80

Section 22

Orrin CARTWRIGHT	Monroe	NY	Apr. 1,1836	SE/SE	40
James LEWIS	Erie	NY	May 2,1836	W$\frac{1}{2}$/NE & E$\frac{1}{2}$/NW	160
Alfred WHITE	Livingston	NY	May 24,1836	W$\frac{1}{2}$/SW	80
Abram FAIRCHILDS	Wayne	NY	June 14,1836	E$\frac{1}{2}$/NE	80
Rensellor POMEROY	Wayne	NY	June 14,1836	E$\frac{1}{2}$/SW	80
Charles D TOPPING	Washtenaw	MI	June 20,1836	W$\frac{1}{2}$/NW	80
Thomas C SMITH		NY	Aug. 2,1836	W$\frac{1}{2}$/SE & NE/SE	120

Section 23

Joseph WELCH & George GREEN	Washtenaw	MI	Mar. 9,1836	E$\frac{1}{2}$/SE	80
Orrin CARTWRIGHT	Monroe	NY	Apr. 1,1836	SW/SW	40
Abram FAIRCHILDS	Wayne	NY	June 14,1836	W$\frac{1}{2}$/NW	80
William J SPALDING	Cayuga	NY	June 27,1836	W$\frac{1}{2}$/NE & E$\frac{1}{2}$/NW	160
Charles KELLOGG	Cayuga	NY	July 16,1836	E$\frac{1}{2}$/NE	80
Hall DELAND	Genessee	NY	Aug. 2,1836	W$\frac{1}{2}$/SE & E$\frac{1}{2}$/SW	160
Thomas C SMITH		NY	Aug. 2,1836	NW/SW	40

Section 24

Joseph WELCH & George GREEN	Washtenaw	MI	Mar. 9,1836	W$\frac{1}{2}$/SW	80
David BANGS	Monroe	NY	May 5,1836	NE$\frac{1}{4}$	160
Thomas LEWITT	Washtenaw	MI	May 16,1836	E$\frac{1}{2}$/SW	80
James TYLER	Tompkins	NY	June 2,1836	W$\frac{1}{2}$/NW	80
Sophia SMALLEY	Washtenaw	MI	June 3,1836	NE/NW	40
Charles WRIGHT	Jefferson	NY	June 6,1836	SE$\frac{1}{4}$	160
Adam BAYLEY	Livingston	MI	May 5,1837	SE/NW	40

*(not recorded in tract index)

Deerfield township

Section 25

Russell MORTON	Washtenaw	MI	Jan. 11,1836	SW¼	160
Dennis McCARTHY	Wayne	MI	Feb. 29,1836	W½/SE & W½/NE	160
Joseph WELCH &					
George GREEN	Washtenaw	MI	Mar. 9,1836	W½/NW	80
Joseph CHAMBERLIN	Livingston	NY	May 3,1836	E½/SE	80
David BANGS	Monroe	NY	May 5,1836	E½/NW	80
Philo H MUNSON	Livingston	NY	June 6,1836	E½/NE	80

Section 26

Eli H EVANS	Washtenaw	MI	Feb. 29,1836	W½/NE & W½/SE	160
Elisha G MAPES	Washtenaw	MI	Feb. 29,1836	E½/NE & E½/SE	160
Orrin CARTWRIGHT	Monroe	NY	Apr. 1,1836	W½/NW	80
Charles KELLOGG	Cayuga	NY	July 16,1836	SW¼	160
Samuel L WALDEN		NY	Aug. 2,1836	E½/NW	80

Section 27

Joseph GILLMAN	Monroe	NY	Apr. 1,1836	W½/NE & E½/NW	160
Orrin CARTWRIGHT	Monroe	NY	Apr. 1,1836	E½/SE	80
James HENRY	Wayne	MI	June 7,1836	W½/NW & NW/SW	120
Friend BURT	Genessee	NY	June 13,1836	E½/SW	80
Preston H SMITH	Madison	NY	June 20,1836	E½/SE	80
Nelson A SMITH	Madison	NY	June 20,1836	W½/SE	80
Joseph WELCH &					
George GREEN	Livingston	MI	Nov. 5,1836	SW/SW	40

Section 28

William P FINCH	Saratoga	NY	May 21,1836	SW¼ & W½/SE	240
David S IRELAND	Monroe	NY	May 21,1836	NE¼ & NW¼	320
Rhoda DAVIS	Washtenaw	MI	May 30,1836	E½/SE	80

Section 29

William PIKE	Monroe	NY	May 21,1836	E½/SE	80
Robert CHAMBERS	Monroe	NY	May 21,1836	E½/NE	80
William JUBB	Monroe	NY	May 24,1836	W½/NW	80
Myron H WARNER	Washtenaw	MI	June 3,1836	E½/NW	80
George GRANT	St. Lawrence	NY	June 3,1836	W½/SW	80
Austin DELAND	Livingston	NY	June 3,1836	W½/NE	80
Robert SOWDERS	Livingston	NY	June 3,1836	W½/SE	8-
Montgomery P ADAMS	Madison	NY	Nov. 14,1836	E½/SW	80

Deerfield township

Section 30

William JUBB	Monroe	NY	May 24,1836	NE/NE	40
William B WRIGHT	Livingston	MI	June 11,1836	E½/SE	80
John H SANFORD	Livingston	MI	July 8,1836	Ep/NW	80
			Sept. 23,1836	NE/SW	40
B B KERCHIVAL	Wayne	MI	Oct. 29,1836	W½/NE & SE/NE	120
Daniel MILLER	Washtenaw	MI	Oct. 28,1836	W½/SE	80
Daniel BOUTELL Jr.	Onondaga	NY	Nov. 5,1836	Wp/NWf	61
Margaret COOPER	Madison	NY	Nov. 14,1836	SE/SW	40
Dennis MURPHY	Wayne	MI	Nov. 26,1836	Wp/SWf	62

Section 31

Joseph HOSLEY	Wayne	MI	June 1,1836	NWf¼ & SWf¼	291
	Livingston	NY	Sept. 23,1836	W½/NE	80
			Nov. 14,1836	NW/SE	40
Myron H WARNER	Washtenaw	MI	June 3,1836	E½/SE & SW/SE	120
George GRANT	St. Lawrence	NY	June 3,1836	NE/NE	40
Isaac N HEDDEN	Livingston	MI	Sept. 24,1836	SE/NE	40

Section 32

James MILLAR	Oakland	MI	Apr. 1,1836	SE¼	160
Harry H NEFF	Livingston	MI	June 11,1836	NW/SW	40
William B WRIGHT	Livingston	MI	June 11,1836	W½/NW	80
John CRANE	Erie	NY	June 28,1836	E½/SW & SW/SW	120
Dennis J ROCKWELL	Wayne	MI	Oct. 27,1836	NE¼	160
David F ROCKWELL	Wayne	MI	Oct. 27,1836	E½/NW	80

Section 33

Ezel MERRILL	Oakland	MI	May 2,1836	SE/SW	40
Stephen C GOFF	Wayne	MI	May 11,1836	SE¼	160
George FAUSSETT	Seneca	NY	May 12,1836	E½/NW	80
Henry FAUSSETT	Seneca	NY	May 12,1836	W½/NW	80
Thomas FAUSSETT	Seneca	NY	May 12,1836	NE¼	160
Benjamin MERRILL	Wayne	MI	Sept. 23,1836	NE/SW	40
Hiram MERRILL			(May 30,1837)	W½/SW	80

Deerfield township

Section 34
Henry LOWN	Genessee	NY	Apr. 18,1836	SW¼	160
Michael BENNET	Washtenaw	MI	June 4,1836	NE¼ & NW¼	320
Richard H CANIFF	(New York city)		Aug. 4,1836	SE¼	160

Section 35
Elijah CRANE	Wayne	MI	Mar. 4,1836	E½/NE	80
Joseph WELCH & George GREEN	Washtenaw	MI	Mar. 18,1836	W½/NE	80
William PAYNE	Washtenaw	MI	May 16,1836	E½/SE	80
Garret MARTIN	Yates	NY	May 21,1836	W½/SE	80
John VAN TUYL	Yates	NY	May 27,1836	S½/SW	80
Hugh GILSHANNAN	Washtenaw	MI	June 4,1836	NW¼	160
Electa A HEDDEN	Livingston	MI	Sept. 24,1836	N½/SW	80

Section 36
Thales DEAN	Washtenaw	MI	Jan. 11,1836	E½/SE	80
Dennis McCARTEY	Wayne	MI	Feb. 29,1836	W½/NE & E½/NW	160
Elijah CRANE	Wayne	MI	Mar. 4,1836	W½/NW	80
John WINTER	Genessee	NY	May 3,1836	E½/NE	80
Thomas LEWITT	Washtenaw	MI	May 16,1836	W½/SW	80
Garret MARTIN	Yates	NY	May 21,1836	W½/SE & E½/SW	160

34

NAME	COUNTY & STATE		DATE	LAND	ACRES
Section 1					
William PLACEWAY	Livingston	MI	Jan. 4,1837	NW/NEf	41
Alvin F BENJAMIN	Washtenaw	MI	July 9,1835	SE/SE	40
William S CONELY	(New York city)		Aug. 1,1835	NE/SE	40
Peter DUROSS	Washtenaw	MI	Feb. 3,1836	E½/SW	80
Erastus KELLOG	Washtenaw	MI	Feb. 17,1836	Np/NWf	78
Alvin NORTON	Wayne	MI	Mar. 28,1836	W½/SW	80
Andrew LAMB	Wayne	MI	Mar. 28,1836	SW/SE	40
John W WILLIAMS	Allegeny	NY	May 2,1836	Sp/NWf	80
Valentine STRACK	Wayne	MI	June 7,1836	NE/NEf	41
Horace R HUDSON	(New York city)		Sept. 24,1836	S½/NE & NW/SE	120
Section 2					
Chester HAZARD	Stueben	NY	Nov. 3,1835	SW/SW	40
James M MURRAY	Washtenaw	MI	Jan. 21,1836	E½/SE	80
Erastus KELLOG	Washtenaw	MI	Feb. 17,1836	Np/NEf	76
Abram HANKINS	Washtenaw	MI	Apr. 14,1836	Sp/NE	80
Joseph PLACEWAY	Allegeny	NY	May 2,1836	W½/SE & E½/SW	
				& SE/NW	200
John WHYTE	Wayne	MI	Dec. 26,1836	NW/SW	40
Amasa DEAN	Oakland	MI	Jan. 9,1837	Np/NWf	77
John CLARK	Ontario	NY	Mar. 2,1838	SW/NW	40
Section 3					
John L MARTIN	Livingston	NY	Oct. 17,1835	SW/NW	40
Benjamin EARL	Washtenaw	MI	Feb. 16,1836	NW/NWf	39
Benjamin J BONIWELL	Wayne	MI	Mar. 28,1836	E½/NWf	79
Erastus WATROUS	Genessee	NY	June 4,1836	E½/SW	80
Richard BROWN	Livingston	MI	July 13,1836	NW/SW	40
John WHITE	Wayne	MI	Dec. 24,1836	SE¼	160
William JACOBS	Erie	NY	Feb. 23,1837	Np/NEf	78
	Livingston	MI	Dec. 22,1837	SE/NE	40
Charles P BUSH	Ingham	MI	Oct. 6,1853	SW/SW	40
J J BUSH	Ingham	MI	Oct. 13,1853	SW/NE	40

Genoa township

Section 4

Samuel WEST	Wayne	NY	June 8,1835	S½/SW	80
John ELLIS	Albany	NY	June 22,1835	N½/SW	80
John L MARTIN	Livingston	NY	Oct. 17,1835	Sp/NE	80
Benjamin EARL	Washtenaw	MI	Mar. 11,1836	Np/NEf	77
John ELLIS	Albany	NY	Aug. 1,1836	Sp/NW	80
John F LAWSON	Livingston	NY	Sept. 22,1836	NE/SE & W½/SE	120
Cornelius N BURWELL	Livingston	NY	Jan. 18,1851	NW/NWf	39
Claude W CASE				SE/SE	40

Section 5

Cornelius W BURWELL	Livingston	MI	Apr. 5,1837	NW/NE	40
John DREW	(Detroit)	MI	Aug. 13,1835	SW¼	160
			Nov. 4,1835	W½/SE	80
John ELLIS	Albany	NY	June 22,1835	E½/SE	80
Asahel DIBBLE	Livingston	MI	Sept. 15,1835	SW/NW	40
			May 2,1836	Np/NW & SE/NW	120
John ELLIS	Albany	NY	Aug. 1,1836	Sp/NE	80
Orson ELLIOT	Wayne	MI	Feb. 21,1837	NE/NEf	40

Section 6

Asa COBB	Crawford	OH	June 23,1835	Sp/NE	80
William SHAFT	Washtenaw	Mi	July 27,1835	SE/SE	40
Asahel DIBBLE	Livingsron	MI	Sept. 15,1835	W½/SE & NE/SE	120
Flavius B CRANE	Livingston	MI	Nov. 9,1835	NE/NWf	107
			Nov. 26,1835	Np/NEf	89
Horace H COMSTOCK	Kalamazoo	MI	Aug. 27,1836	Sp/NWf	84
Mark HEALY &					
B B KERCHIVAL	(U. S.)		May 28,1836	SWf¼	168

Section 7

Ely BARNARD	Madison	NY	Dec. 23,1834	E½/SE	80
Edward LATSON	Genessee	NY	Nov. 9,1835	Ep/SW & NW/SE	
				& SW/NE	160
William SHAFT	Madison	NY	Nov. 19,1835	NE/NE	40
William Burr CURTIS	Livingston	MI	July 2,1836	SW/SE	40
Peter SHAFT	Livingston	MI	July 11,1836	SE/NE	40
Asahel DIBBLE	Livingston	MI	Nov. 3,1836	SW/NWf	44
			Apr. 11,1837	Wp/SWf	92
			June 16,1838	Ep/NW & NW/NE	120
David PARKER	Livingston	MI	Mar. 21,1837	NW/NWf	44

36

Genoa township

Section 8

Ely BARNARD	Madison	NY	Dec. 23,1834	$W\frac{1}{2}$/SW	80
John ELLIS	Albany	NY	June 22,1835	$NE\frac{1}{4}$ & $E\frac{1}{2}$/NW	240
Asa COBB Jr.	Crawford	OH	June 23,1835	$SE\frac{1}{4}$ & $E\frac{1}{2}$/SW	240
Jacob VANDEWALKER	Washtenaw	MI	Sept. 5,1835	$W\frac{1}{2}$/NW	80

Section 9

Zachariah SUTTON	Oakland	MI	Oct. 24,1834	$W\frac{1}{2}$/NE	80
Samuel WEST	Wayne	NY	June 8,1835	$NW\frac{1}{4}$	160
Neil F BUTTERFIELD	Wayne	NY	June 22,1835	$W\frac{1}{2}$/SE & $E\frac{1}{2}$/SW & NE/SE	200
			Oct. 12,1835	$W\frac{1}{2}$/SW	80
Lucius H PEET	Livingston	MI	Oct. 12,1835	SE/NE	40
William P PATRICK	Wayne	MI	Sept. 20,1837	SE/SE	40
John F LAWSON	Livingston	MI	Feb. 27,1837	NE/SE	40

Section 10

John WHYTE	Wayne	MI	July 22,1833	$SE\frac{1}{4}$	160
			Oct. 15,1835	$E\frac{1}{2}$/NE & NW/NE	120
Jehial BARRON	Hampshire	MA	May 11,1834	$E\frac{1}{2}$/SW	80
Horace H COMSTOCK	Kalamazoo	MI	Jan. 27,1836	$W\frac{1}{2}$/SW	80
Steward H HAZARD	Wayne	MI	Mar. 10,1837	SW/NW	40
Charles P BUSH	Ingham	MI	July 31,1853	SW/NW	40
			Nov. 17,1854	NE/NW	40
Asa VAN KLEEK	Livingston	MI		SE/NW	40
Ezra W MILLER				NW/NW	40

Section 11

Steward HAZARD	Wayne	MI	Dec. 26,1836	NE/NE	40
Oren RHOADES	Washtenaw	MI	Sept. 20,1836	SE/NE	40
Jacob EULER	Livingston	MI	Aug. 5,1835	SE/SE	40
			Dec. 14,1835	NE/SE	40
Lavina ROBBINS	Broome	NY	Oct. 5,1835	SW/NW	40
Thomas PINCKNEY	Livingston	MI	Oct. 26,1835	SW/NW	40
Chester HAZARD	Stueben	NY	Nov. 3,1835	$W\frac{1}{2}$/SE & $E\frac{1}{2}$/SW	160
Lucius H PEET	Livingston	MI	Jan. 21,1836	SE/NW	40
Pamelia & Lavina & Jane WOOD	Ontario	NY	May 23,1836	$W\frac{1}{2}$/NE	80
			June 3,1836	$N\frac{1}{2}$/SW	80
John WHITE	Wayne	MI	Dec. 26,1836	NW/SW	40

37

Genoa township

Section 12

Alvin F BENJAMIN	Washtenaw	MI	July 9,1835	SE¼		160
George Henry ZULAUF	Livingston	MI	Aug. 5,1835	E½/SW		80
Peter EULER	Montgomery	NY	Aug. 5,1835	W½/SW		80
Aaron H KELLY	Washtenaw	MI	Dec. 18,1835	NE/NE		40
John EULER	Momtgomery	NY	Dec. 28,1835	NW/NW		40
Peter DUROSS	Washtenaw	MI	Feb. 3,1836	NE/NW		40
John J BROWN	Orleans	NY	Aug. 1,1836	S½/NE		80
Elisha HODGEMAN	Onondaga	NY	Nov. 16,1836	NW/NE		40
Lawrence EULER	Livingston	MI	Jan. 6,1837	SE/NW		40
			Nov. 26,1847	SW/NW		40

Section 13

Alexander FRASER	(New York city)		Aug. 9,1834	E½/SE		80
Thomas PINCKNEY	Washtenaw	MI	Sept. 31,1834	W½/NW		80
Charles A GREEN	Washtenaw	MI	Nov. 22,1834	SW/NE		40
Mansing HATHAWAY	Washtenaw	MI	July 9,1835	E½/NW & NE/SW		120
Alvin F BENJAMIN	Washtenaw	MI	July 9,1835	E½/NE		80
Roswell BARNES	Genessee	NY	Sept. 29,1835	W½/SW		80
Horace H COMSTOCK	Kalamazoo	MI	May 27,1836	NW/NE		40
Benjamin J BONTWELL	Wayne	MI	Feb. 3,1836	NW/NE		40
Nehemiah BONTWELL	Hillsborough	NH	June 16,1836	SE/SW		40

Section 14

Lucius H PEET	Washtenaw	MI	June 10,1835	E½/NE		80
Neil F BUTTERFIELD	Wayne	NY	June 22,1835	E½/NW & W½/NE		160
Isaiah P ROBBINS	Broome	NY	Oct. 5,1835	NW/NW		40
Abigail A R PINCKNEY	Washtenaw	MI	Nov. 9,1835	NE/SE		40
Mark HEALY &						
B B KERCHIVAL	(U. S.)		May 28,1836	SW¼ & W½/SE		
				& SE/SE		280
Phillip COON	Livingston	MI	July 25,1837	SW/NW		40

Section 15

Isaiah P ROBBINS	Broome	NY	Oct. 5,1835	NE/NE		40
Peter McDERBY	Wayne	MI	Oct. 31,1835	SW/SE		40
William MILLER	Livingston	MI	Apr. 4,1836	SW/SW		40
Mark HEALY &						
B B KERCHIVAL	(U. S.)		May 28,1836	NW¼		160
Jacob FISHBECK	Livingston	MI	July 13,1836	N½/SW		80
Charles BENEDICT	Livingston	MI	Aug. 4,1836	SE/SW		40
Patrick BOGAN	Wayne	MI	Nov. 15,1836	NE/SE		40
Samuel SEWALL	(Boston)		Dec. 2,1836	NW/SE		80
B B KERCHIVAL	Wayne	MI	Dec. 6,1836	SE/NE		120

Genoa township

Section 16 (School section)

Freeman FISHBECK		Jan. 8,1846	SE/SE	40
		Dec. 27,1853	Se/NW	40
Jacob FISHBECK		Apr. 7,1851	SW/SE	40
Charles BENEDICT		Apr. 25,1851	$S\frac{1}{2}$/SW	80
		Aug. 16,1854	NE/SW	40
Hans RUSSELL		Mar. 17,1853		
William GROSTICK		Aug. 24, 1853	$S\frac{1}{2}$/NE	80
John E DORA		Sept. 13,1853	NW/NW	40
William VAN BLAIRCUM		Nov. 15,1853	SW/NW & NW/NE	80
James O'HARA		Nov. 16,1853	NW/SW	40
John DUFFY		Dec. 20,1853	NW/SE	40
John BOGAN		Dec. 20,1853	NE/NW	40
Catherine McGARK		Mar. 16,1856	NE/NE	40

Section 17

Ely BARNARD	Madison	NY	Dec. 23,1834	NW/NW	40
Asa COBB	Crawford	OH	June 23,1835	Ne/NW	80
Pardon BARNARD	Madison	NY	June 24,1835	SW/NW	40
Elias DAVIS	Livingston	MI	July 16,1835	SE/NW	200
Joseph RIDER	Oakland	MI	Dec. 15,1835	NE/SE & $W\frac{1}{2}$/SE	120
Isaac MORSE	Wayne	NY	Feb. 10,1836	SE/NE	80
David PERCE	Oakland	MI	Apr. 25,1836	NE/NE	40
Henry WILLIAMS	Lenewee	MI	June 1,1836	SW/NE	40

Section 18

Ely BARNARD	Madison	NY	Dec. 23,1834	NE/NE	40
Pardon BARNARD	Madison	NY	June 24,1835	SE/NE	40
Josiah WARD	Washtenaw	MI	Nov. 19,1835	NW/SW & SE/NWf	87
George BABCOCK	Livingston	MI	June 6,1836	$E\frac{1}{2}$/SE	80
Timothy R BENNET	Livingston	MI	June 17,1836	SW/NWf	47
William P CURTIS	Livingston	MI	July 2,1836	SW/SWf & $W\frac{1}{2}$/NE	127
Laurence NOBLE	Washtenaw	MI	Oct. 26,1836	Ep/Sf & NW/SE	120
Asahel DIBBLE	Livingston	MI	Nov. 3,1836	$N\frac{1}{2}$/NW	87
Richard BRITTEN	Livingston	MI	Nov. 24,1854	SW/SE	40

39

Genoa township

Section 19

Timothy R BENNET	Livingston	MI	July 24,1835	E½/NW	80
Rueben MOORE	Washtenaw	MI	Oct. 27,1835	Ep/SW	80
Richard BRITTEN	Livingston	MI	May 17,1836	SW/SE	40
John TOMPKINS	Livingston	MI	June 15,1836	NE/SE	40
Enoch WEBSTER	Stueben	NY	June 22,1836	E½/NE	80
Samuel W BALDWIN	Madison	NY	Sept. 24,1836	Wp/NWf	94
Joseph BOWEN	Livingston	MI	Sept. 24,1836	Wp/SWf	74
Laurence NOBLE	Washtenaw	MI	Oct. 26,1836	NW/NE	40
Samuel SEWALL	Wayne	MI	Dec. 19,1836	NW/SE	40
Consider CRAPO	Cayuga	NY	Jan. 9,1837	SW/NE	40

Section 20

James H COLE	Yates	NY	Nov. 16,1835	E½/NE	80
Elias DAVIS	Livingston	MI	Jan. 21,1836	NW/NW	40
Amariah HAMMOND	Washtenaw	MI	May 21,1836	W½/SW	80
Hubbard McCLOUD	Ontario	NY	May 23,1836	W½/NE	80
Henry S LISK	Ontario	NY	May 23,1836	E½/NW & SW/NW	120
Margaret CANTINE	Ulster	NY	June 18,1836	E½/SE	80
Caleb CURTIS	Stueben	NY	July 15,1836	SE/SW	40
William P CURTIS	Livingston	MI	Dec. 5,1838	W½/SE	80
James WELCH	Wayne	MI	Nov. 18,1854	NE/SW	40

Section 21

Freeman FISHBECK	Oakland	MI	Oct. 23,1835	W½/NE	80
	Livingston	MI	Sept. 20,1836	SE/NE	40
David PERCE	Oakland	Mi	Oct. 23,1835	W½/NW	80
Jemina FISHBECK	Livingston	MI	Nov. 5,1835	NE/NE	40
William B YANGER	Washtenaw	MI	Apr. 16,1836	SW/SW	40
Charles BENEDICT	Washtenaw	MI	May 30,1836	E½/NW & N½/SW	160
Abram CANTINE	Orleans	NY	June 18,1836	SE/SW	40
Phillip FISHBECK	Livingston	MI	Sept. 20,1836	NW/SE	40
William SUHR	Livingston	MI	Nov. 15,1854	NE/SE	40
Alexander CARPENTER	Livingston	MI	Dec. 22,1854	SW/SE	40
Jacob CONRAD	Livingston	MI		SE/SE	40

Genoa township

Section 22

Peter McDERBY	Wayne	MI	Oct. 31,1835	NE/NW	40
Chancey SYMONDS	Livingston	MI	May 31,1836	E½/NE & NW/NE	120
Laurence EULER	Wayne	MI	June 7,1836	NW/NW	40
John MAGEE	Stueben	NY	July 6,1836	E½/SW & SE/NW	120
Gardner CARPENTER	Livingston	MI	Oct. 30,1836	SW/SW	40
Daniel JONES	Livingston	MI	Aug. 1,1837	E½/SW	80
Rodman STODDARD	Wayne	MI	Mar. 12,1840	NW/SE	40
Lewis DORR	Livingston	MI	Aug. 22,1850	SW/NE	40
William SUHR	Livingston	MI	Nov. 15,1854	NW/SW	40
Joseph M GILBERT	Livingston	MI	Feb. 8,1854	SW/NW	40

Section 23

Moses O JONES	Livingston	MI	June 21,1838	NW/SW	40
Henry BUSH	Livingston	MI	Dec. 10,1839	NW/SE	40
Henry SMITH	Wayne	MI	June 6,1836	SW/NE	40
Charles HARTMAN	Wayne	MI	June 6,1836	E½/NW	80
Charles CONRAD	Wayne	MI	June 6,1836	W½/NW	80
Hazard NEWTON	Allegeny	NY	June 7,1836	E½/NE	80
Henry SMITH	Wayne	MI	Jan. 5,1837	NW/NE	40
George RAUSHER	Wayne	MI	Feb. 1,1837	E½/SE	80
Catherine HARTMAN	Wayne	MI	Jan. 31,1837	NE/SW	40
Henry FOSTER	Wayne	MI	Feb. 1,1837	SW/SE	40
William HACKER	Livingston	MI	Oct. 4,1837	SE/SW	40
Jacob CONRAD	Livingston	MI	July 1,1852	SW/SW	40

Section 24

Chester HAZARD	Stueben	NY	Nov. 3,1835	E½/SW & SW/SW	120
Benjamin J BONTWELL	Wayne	MI	Jan. 26,1836	E½/NE	80
Mark HEALY & B B KERCHIVAL	(U. S.)		May 28,1836	NW¼ & SE ¼ & W½/NE	400
Charles S EMERSON	Monroe	MI	Dec. 26,1836	NW/SW	40

Section 25

Almon MALTBY	Washtenaw	MI	May 13,1835	SE/SW	40
Joseph BOWEN Jr.	Cayuga	NY	July 20,1835	S½/SE	80
Mark HEALY & B B KERCHIVAL	(U. S.)		May 28,1836	NE¼ & NW¼	320
Hiram OLDS	Oakland	MI	Sept. 20,1836	NW/SW	40
Trumen B WORDEN	Livingston	MI	Feb. 21,1837	NE/SE	40
			Apr. 5,1837	NE/SW	40
Grace THOMPSON	Livingston	MI	Mar. 12,1839	SW/SW	40
John CUSHING	Livingston	MI	May 6,1847	NW/SE	40

Genoa township

Section 26

Name	County	State	Date	Description	Acres
Nathaniel CARR	Washtenaw	MI	July 6,1836	E½/SE & SE/NE	120
	Livingston	MI	Sept. 3,1840	SW/NE	40
Henry EARL	Washtenaw	MI	July 6,1836	W½/SE & E½/SW	160
Justin WILLEY	Monroe	MI	Nov. 20,1838	W½/NW	80
Francis W BROWN	Livingston	MI	Nov. 20,1838	SW/SW	40
Daniel S O'NEAL	Livingston	MI	Aug. 27,1839	NE/NW	40
John BAUER	Livingston	MI	Apr. 25,1854	N½/NE	80
Gustav BAETCKE	Livingston	MI	May 1,1854	SE/NW	40
			Nov. 21,1854	NW/SW	40

Section 27

Name	County	State	Date	Description	Acres
Herman C HAUSE	Stueben	NY	Oct. 31,1835	W½/SW	80
	Livingston	MI	June 8,1836	SE/SW	40
Nathan HAWLEY	Lenewee	MI	June 25,1836	W½/SE & SE/SE	120
John D ROBINSON	Livingston	MI	Dec. 5,1836	SW/NW	40
Luther H HOVEY	Monroe	NY	Dec. 23,1836	E½/NE	80
Henry WARD				NE/SW	40
Charles WELLER	Stueben	NY	Mar. 1,1837	E½/NW	80
Moses O JONES	Huron	OH	Apr. 16,1838	W½/NE	80
Betsey McMULLING	Livingston	MI	Aug. 7,1838	NE/SE	40
Philip CONRAD	Livingston	MI	Nov. 7,1856	NW/NW	40

Section 28

Name	County	State	Date	Description	Acres
Nicholas KRISTLER	Stueben	NY	June 4,1835	S½/SW	80
William HARMON	Genessee	NY	June 26,1835	N½/SW	80
Herman C HAUSE	Stueben	NY	Oct. 31,1835	E½/SE	80
Justus J BENNET	Livingston	MI	Mar. 24,1836	NW/SE	40
Amariah HAMMOND	Washtenaw	MI	May 20,1836	SW/NE	40
Daniel B HARMON	Livingston	NY	May 20,1836	SW/SE	40
Norman L GASTON	Wayne	MI	May 21,1836	SE/NW	40
Abner ORMSBY	Washtenaw	MI	June 15,1836	SW/NW	40
Margaret CANTINE	Ulster	NY	June 18,1836	N½/NW	80
Alexander CARPENTER	Livingston	MI	Dec. 22,1854	NW/NE	40
Edward N H BODE	Livingston	MI	Apr. 9,1857	E½/NE	80

Genoa township

Section 29

Name	County	State	Date	Description	Acres
Nicholas KRISTLER	Stueben	NY	June 4,1835	E½/SE	80
David HIGHT	Stueben	NY	June 15,1835	NW/SE & SW/NE	80
Daniel JESSUP	Stueben	NY	Nov. 9,1836	W½/NW & NE/NW	120
Rueben HAIGHT	Livingston	MI	June 15,1836	SE/NW	40
Ira WHITE	Stueben	NY	July 7,1836	E½/NE	80
Caleb CURTIS	Stueben	NY	July 15,1836	NW/NE	40
Byran SIMMONS	Washtenaw	MI	Aug. 5,1836	SW/SW & E½/SW	120
Patrick SMITH	Washtenaw	MI	Aug. 5,1836	NW/SW	40
Asahel DIBBLE	Livingston	MI	Nov. 3,1836	SW/SE	40

Section 30

Name	County	State	Date	Description	Acres
Rueben MOORE	Washtenaw	MI	Oct. 27,1835	W½/NE	80
Richard BRITTEN	Washtenaw	MI	Mar. 26,1836	E½/NE	80
John JENNINGS	Washtenaw	MI	June 17,1836	NE/NW	40
Enoch WEBSTER	Stueben	NY	June 22,1836	SE/NW	40
Patrick SMITH	Washtenaw	MI	Aug. 5,1836	E½/SE	80
Samuel SEWALL	Wayne	MI	Dec. 19,1836	W½/SE	80
William L TOMPKINS	Livingston	MI	Dec. 29,1836	NE/SW	40
Jonathan P KING	Mackinaw	MI	Jan. 11,1837	Wp/SWf	95
Nicholas FISHBECK	Livingston	MI	Jan. 20,1836	SE/SW	40
Jacob D GALL	Livingston	MI	Aug. 24,1846	W½/NWf	94
Mathew BRADY	Livingston	MI	Nov. 25,1854	SW/NE & SW/NWf	87

Section 31

Name	County	State	Date	Description	Acres
John B BRITTEN	Wayne	MI	Feb. 15,1837	SE/NE	40
Samuel DEAN	Oakland	MI	Nov. 28,1837	NW/NE	40
Michael FUHAY	Livingston	MI	Dec. 12,1837	SW/SE & SE/SW	80
James COLLINS	Washtenaw	MI	Nov. 7,1837	Ep/NW	80
Joseph GROVER	Washtenaw	MI	Nov. 27,1838	NE/NE	40
Semoyer PHILIPS	Livingston	MI	Oct. 26,1838	SE/SE	40
Mathew BRADY	Livingston	MI	Jan. 2,1847	SW/SWf	45
			May 7,1850	N½/SE & N½/SWf	165
Phillip BRADY	Livingston	MI	Sept. 12,1853	NW/NWf	47

43

Genoa township

Section 32

Parley PHILLIPS	Washtenaw	MI	July 6,1836	W½/SW	80
Henry PHILLIPS	Washtenaw	MI	Aug. 2,1836	SE/SE	40
David HIGHT	Livingston	MI	Oct. 27,1836	E½/NW	80
David WELLS	Fairfield	CN	Nov. 17,1836	E½/NE	80
William BLOODWORTH	Washtenaw	MI	Jan. 16,1837	W½/NE	80
John B BRITTEN	Wayne	MI	Feb. 15,1837	NE/SE	40
Dennis TISDALE	Oakland	MI	Mar. 9,1837	E½/SW	80
Josepg GROVER	Washtenaw	MI	Nov. 27,1838	NW/NW	40
Timothy PHILLIPS	Livingston	MI	Aug. 12,1853	SW/NW	40

Section 33

Gardner CARPENTER	Washtenaw	MI	Mar. 13,1835	SE/SE	40
Easman GRIFFETH	Stueben	NY	May 18,1835	SE/SW	40
Daniel B HARMON	Livingston	NY	May 20,1836	NW/NE	40
Miltetus H SNOW	Portage	OH	May 26,1836	NE/NW	40
Fanny L SNOW	Livingston	MI	June 8,1836	SW/NE	40
Easman GRIFFITH & Rueben BENNET	Livingston	MI	June 8,1836	NE/SW	40
Christopher HOAGLAND	Livingston	MI	June 8,1836	SW/SE	40
Caleb CURTIS	Stueben	NY	July 15,1836	S½/NW	80
Jonathan STONE	Livingston	MI	June 29,1836	NW/NW & NW/SW	80
Rodney HILL	Wayne	MI	Nov. 1836	E½/NE & N½/SE	160
Dennison TISDALE Jr.	Oakland	MI	Mar. 9,1837	SW/SW	40

Section 34

Nelson HAWLEY	Lenewee	MI	June 25,1836	E½/NE	80
David WHITHEY	Ontario	NY	June 25,1836	W½/NE & E½/NW	160
Rodney HILL	Wayne	MI	Nov. 17,1836	W½/NW	80
B B KERCHIVAL	Wayne	MI	Dec. 24,1836	SW¼	160
Luther HOVEY	Monroe	MI	Dec. 23,1836	W½/SE	80
George MOON	Livingston	MI	Apr. 1837	E½/SE	80

Section 35

Samuel E CHAPMAN	Hartford	CN	Jan. 21,1836	S½/NE	80
Levi HANLEY Jr.	Lenewee	MI	June 25,1836	W½/NW	80
Joseph CHARLES	Washtenaw	MI	Nov. 22,1836	NE/NE	40
			Mar. 31,1837	NW/NE	40
*Otis WHITNEY	Ontario	NY	(Aug. 12,1837)	SE¼ & SW¼ & E½/NW	360

*(Not in tract, date is when patent given)

44

Genoa township

Section 36

Elijah FITCH	Washtenaw MI	July 29,1835	N½/NE	80
William TOWNSEND	(New York city)	Aug. 5,1835	SW¼	160
		Oct. 15,1835	W½/SE & E½/NW	160
Philip STEWERT	Livingston MI	Oct. 29,1835	S½/NE	80
Amy HAWKSHURST	(New York city)	Nov. 4,1835	E½/SE	80
George MOON	Livingston MI	Aug. 17,1837	SW/NW	40
		Dec. 14,1854	NW/NW	40

Genoa township became the home of a large German
population, mostly of the Lutheran faith.

GREEN OAK township–FIRST Land Owners

NAME	COUNTY & STATE		DATE	LAND	ACRES
Section 1					
Joel REDWAY	Allegeny	NY	Oct. 29,1832	Np/NWf	87
Ruth ALEXANDER,heirs	Washtenaw	MI	Jan. 15,1833	E½/SE	80
George W GLOVER	Allegeny	NY	May 21,1833	NEf¼ & W½/SE	242
Guy N ROBERTS	Tioga	NY	May 1,1834	W½/SW	80
	Livingston	MI	May 22,1835	SW/NW	40
John Peter CLEMENT	Washtenaw	MI	MAY 17,1834	E½/SW	80
Alexander G MELVIN	Washtenaw	MI	Oct. 19,1835	SE/NW	40
Section 2					
Joel REDWAY	Allegeny	NY	Oct. 29,1832	Np/NEf	89
John W PEAVY	Allegeny	NY	May 27,1833	Np/NWf	88
James GAGE	Oakland	MI	Oct. 1,1833	E½/SE & SE/NE	120
John S BEACH	Livingston	MI	Aug. 3,1835	SW/NE	40
William S RUSSEL	Livingston	MI	Oct. 20,1835	SE/NW	40
Joseph COLE	Potter	PA	Oct. 24,1835	W½/SW	80
Elihu RUSSELL	Washtenaw	MI	Nov. 21,1835	SW/NW	40
Erastus RADE	Albany	NY	July 15,1836	E½/SW & W½/SE	160
Section 3					
Joseph L BRIGGS	Stueben	NY	May 6,1833	NWf¼	168
William S RUSSEL	Monroe	NY	May 6,1833	NEf¼	168
Samuel COLE	Oakland	MI	May 18,1835	SE¼	160
Alonso BENNETT	Oakland	MI	May 26,1835	NE/SW	40
Ansel CLARK	Wayne	MI	July 22,1835	SW/SW	40
			July 29,1835	SE/SW	40
Harrison COE	Livingston	NY	May 14,1836	NW/SW	40
Section 4					
John DALLY	(New York city)		Apr. 13,1833	W½/SE & S½/SW	160
John C MUNDY	Washtenaw	MI	July 27,1833	NW/NWf	44
Harrison COE	Livingston	NY	May 14,1836	NE/SE	40
Rhebe BURNETT	Ontario	NY	July 6,1836	NE/NWf	44
Ira JENNINGS	Livingston	MI	Dec. 6,1836	NW/SW & SE/SE	80
Charles W PENNY	Wayne	MI	Feb. 7,1837	NEf¼	169
Thomas B EDMONDS	Wayne	MI	Feb. 28,1837	SW/NW	40
			Mar. 20,1837	SE/NW	40
John SOWLE	Livingston	MI	Dec. 8,1854	NE/SW	40

Green Oak township

Section 5

Ephriam B CORNISH	Washtenaw	MI	July 3,1832	NWf¼	166
			Aug. 7,1832	NW/NEf	43
William C RUMSEY	Washtenaw	MI	Apr. 11,1833	E½/SW & NW/SW	120
Royal C RUMSEY	Washtenaw	MI	Nov. 14,1834	W½/SE	80
	Livingston	MI	June 8,1836	E½/SE	80
Caleb M ETSON	Washtenaw	MI	May 11,1835	SW/SW	40
Augustus COTTON	Livingston	MI	May 11,1835	SW/NE	40

Section 6

William C RUMSEY	Washtenaw	MI	Apr. 11,1833	W½/Sp/NE	40
Ambrose ALEXANDER	Washtenaw	MI	June 18,1834	E½/SE	80
David KINGSBURY	Washington	VT	Oct. 29,1834	SW/SE	40
			Sept. 1,1835	NW/SE	40
Florus A HOUSE	Washtenaw	MI	Nov. 28,1834	Ep/SW	80
William B HOPKINS	Washtenaw	MI	Dec. 23,1834	E½/NEf	82
Stephen CURTIS	Washtenaw	MI	June 17,1836	SE/NW	40
Ira JENNINGS	Rutland	VT	June 22,1836	NW/NE	40
Ebenezer THOMAS	Stueben	NY	June 22,1836	E½/Wp/SWf	67
John FARNSWORTH	Washtenaw	MI	July 15,1836	SW/NWf	67
Harry MEECH	Livingston	MI	Apr. 8,1837	W½/Np/SWf	67
John CHARLES	Washtenaw	MI	Dec. 16,1836	NE/NWf	57
Horace CUTLER	Livingston	MI	Oct. 31,1836	NW/NWf	57

Section 7

Horace CUTLER	Orleans	NY	Oct. 29,1834	E½/NE	80
Mary FULLER	Oneida	NY	June 29,1835	W½/NE	80
Orlando A FULLER	Oneida	NY	June 29,1835	Ep/NWf & SW/SWf	147
James HARWICK	Orleans	NY	Apr. 28,1836	N½/SE	80
Jefferson J M NEWCOMB	Livingston	MI	July 2,1836	SE/SE	40
Harry MEECH	Livingston	MI	Apr. 8,1837	N½/SWf	107
Ephriam MEECH	Livingston	MI	Apr. 21,1837	SE/SW	40
William CASE	Washtenaw	MI	May 19,1840	W½/NWf	67
Samuel McCOSKRY	Wayne	MI	Jan. 2,1845	SW/SE	40
Henry S THOMAS	Livingston	MI	June 23,1847	E½/NWf	67

Green Oak township

Section 8

Isaac SMITH Jr.	Washtenaw	MI	Dec. 10,1832	SE/SE	40
Samuel HUBBARD	Washtenaw	MI	June 20,1833	NE/SE	40
Elon FARNSWORTH	(Detroit, MI)		Nov. 16,1833	E½/NW	80
Nehemiah O SARGENT	Wayne	MI	Dec. 4,1833	SW¼	160
Ambrose ALEXANDER	Wayne	MI	Dec. 4,1833	N½/NW	80
Ira JENNINGS	Rutland	VT	June 23,1836	E½/NE	80
H HAWKINS &					
V R HAWKINS	Genessee	NY	July 5,1836	W½/NE & W½/SE	160

Section 9

Isaac SMITH	Washtenaw	MI	Dec. 10,1832	SW/SW	40
Asahel HUBBARD	Washtenaw	MI	May 28,1834	NW/SW	40
Jason CLARK	Livingston	MI	June 3,1835	E½/NW & NW/NE	
				& SE/NE	160
			Nov. 25,1835	SW/NE	40
Katherine SMITH	Livingston	MI	Feb. 6,1836	SE/SW	40
Ira JENNINGS	Rutland	VT	June 8,1836	NE/NE	40
			June 23,1836	W½/NW	80
Mathew BRADY	Livingston	MI	July 8,1836	E½/SE	80
Bridget CRAIGHAM	Livingston	MI	Aug. 5,1836	SW/SE	40
Terence ROE	Washtenaw	MI	Oct. 27,1836	NE/SW & NW/SE	80

Section 10

Terence ROE	Washtenaw	MI	Oct. 27,1836	NW/SW & SE/NW	80
Patrick ROE	Genessee	NY	June 13,1832	SE¼	160
Michael ROCHE	Livingston	MI	Aug. 14,1832	E½/SW	80
Royal C RUMSEY	Livingston	MI	Nov. 14,1834	NW/NW	40
	Washtenaw	MI	Jan. 30,1836	SW/NW	40
Charles STEWARD	Livingston	MI	Nov. 17,1834	E½/NE	80
Richard TONCRAY	Livingston	MI	Dec. 23,1834	SW/NE	40
Ansel CLARK	Wayne	MI	July 22,1835	NE/NW	40
John A VAN CAMP	Livingston	MI	Sept. 21,1835	SW/NE	40
Patrick McNAMEE	Livingston	MI	Aug. 2,1836	SW/SW	40

Green Oak township

Section 11

Name	County	State	Date	Description	Acres
Warren PARKER	Wayne	MI	June 8,1832	E½/NE & NE/SE	120
Thomas HAMMER	Wayne	MI	June 13,1832	SW¼	160
Alanson GLAZIER	Washtenaw	MI	June 27,1832	SW/NE & NW/SE	80
Michael CARRIGAN	Wayne	MI	May 5,1834	SW/SE	40
Enos COLE	Livingston	MI	Nov. 2,1835	NE/NW	40
Gilbert C BEDELL	Washtenaw	MI	Nov. 3,1835	SE/SE	40
			Jan. 25,1836	SE/NW	40
Oliver CARPENTER	Livingston	MI	May 12,1836	W½/NW	80
Erastus SLADE	Albany	NY	July 15,1836	NW/NE	40

Section 12

Name	County	State	Date	Description	Acres
Jay OLMSTED	Onondaga	NY	June 7,1832	W½/of Sec.	320
Pelig COREY	Onondaga	NY	June 8,1832	SE¼	160
Joseph LOREE	Stueben	NY	June 8,1832	NE¼	160

Section 13

Name	County	State	Date	Description	Acres
Elihu GUNNISON	Washtenaw	MI	June 27,1832	E½/NE & SW/NE	120
Sylvester SCOTT	Washtenaw	MI	Nov. 29,1832	W½/SE	80
Nathan LELAND	Washtenaw	MI	May 23,1833	NE/SW	40
John HAGADOME	Stueben	NY	May 15,1834	E½/SE	80
Asa BLY Jr.	Madison	NY	July 12,1834	NW/SW & SE/SW	80
Joseph LOREE	Washtenaw	MI	Oct. 20,1835	NW/NE	40
Robert WARDEN	Livingston	MI	Oct. 27,1835	NW/NW	40
Kingsley S BINGHAM	Livingston	MI	Oct. 27,1835	NE/NW	40
John HERRINGTON	Livingston	MI	Nov. 10,1835	S½/NW	80
John GATES	Oakland	MI	Aug. 2,1836	SW/SW	40

Section 14

Name	County	State	Date	Description	Acres
Terence ROE	Livingston	MI	Nov. 13,1833	SW/NW & NE/NW	80
Isaac CARMER	Ontario	NY	Mar. 6,1834	SE/NW	40
Cornelius CORSON	Ontario	NY	Mar. 6,1834	N½/SW	80
Arnold HAYS	Oakland	MI	May 19,1834	S½/SW	80
	Livingston	NY	June 18,1834	W½/SE	80
Asa BLY Jr.	Madison	NY	July 12,1834	E½/NE	80
Michael CORRIGAN	Livingston	MI	Dec. 11,1835	NW/NW	40
Benjamin ROGERS	Dutchess	NY	June 14,1836	E½/SE	80
Kingsley S BINGHAM & Robert WARDEN Jr.	Washtenaw	MI	Nov. 23,1835	W½/NE	80

49

Green Oak township

Section 15

Name	County	State	Date	Description	Acres
Kingsley S BINGHAM &					
Robert WARDEN	Livingston	MI	Dec. 29,1835	SW/SE	40
			Aug. 2,1836	SW/NW	40
Ammon BLAIN	Washtenaw	MI	Aug. 23,1832	SE/NW	40
Thomas CASEY	Washtenaw	MI	Sept. 5,1832	E½/SW	80
Roger HADICAN	Washtenaw	MI	Sept. 12,1832	W½/SW	80
John SHEARLIN	Washtenaw	MI	Sept. 13,1832	NW/NW	40
John AIKIN	Washtenaw	MI	July 30,1833	SW/NE	40
Elizabeth AIKEN	Washtenaw	MI	July 30,1833	E½/NE	80
Patrick McNAMEE	Wayne	MI	May 12,1834	NW/NE & NE/NW	80
Michael CASEY	Wayne	MI	May 24,1834	NW/SE	40
Patrick BRADY	Washtenaw	MI	Oct. 11,1834	E½/SE	80

Section 16

Name	County	State	Date	Description	Acres
James HEMMEL			July 18,1840	NE/NE	40
N F McCABE			Oct. 29,1842	W½/NE	80
John HANNAN			July 6,1843	SE/NE	40
Thomas ANDERSON			Nov. 26,1845	SE/NW	40
			Jan. 12,1848	SW/NW	40
R HEDICAN			July 6,1847	SE/SE	40
Daniel CAMP			July 26,1847	NW/SW	40
M McCABE			July 25,1848	NE/NW	40
James ANDREWS			Sept. 19,1848	NW/SE	40
J J RYAN			Dec. 4,1849	SW/SE	40
Patrick McCABE			May 5,1852	NE/SE	40
F ANDREWS			June 29,1853	MW/NW	40
H M McCABE			Apr. 17,1848	NE/SW	40
Mary KELLEY			Apr. 11,1855	SW/SW & SE/SW	80

Section 17

Name	County	State	Date	Description	Acres
Isaac APPLETON	Tompkins	NY	Oct. 26,1830	SWf¼	127
Henry D BARTO	Washtenaw	MI	June 16,1831	Ep/SEf	77
Sherman D DIX	Washtenaw	MI	May 14,1832	Ep/NWf	82
Nathaniel POTTER Jr.	Erie	NY	Aug. 6,1832	NW/NE	40
Benjamin DIX	Middlesex	MA	July 11,1833	Wp/NWf	78
Robert CALDER Jr.	Middlesex	MA	May 30,1834	Wp/SEf	96
Harvey P SMITH	Washtenaw	MI	July 9,1834	NE/NE	40
Charles C TROWBRIDGE	Wayne	MI	June 14,1836	SW/NE	40
Horace BARNUM	Livingston	MI	Sept. 24,1836	SE/NE	40

Green Oak township

Section 18

Name	County	State	Date	Description	Acres
Nehemiah O SARGENT	Wayne	MI	Dec. 4,1833	NEf$\frac{1}{4}$ & NW/SE	238
			Dec. 16,1833	Ep/NWf & N$\frac{1}{2}$SW	186
Robert CALDER Jr.	Middlesex	MA	May 30,1834	Sp/of SEC.	153
Charles C TROWBRIDGE	Wayne	MI	June 14,1836	Wp/NWf	67
William B HOPKINS	Livingston	MI	July 2,1836	Center NWf	67

Section 19

Name	County	State	Date	Description	Acres
Moses GLEASON	Tompkins	NY	June 14,1831	Ep.NW	80
Daniel APPLETON	Tompkins	NY	June 14,1831	NE$\frac{1}{4}$	160
Johnathan BURNET	Livingston	MI	May 30,1834	SE/SW & SW/SE	80
Jason G DEWOLF	Livingston	MI	June 3,1834	SW/SWf	66
Thomas SARGENT	Middlesex	MA	Sept. 23,1834	Wp/NWf	135
Grace PENOYER	Washtenaw	MI	Nov. 21,1834	NE/SW	40
			Mar. 25,1835	NW/SE	40
Phebe BURNET	Ontario	NY	July 6,1835	E$\frac{1}{2}$/SE	80
Nancy PENOYER	Washtenaw	MI	Feb. 13,1837	NW/SWf	66

Section 20

Name	County	State	Date	Description	Acres
Stephen LEE	Washtenaw	MI	Oct. 6,1830	E$\frac{1}{2}$/NWf	79
Benjamin CURTIS	Washtenaw	MI	Oct. 6,1830	W$\frac{1}{2}$/NEf	67
Henry D BARTS	Washtenaw	MI	June 16,1831	Np/NEf	14
James LOVE	Washtenaw	MI	Dec. 10,1832	Ep/NEf	71
George H EMONS	Washtenaw	MI	July 2,1833	SW/NW	40
George BURNETT	Livingston	MI	June 11,1836	W$\frac{1}{2}$/SW	80
Clarissa SEARS	Wayne	MI	June 15,1836	E$\frac{1}{2}$/SE	80
Paul SEARS	Wayne	MI	June 15,1836	W$\frac{1}{2}$/SE	80
George BUTLER	Livingston	MI	July 7,1836	NW/NW	40
Phebe BURNETT	Ontario	NY	July 7,1836	E$\frac{1}{2}$/SW	80

Section 21

Name	County	State	Date	Description	Acres
Nathaniel GOTT	Washtenaw	MI	Oct. 13,1831	E$\frac{1}{2}$/SE	80
John D BORDEN	Montgomery	NY	Feb. 16,1832	E$\frac{1}{2}$/NE	80
Oliver CARPENTER	Washtenaw	MI	Sept. 14,1832	NW/NE	40
Arnold PAYNE	Washtenaw	MI	Nov. 13,1832	SW/SW	40
Epenetus HOWE	Cayuga	NY	June 30,1835	NW$\frac{1}{4}$	160
Betsey ORTON	Washtenaw	MI	Oct. 20,1835	NW/SW	40
Timothy LYON	Wayne	MI	Mar. 22,1836	W$\frac{1}{2}$/SE & E$\frac{1}{2}$/SW	
				& SW/NE	200

Green Oak township

Section 22

Nathaniel GREEN	Sullivan	NY	Aug. 29,1832	NE/SW	40
Ammon BLAIN	Washtenaw	MI	June 4,1833	NE/NW	40
Moses THOMPSON	Herkimer	NY	June 12,1833	E½/NE	80
Sally Ann BOWEN	Wayne	MI	Oct. 20,1835	N½/SE	80
Lucy BLAIN	Washtenaw	MI	Nov. 23,1835	NW/NE	40
William W DEAN	Livingston	NY	July 16,1836	SW/NE & SW/SW	80
James P CLEMENTS	Washtenaw	MI	Sept. 21,1836	SE/SW	40
			Mar. 2,1837	SW/SE	40
John E SCHWARZ	Wayne	MI	Sept. 23,1836	NW/NW	40
George MENZIE	Madison	NY	June 27,1837	S½/NW	80
Alonzo W OLDS	Livingston	MI	June 29,1849	SE/SE	40
Stephen TINKER	Livingston	MI	Nov. 25,1855	NW/SW	40

Section 23

Moses THOMPSON	Herkimer	NY	June 12,1833	W½/NW	80
			July 18,1833	E½/SW & E½/NE & SW/NE	200
Ives SMITH	Oakland	MI	July 2,1833	SE¼	160
			May 25,1836	E½/NW	80
James M BROWN	Oakland	MI	Apr. 9,1836	SW/SW	40
William W DEAN	Livingston	NY	July 16,1836	NW/SW	40
William HANNON	Livingston	MI	Nov. 21,1836	NW/NE	40

Section 24

Alexander DUNCAN	Wayne	MI	Jan. 1,1834	NE/NE	40
Nathan LELAND	Livingston	MI	July 31,1834	NE/NW	40
Orange SEARS	Washtenaw	MI	Jan. 29,1833	SE/SW	40
Mary BROWN	Oakland	MI	June 4,1835	SW/SE	40
Richard TURNEY	Livingston	MI	June 4,1836	SE/SE	40
Joseph BERRY	Cayuga	NY	June 22,1836	N½/SW	80
Henry H BINGHAM	Livingston	MI	Aug. 2,1836	NW/NW	40
Charles BORDEN	Oakland	MI	Nov. 29,1836	SW/NW	40
William HAGADOME	Livingston	MI	Jan. 3,1837	NW/NE	40
Mary LELAND	Livingston	MI	Jan. 20,1837	SE/NW	40
William SLYFIELD	Livingston	MI	July 29,1838	SW/SW	40
			May 16,1838	NW/SE	40
William L WEBB	Oakland	MI	Jan. 23,1855	SW/NE & NE/SE	80
John SAYRES	Livingston	MI	Dec. 13,1853	SE/NE	40

Green Oak township

Section 25

Allen W DAILEY	Stueben	NY	Oct. 5,1833	E½/NE	80
James GREADY	Oakland	MI	Nov. 1,1833	NE/SE	40
Robert R THOMPSON	Washtenaw	MI	Dec. 10,1833	NE/SW	40
Ambrose W BORDEN	Stueben	NY	May 28,1835	W½/NE	80
John HOOPER	Wayne	MI	July 2,1835	W½/NW	80
			Aug. 11,1835	NW/SW	40
James DEFORREST	Livingston	MI	Nov. 7,1835	SW/SW	40
Jonas MANTERSTOCK	Livingston	MI	Dec. 30,1836	SE/SE	40
William W DEAN	Livingston	MI	Jan. 21,1837	SE/NW	40
James HANCHETT	Livingston	MI	June 13,1837	SE/SW	40
William SLYFIELD	Oakland	MI	June 27,1837	NE/NW	40
George GREADY	Livingston	MI	Nov. 28,1854	SW/SE	40

Section 26

David MEECH	Cayuga	NY	June 6,1831	E½/NW & W½/NE	
				E½/SW & W½/SE	320
	Wayne	MI	July 20,1831	W½/SW	80
John CUMMINGS	Cayuga	NY	June 18,1833	E½/SE	80
Ives SMITH	Oakland	MI	July 2,1833	NW/NW	40
Seymour GOODALE	Ontario	NY	May 15,1834	E½/NE	80
Alonzo W OLDS	Livingston	NY	May 29,1840	SW/NW	40

Section 27

Ariel Y OLDS	Oakland	MI	Aug. 30,1833	NW/SW	40
Alonzo W OLDS	Livingston	MI	Dec. 25,1833	NE/SE	40
Harry MEECH	Washtenaw	MI	Feb. 13,1834	NW/SE	40
Webster TOMER	Stueben	NY	June 4,1835	NE/NE	40
George MEECH	Washtenaw	MI	Oct. 9,1835	SE/SE	40
John S BENNET	Livingston	MI	June 18,1836	SE/SW	40
Ezra ROBINSON	Washtenaw	MI	June 18,1836	SW/SW	40
Nelson H WING	Washtenaw	MI	July 1,1836	NW¼	160
Patrick HANNAN	Livingston	MI	Nov. 21,1836	SW/SE	40
Warren CLARK	Livingston	MI	Apr. 6,1853	NW/NE	40
Stephen TINKER Jr.	Livingston	MI	Jan. 3,1854	NE/SW	40

Green Oak township

Section 28

Jared HAINES	Morris	NY	Apr. 22,1831	NW$\frac{1}{4}$	160
Nathaniel GOTT	Washtenaw	MI	Aug. 7,1832	NW/NE	40
Ariel Y OLDS	Oakland	MI	Aug. 30,1833	NE/SE	40
Edward F OLDS	Oakland	MI	Aug. 30,1833	W$\frac{1}{2}$/SE & SE/NE	120
Frederick SMITH	Washtenaw	MI	Dec. 3,1836	SW/NE	40
Gilbert G BEDELL	Washtenaw	MI	Jan. 25,1836	E$\frac{1}{2}$/SW	80
Henry STANSELL	Livingston	MI	July 16,1836	NE/NE	40
James HANCHETT	Livingston	MI	Sept. 23,1836	W$\frac{1}{2}$/SW	80
Leroy H BURT	Washtenaw	MI	Sept. 23,1836	SE/SE	40

Section 29

William KERNAN	Stueben	NY	Apr. 24,1832	SW$\frac{1}{4}$ & W$\frac{1}{2}$/SE	240
Ambrose ALEXANDER	Washtenaw	MI	June 18,1834	SW/NE	40
James TOMPKINS	Niagara	NY	June 19,1834	E$\frac{1}{2}$/NE & NW/NE	120
Parley GARDNER	Niagara	NY	June 24,1836	SW/NW	40
William H MOORE	Oakland	MI	Aug. 6,1836	NW/NW	40
James HANCHETT	Livingston	NY	Sept. 23,1836	SE/SE	40
Levi KNIGHT	Livingston	MI	Oct. 31,1836	E$\frac{1}{2}$/NW	80
*(James D TUTTLE)				NE/SE	40

Section 30

William KERNAN	Stueben	NY	Apr. 24,1832	E$\frac{1}{2}$/SE	80
Johnathan HAIGHT	Stueben	NY	Oct. 15,1833	SW/SE & SE/SW	80
Eliza W BROCKWAY	Washtenaw	MI	Nov. 4,1833	SW/SWf	66
Caleb SAWYER	Cataragus	NY	May 16,1834	NW/NWf	66
Jason G DEWOLF	Livingston	MI	Oct. 15,1834	NE/NW	40
Isaac PENOYER	Washtenaw	MI	Mar. 25,1835	NW/SE	40
Stephen DRAPER	Livingston	MI	May 4,1836	SW/NWf	66
James BURNETT	Livingston	MI	June 5,1836	Np/SWf	106
George BURNETT	Livingston	MI	June 11,1836	SE/NW	40
Parley GARDNER	Livingston	MI	June 24,1836	SE/NE	40
Michael CARBERY	Wayne	MI	Oct. 27,1836	W$\frac{1}{2}$/NE	80
Zelotes TRUENDALE	Livingston	MI	Dec. 25,1854	NE/NE	40

*(he was of Green Oak township)

Green Oak township

Section 31

Name	County	State	Date	Description	Acres
William LEMON	Livingston	NY	May 24,1834	SWf¼ & W½/SE	293
	Livingston	MI	Jan. 14,1836	SW/NE	40
George W DEXTER	Washtenaw	MI	Aug. 12,1834	E½/SE	80
Cornelius W MILLER	Stueben	NY	Oct. 7,1834	W½/Wp/NWf	66
Thomas TUTHILL	Cayuga	NY	May 20,1833	SE/NW	40
				Ep/Np/NWf	66
	Livingston	MI	Oct. 18,1833	NE/NW	40
George GALLOWAY	Livingston	MI	Oct. 7,1833	N½/NE	80
Eldad S FIELD	Livingston	MI	Nov. 29,1836	SE/NE	40

Section 32

Name	County	State	Date	Description	Acres
Thomas F PETTIS	Chenango	NY	Sept. 16,1835	W½/SW	80
John L TUTHILL	Washtenaw	MI	Aug. 31,1832	NE/NW & NW/NE	80
Thomas DOSSET	(Detroit,Mi)		May 22,1833	NE/SW	40
Isaac ELA	Wayne	MI	May 20,1834	SE/NW	40
James TOMPKINS	Niagara	NY	June 19,1834	NW/NW	40
Arthur B PERRY	Wayne	MI	Dec. 1,1835	NE/NE	40
Eldad S FIELD	Livingston	MI	Nov. 29,1836	SW/NW	40
Joseph ROBINSON	Wayne	MI	Jan. 17,1837	NW/SE	40
John GARRISON	Wayne	MI	Jan. 17,1837	S½/NE & SE/SW	120
George S WHEELER	Livingston	MI	June 10,1862	SE/SE	40

Section 33

Name	County	State	Date	Description	Acres
Stephen DEXTER	Wayne	MI	Sept. 4,1830	W½/SW	80
Sylvester R PERRY	Washtenaw	MI	Aug. 26,1833	SW/NW	40
John BOYLE	Hampden	MA	Nov. 2,1833	NE¼ & E½/NW	240
James McMAHON	Livingston	MI	Nov. 28,1833	NE/SE	40
Dennis BURNS	Susquehanna	PA	May 30,1834	NW/SE	40
Patrick GILLIGAN	Wayne	MI	Aug. 30,1834	SE/SE	40
James HANCHET	Livingston	NY	Sept. 23,1836	NW/NW	40
John McGOIREN	Washtenaw	MI	Aug. 13,1838	SE/SW	40
Emery BEAL	Livingston	MI	Oct. 12,1839	SW/SE	40
James CONLAN	Livingston	MI	Sept. 13,1847	SE/SW	40

Green Oak township

Section 34

John B HAMMOND	Livingston	NY	May 23,1831	E½/SE	80
Amsley S AMES	Oakland	MI	May 24,1833	E½/NE	80
James HYNES	Luzerne	PA	Sept. 21,1833	W½/SW	80
John S BENNET	Washtenaw	MI	Dec. 6,1833	W½/SE & W½/NE	160
Timothy McCARTHY	Newport	RI	Apr. 28,1834	NW¼ & E½/SW	240

Section 35

John B HAMMOND	Livingston	NY	May 23,1831	SW¼	160
Micajah WILLITS	Wayne	NY	June 18,1831	E½/SE	80
Henry HAYWARD	Ontario	NY	June 18,1831	W½/SE	80
Manly SMITH	Wayne	MI	Nov. 11,1831	E½/NE	80
Ephriam MEECH	Wayne	MI	June 25,1832	W½/NE & E½/NW	160
John STARKWEATHER	Wayne	MI	Nov. 24,1832	W½/NW	80

Section 36

Benjamin WELCH	Wayne	MI	June 15,1831	W½/SW	80
John H CARLETON	Wayne	MI	June 8,1832	W½/NW	80
Luzen TOWZEY	Wayne	MI	June 23,1832	W½/SE	80
Elias DEAN	Cayuga	NY	Aug. 20,1832	SE/SE	40
Ansley S AMES	Oakland	MI	May 24,1833	E½/SW	80
Henry MEECH	Cayuga	NY	June 24,1833	E½/NW	80
Alonzo W OLDS	Oakland	MI	July 12,1833	NE/NE	40
Thomas MALONE	Wayne	MI	Oct. 27,1836	W½/NE & SE/NE	120
Adam J COONS	Washtenaw	MI	June 10,1839	NE/SE	40

HAMBURG township-FIRST Land Owners

NAME	COUNTY & STATE		DATE	LAND	ACRES
Section 1					
Amrod MOON	Niagara	NY	Apr. 25,1836	SEf¼	137
Robert L SPEAR	Wayne	MI	July 1,1836	E½/SW	80
Nelson H WING	Washtenaw	MI	July 15,1836	SE¼	160
Sanford BRITTON	Wayne	MI	Mar. 8,1837	W½/SW	80
George WALKER	Livingston	MI	Mar. 22,1837	NWf¼	160
Section 2					
Franklin HOPKINS	Oakland	MI	July 13,1836	SW/SW	40
Joseph BROWN	Livingston	MI	Feb. 6,1838	SW/SE	40
Joseph NUTE	Stueben	NY	June 11,1838	SE/NEf &	
				NE/NEf	70
Ezekial CASE	Washtenaw	MI	Sept. 29,1840	NE/SE	40
	Livingston	MI	Oct. 16,1845	NW/SE	40
			July 8,1847	NE/SW	40
			Nov. 9,1849	SW/NE	40
William PURVIS	Livingston	MI	Nov. 10,1840	SE/SE	40
Isaac W APPLETON	Washtenaw	MI	Mar. 15,1845	SW/NW	40
			May 3,1845	Np/NWf	60
			Dec. 8,1854	SE/NW	40
Timothy PHILIPS	Livingston	MI	Aug. 12,1853	SE/SW	40
John S BENNETT	Livingston	MI	Nov. 15,1854	NW/NE	40
Luther JEFFERD	Livingston	MI	Dec. 8,1854	NW/SW	40
Section 3					
John STEWART	Livingston	MI	Mar. 16,1836	NW/NEf &	
				NE/NWf	60
Mary STEWART	Livingston	MI	May 26,1836	SE/NW	40
Horace GRIFFETH	Stueben	NY	June 22,1836	NE/SE	40
Ralph SWARTHOUT	Livingston	MI	Aug. 1,1836	W½/SW & NE/SW	
				SW/NW	160
Jabez HOPKINS	Wayne	MI	Sept. 25,1837	NW/SE	40
Luther JEFFERDS	Washtenaw	MI	Aug. 9,1842	SW/NE	40
	Livingston	MI	Sept. 20,1848	SW/SE	40
			Dec. 8,1854	SE/NE	40
James HUMPHREYS	Livingston	MI	Sept. 23,1850	SE/SW	40
Chancey A STEWART	Livingston	MI	Mar. 27,1845	NE/NEf	30
			June 12,1854	NW/NWf	30

Hamburg township

Section 4

Name	County	State	Date	Description	Acres
Justus J BENNETT	Washtenaw	MI	Oct. 2,1834	E½/SW	80
			May 13,1835	W½/SE	80
	Livingston	MI	Aug. 2,1835	E½/SE	80
Timothy A PETTIT	Livingston	MI	May 7,1835	Sp/NEf	80
Eastman GRIFFITH	Stueben	NY	May 18,1835	NWf¼	138
Christopher HOAGLAND	Washtenaw	MI	July 21,1835	Np/NEf	60
John SPAULDING	Livingston	MI	July 18,1837	SW/SW	40
Mitchel C CASE	Wayne	MI	Aug. 22,1838	NW/SW	40

Section 5

Name	County	State	Date	Description	Acres
Joseph CASE	Oswego	NY	May 9,1836	NEf¼	135
Elisha CASE	Oswego	NY	May 9,1836	Np/NWf &	
				SE/NWf	90
	Livingston	MI	Sept. 21,1836	SW/NW	40
			Sept. 22,1841	NW/SW	40
Samuel CASE	Livingston	MI	Jan. 26,1838	NE/SW	40
Simeon D SALMON	Washtenaw	MI	May 24,1838	SE/SW	40
	Livingston	MI	Sept. 20,1838	SW/SW	40
Spaulding M CASE	Wayne	MI	Aug. 22,1838	NW/SE	40
Daniel HALLECK	Genessee	NY	Sept. 17,1838	E½/SE	80
Rodman CASE	Ontario	NY	Sept. 22,1838	SW/SE	40

Section 6

Name	County	State	Date	Description	Acres
William WHITE	Ontario	NY	Aug. 6,1836	SW/SWf	49
Samuel TAYLOR	Wayne	MI	Jan. 23,1837	NEf¼	130
	Washtenaw	MI	Feb. 27,1837	NE/SE	40
Lorenzo JORDEN	Livingston	MI	Dec. 16,1838	SW/SE	40
			Oct. 2,1838	NE/SW	40
James V SIMONS	Wayne	MI	Apr. 16,1839	Np/NWf	63
Joseph CASE	Livingston	MI	Oct. 6,1841	SE/SW	40
Simeon D SALMON	Livingston	MI	June 3,1849	NW/SE & SE/SE	80
James HAYNES	Livingston	MI	July 28,1853	SE/NW	40
William H PROME	Montgomery	NY	Aug. 12,1853	NW/SW	40
(Elisha CASE)				SW/NWf	49

Hamburg township

Section 7
William H BENNETT	Washtenaw	MI	Jan. 7,1835	E½/SE & SW/SE	120
Henry FARRELL	Washtenaw	MI	May 17,1836	E½/NE	80
Richard BURKE	Wayne	MI	May 17,1836	W½/NE	80
Amariah HAMMOND	Washtenaw	MI	May 20,1836	NW/SE	40
David BENNETT	Stueben	NY	June 4,1836	SW/NWf & NW/SWf	97
Elizabeth M WHITE	Orleans	NY	Aug. 6,1836	Ep/NWf & NW/SWf	129
Anna PORTER	Orleans	NY	Aug. 6,1836	Ep/SWf	80
Jesse D HAUSE	Livingston	MI	Sept. 6,1838	SW/SWf	48

Section 8
Justus J BENNETT	Washtenaw	MI	Oct. 2,1834	E½/SE	80
John DAVIS	Washtenaw	MI	Mar. 13,1835	W½/SE & SW/NE & SE/NE	160
Elijah BENNETT	Livingston	MI	July 14,1835	E½/SE	80
	Livingston	NY	May 26,1835	SE/NW	40
George MERCER	Livingston	MI	Aug. 3,1835	E½/NE	80
Robert SAUNDERS	Wayne	MI	Dec. 5,1835	NW/NE	40
Henry A WELLER	Wayne	MI	Jan. 7,1837	NE/NW	40
Simeon D SALMON	Livingston	MI	SEpt. 28,1838	NW/NW	40
Henry FARRELL	Livingston	MI	Oct. 2,1839	NW/SW	40
Elias DAVIS	Livingston	Mi	Apr. 10,1854	SW/SW	40

Section 9
Justus J BENNETT	Washtenaw	MI	Oct. 2,1834	W½/SW & SE/NW	120
			Mar. 13,1835	W½/NE	80
			June 5,1846	NE/NE	40
Daniel HARMON	Washtenaw	MI	Oct. 2,1834	E½/SW	80
Rueben H BENNETT	Washtenaw	MI	Mar. 13,1835	NE/NW	40
George MERCER	Livingston	MI	Nov. 23,1835	NW/SE	40
			June 10,1836	SW/SW	40
William H BENNETT	Livingston	MI	July 16,1836	E½/SE	80
Cornelius WICKWARE	Wayne	MI	Aug. 8,1836	SW/SE	40
*Edward M CUST	Livingston	MI	Mar. 5,1845	NW/NW	40
Daniel S BENNETT	Livingston	MI	June 20,1854	SE/NE	40

*(Michigan State Senator, 1848; born England)

Hamburg township

Section 10

Edward BISHOP	Yates	NY	July 15,1836	E½/NE	80
Spaulding M CASE	Wayne	NY	Aug. 2,1836	W½/NE	80
John WEBBER	Wayne	MI	Sept. 24,1836	SW/SW	40
Thomas LOOMIS	Yates	NY	Oct. 27,1836	SE¼	160
William COOLBAUGH	Yates	NY	Oct. 27,1836	E½/SW	80
William B SCOTT	Livingston	MI	May 18,1847	E½/NW	80
Edwin M CUST	Livingston	MI	Jan. 20,1851	NW/SW	40
Isaac T VANDUSEN	Livingston	MI	June 20,1854	W½/NW	80

Section 11

David PARKER	Washtenaw	MI	July 27,1835	E½/SE	80
John BASSET	Cayuga	NY	May 27,1836	NE¼	160
Rueben NEWLAND	Cayuga	NY	May 27,1836	E½/SW	80
Franklin HOPKINS	Oakland	MI	July 13,1836	NW/NW	40
Daniel C KINGSLAND	(New York city)		Oct. 27,1836	W½/SE & W½/SW	
				E½/NW & SW/NW	280

Section 12

Abraham D PECK	Washtenaw	MI	Sept. 26,1832	SE/NW	40
	Livingston	MI	Nov. 2,1836	SW/NW	40
Abraham BENNETT	Washtenaw	MI	July 10,1835	SW/SE	40
David PARKER	Washtenaw	MI	July 27,1835	SW¼ & SE/SE	200
Joseph H BENNETT	Washtenaw	MI	June 20,1836	W½/NE & NW/SE	120
Conrad HANER	Washtenaw	MI	June 24,1836	NE/NE	40
Henry KELLOG	Livingston	MI	Aug. 2,1836	NE/NW	40
Gary SPENCER	Wayne	MI	Mar. 8,1837	NW/NW	40
David A PARKHILL	Livingston	MI	Apr. 1,1837	NE/SE	40
Bradford CAMPBELL	Livingston	MI	May 31,1853	SE/NE	40

Section 13

George J GRISSON	Livingston	MI	Oct. 22,1834	SE/SEf	23
Alonzo GUNN	Livingston	MI	Feb. 17,1835	E½/NW	80
David PARKER	Livingston	MI	Oct. 16,1836	E½/SW	80
			May 6,1842	NW/NE	40
Miner KELLOG	Livingston	MI	Dec. 16,1836	SW/SW	40
Jacob C HANER	Livingston	MI	May 30,1837	NW/NW	40
John PICHARD	Livingston	MI	Oct. 3,1837	SW/SEf	30
Benjamin F FOSTER	Livingston	MI	June 21,1838	SW/NW	40
Russell F HANER	Livingston	MI	Apr. 15,1854	NW/SW	40
George E HALL	Wayne	MI	Nov. 15,1854	Sp/NEf &	
				Np/SEf	178
J Louis FASQUELLE	Washtenaw	MI	Oct. 26,1859	NE/NE	40

Hamburg township

Section 14

Name	County	State	Date	Description	Acres
Conrad HANER	Livingston	MI	June 2,1835	SW/SE	40
Sophronia PERRY	Washtenaw	MI	Nov. 4,1835	SW/NE	40
			Feb. 6,1836	NE/NE	40
Emory RICHARDSON	Washtenaw	MI	Apr. 26,1836	NW/SE & SE/SW	80
Miner KELLOG	Livingston	MI	Dec. 18,1836	SE/SE	40
Levi TOWNSEN	Washtenaw	MI	Feb. 2,1837	NW¼	160
David WILKIE	Livingston	MI	Aug. 4,1842	SE/NE	40
George GALLOWAY	Washtenaw	MI	Mar. 8,1851	NE/SW	40
Thomas FEATHERLY	Livingston	MI	July 25,1851	NE/SW	40
Deborah Ann COLE	Livingston	MI	Aug. 19,1851	NW/NE	40
Russell S HANER	Livingston	MI	Dec. 1,1854	NE/SE	40
(Simeon FREEDMAN)				NW/SW	40

Section 15

Name	County	State	Date	Description	Acres
George GALLOWAY	Washtenaw	MI	July 3,1834	W½/SE	80
	Livingston	MI	Oct. 31,1836	NE/SW	40
Susan GALLOWAY	Washtenaw	MI	July 3,1834	SE/SW	40
Adonijah HARMON	Genessee	NY	June 26,1835	SE/SE	40
Eleaner COLYER	Wayne	MI	June 18,1836	W½/NW	80
Timothy PETIT	Livingston	MI	Nov. 1,1836	SW/SW	40
Jacob C HANER	Jackson	MI	Nov. 1,1836	SE/NE	40
Edward BISHOP	Wayne	MI	Nov. 5,1836	NW/SW	40
Margaret PEACOCK	Wayne	MI	Nov. 17,1836	E½/NW	80
B B KERCHIVAL	Wayne	MI	Jan. 11,1855	W½/NE & NE/NE	120
Thaddeus S MAPES	Livingston	MI	Jan. 11,1855	NE/SE	40

Section 16 (school section)

Name	Date	Description	Acres
Seth PETTEYS	Oct. 22,1842	SW/NW & NE/NW	80
	May 10,1847	NW/NW	40
L M ROLISON	Dec. 8,1845	SW/SW	40
George HOWARD	May 3,1847	NW/SW	40
E S WHITLOCK	July 23,1847	SE/SW	40
D M ROLLISON	Oct. 8,1847	SW/SE & NE/NE	80
Elisha HESS	Nov. 4,1847	NE/SW	40
William CROWE	July 12,1850	SE/NE & NW/NE	80
John CONNER	Nov. 28,1850	SW/NE	40
Mary MERCER	Feb. 26,1851	SE/SE	40
George MERCER	July 12,1851	NE/SE	40
William MERCER	May 26,1852	SE/NW	40
Robert CONNER	Sept. 7,1853	NW/SE	40

61

Hamburg township

Section 17

Zebolon M DREW	Washtenaw	MI	May 21,1835	NW/SE	40
Gideon CROSS	Washtenaw	MI	May 21,1835	SW/NE	40
Elizabeth C CROSS	Livingston	MI	June 7,1836	NE/SW	40
Daniel BENNET	Livingston	MI	July 1,1836	E½/SE	80
Henry R WHEELER	Wayne	MI	Jan. 1,1837	E½/NE	80
Jarusha PAYNE	Macomb	MI	Sept. 25,1837	SW/SE	40
Tamma BUTTS	Livingston	MI	Jan. 8,1838	NW/NE & NE/NW	80
Norman A ALLEN	Cayuga	NY	Sept. 13,1838	W½/NW	80
Cephus DUNNING	Livingston	MI	Jan. 9,1854	SE/SW	40
Joseph QUINN	Livingston	MI	Mar. 4,1854	SW/SW	40
John DUNN	Livingston	MI	Dec. 13,1853	NW/SW	40

Section 18

William H BENNET	Washtenaw	MI	Jan. 4,1835	SW/NE	40
	Livingston	MI	July 16,1836	Ep/NWf	80
Aaron VANCE	Washtenaw	MI	Nov. 20,1835	SE/SWf	40
Daniel S BENNET	Livingston	MI	Jan. 12,1836	SW/SE	40
Rueben H BENNET	Livingston	MI	May 26,1836	SW/NE	40
David BENNET	Stueben	NY	June 4,1836	NW/SE & NE/SW	80
Timothy R BENNET	Livingston	MI	June 17,1836	SE/NE	40
Mansell HURLBUT	Livingston	MI	June 6,1837	NW/SWf	48
Hezekiah ALLEN	Cayuga	NY	Sept. 13,1838	NE/NE	40
Samuel S FITCH	Livingston	MI	Dec. 18,1838	Wp/NWf	97
John H FORTH	Livingston	MI	May 1,1850	NE/SE	40
Joseph QUINN	Livingston	MI	July 7,1851	SE/SE	40
Thomas DALY				SW/SWf	48

Section 19

Samuel COLE	Ontario	NY	Oct. 20,1835	Wp/NWf & SE/NWf	136
Elijah WHIPPLE	Washtenaw	MI	Nov. 7,1835	SW/NE	40
John MARSH	Washtenaw	MI	Nov. 7,1835	NW/NE	40
Ransom C ROBINSON	Washtenaw	MI	June 30,1836	SE/NE & NE/SE	80
Isreal C TREMBLEY	Livingston	MI	July 15,1836	NE/SW	40
Joseph QUINN	Washtenaw	MI	Dec. 8,1836	NE/NE	40
Henry P ROSEBECK	Washtenaw	MI	Dec. 16,1836	NE/NW	40
John WALLACE	Onondaga	NY	May 22,1837	Wp/SWf	97
Thomas BURNS	Livingston	MI	June 13,1837	SE/SE	40
Ephriam HARGER	Monroe	NY	July 13,1837	SE/SW	40
			July 21,1837	W½/SE	80

Hamburg township

Section 20

Mathew C O'BRIEN	Washtenaw	MI	Nov. 21,1835	SE$\frac{1}{4}$	160
Enoch JONES	Wayne	MI	Feb. 5,1836	SW$\frac{1}{4}$ & E$\frac{1}{2}$/NW	
				& W$\frac{1}{2}$/NE	320
James D W PALMER	Wayne	MI	July 1,1836	SW/NW	40
Erasmus D WHITLOCK	Washtenaw	MI	Oct. 21,1836	E$\frac{1}{2}$/NE	80
Joseph QUINN	Washtenaw	MI	Dec. 8,1836	NW/NW	40

Section 21

Daniel W KELLOGG	Washtenaw	MI	Feb. 4,1836	NW$\frac{1}{4}$	160
Daniel LARKIN	Washtenaw	MI	Nov. 18,1836	NW/SW	40
John LARKIN	Washtenaw	MI	Mar. 3,1837	NW/NE	40
Rueben R DECKER	Livingston	MI	Oct. 28,1848	SW/NE	40
			July 28,1858	E$\frac{1}{2}$/SE	80
			Dec. 30,1858	E$\frac{1}{2}$/SW	80
John F OLIVER	Livingston	MI	Oct. 28,1848	NW/SE	40
William PLACEWAY	Livingston	MI	Dec. 13,1853	E$\frac{1}{2}$/NE	80
John SHAW	Livingston	MI	Jan. 11,1866	SW/SW	40
John N BERGIN				SW/SE	40

Section 22

Christopher L CULVER	Livingston	MI	Nov. 11,1833	SE/SEf	11
Edward BISHOP	Wayne	MI	Nov. 5,1836	NE/NW & NW/NE	80
	Livingston	MI	Dec. 13,1853	NE/SW	40
			Nov. 23,1854	SW/SW	40
			Dec. 20,1855	NW/SW	40
James G CRANE	Wayne	MI	Feb. 2,1837	Wp/SEf	142
Dennis SHEHAN	Livingston	MI	Nov. 2,1837	SE/NW & SW/NW	80
Francis MACKIE	Bristol	MA	June 20,1838	E$\frac{1}{2}$/NE & SW/NE	120
Edwin M CUST	Livingston	MI	Mar. 10,1842	SE/SW	40
George GALLOWAY	Livingston	MI	Dec. 13,1853	NW/NW	40

Hamburg township

Section 23

John HENRY	Madison	NY	May 20,1833	Wp/SEf & SE/NEf	169
Aseneth BURNETT	Washtenaw	MI	Jan. 15,1833	Ep/SEf	53
Edward MUNDY	Washtenaw	MI	June 20,1835	NW/NEf & Sp/NWf	99
			Feb. 26,1836	NE/NW	40
			Feb. 27,1836	NW/SWf	49
Christopher L CULVER	Livingston	MI	Jan. 11,1836	Sp/SWf	63
Miner KELLOGG	Washtenaw	MI	Feb. 26,1836	NE/NE	40
James GILLMAN	Seneca	NY	July 13,1837	NE/SWf	41
Stodard W TWITCHEL	Livingston	MI	Aug. 12,1845	NW/NW	40

Section 24

Thomas SCHOOHOVEN	Stueben	NY	May 22,1833	NWf¼	181
Aseneth BURNETT	Washtenaw	MI	June 15,1833	W½/SWf	56
George G GRISSON	Livingston	MI	June 3,1834	Ep/SWf & SW/NE	108
			Oct. 22,1834	NE/NEf	62
			July 3,1837	SE/NEf	36
George BUTLER	Livingston	MI	June 17,1836	W½/SE	40
			Feb. 13,1837	SE/SE	40
Horace BARNUM	Livingston	MI	Dec. 15,1836	NE/SE	40

Section 25

Calvin JACKSON	Livingston	MI	Sept. 22,1831	E½/SW	80
Jessie HALL	Stueben	NY	Oct. 7,1831	W½/SE & W½/SW	160
Lester BURNETT	Washtenaw	MI	Mar. 29,1832	NW¼	160
James BURNETT	Washtenaw	MI	June 15,1833	W½/NE	80
Jason G DeWOLF	Madison	NY	Oct. 8,1833	E½/NE	80
Ebenezer BLISS	Washtenaw	MI	Nov. 4,1834	E½/SE	80

Section 26

Daniel HALL	Stueben	NY	Oct. 3,1832	NE¼	160
George SESSIONS	Madison	NY	Apr. 26,1833	E½/SW & W½/SE & NE/SE	200
	Washtenaw	MI	Oct. 23,1833	SE/SE	40
Christopher L CULVER	Madison	NY	May 20,1833	NW¼	160
David B POWERS	Madison	NY	May 20,1833	W½/SW	80

Hamburg township

*Section 27
Benjamin LEWITT	Washtenaw	MI	Oct. 10,1832	SWf¼	78
David B POWERS	Madison	NY	May 20,1833	Sp/SEf	75
			Nov. 1,1833	Np/SEf	53
Christopher L CULVER	Livingston	MI	Nov. 11,1833	Ep/NEf	33
B B KERCHIVAL	Wayne	MI	Mar. 3,1837	NWf¼	78
Anson L POWERS	Livingston	MI	July 3,1840	Wp/NEf	84

*Section 28
Cyrus PIERCE	Washtenaw	MI	Mar. 11,1836	SW/NW	40
Daniel SULLIVAN	Wayne	MI	Oct. 25,1836	SE/SEf	41
Patrick GALLAGHER	Livingston	MI	Jan. 11,1837	SWf¼	120
John COURTNEY	Washtenaw	MI	Jan. 11,1837	NW/SEf	49
			Jan. 16,1837	Sp/NEf	48
James GALLAGHER	Livingston	MI	Jan. 20,1837	SW/SEf	35
B B KERCHIVAL	Wayne	MI	Mar. 3,1837	Np/NEf	75

*Section 29
James CORDLEY	Washtenaw	MI	July 17,1835	NE/SW &	
				SW/SEf	77
Robert FINCH	Washtenaw	MI	Oct. 28,1835	W½/SW & SE/SW	120
Andrew SHANAHAN	Livingston	MI	Nov. 17,1835	E½/NW	80
Cornelius O'BRIEN	Washtenaw	MI	Nov. 21,1835	W½/NW	80
Robert CROOKS	Washtenaw	MI	Dec. 24,1835	N½/NE	80
Ann CORDLEY	Livingston	MI	Mar. 31,1836	NW/SE	40
James GALLOWAY	Livingston	MI	Feb. 4,1837	Ep/SEf	64
Robert MARSH	Livingston	Mi	Nov. 8,1837	S½/NE	80

*Section 30
Thomas DALY	Washtenaw	MI	Oct. 7,1837	NW/SWf	49
Orry BUTTS	Monroe	NY	July 31,1837	NW/NE	40
William EDMINISTER	Washtenaw	MI	Sept. 17,1835	SE/SE	40
Cornelius O'BRIEN	Washtenaw	MI	Nov. 21,1836	NE/SE	40
Aaron VANCE	Washtenaw	MI	Dec. 25,1835	SW/SWf	49
Jonathan STONE Jr.	Livingston	MI	Dec. 27,1836	Ep/Sw	80
Nathaniel TEACHWORTH	Washtenaw	MI	Feb. 9,1837	SE/NW	40
Bryan &					
Owen FARLEY	Wayne	MI	May 29,1837	Wp/NWf	98
James FAGAN	Wayne	MI	May 29,1837	W½/SE	80
Ephriam HARGER	Monroe	NY	July 13,1837	NE/NW	40
			July 21,1837	E½/NE	80

* (These sections have large lakes)

Hamburg township

Section 31

Cyrus PIERCE	Washtenaw	MI	May 10,1832	Wp/SEf	39
James W McGRATH	Livingston	MI	Oct. 20,1834	Wp/SWf	89
William W EDMINISTER	Washtenaw	MI	Sept. 17,1835	NE/NE	40
Thomas BURNS	Wayne	MI	Oct. 6,1835	Ep/SWf	48
Mathew BURNS	Wayne	MI	Oct. 6,1835	SW/NE	40
Elias B ROOT	Washtenaw	MI	Nov. 7,1835	NE/NE	40
Asahel SMITH	Washtenaw	MI	Nov. 18,1835	NE/NW	40
	Livingston	MI	Sept. 8,1837	NE/NW	40
John SIMONS	Washtenaw	MI	Nov. 18,1835	NW/NE	40
Cornelius O'BRIEN	Washtenaw	MI	Dec. 11,1835	Ep/SEf	55
Patience NEWTON	Washtenaw	MI	July 15,1836	NW/NWf	49
Luceba PIERCE	Livingston	MI	Aug. 31,1837	SW/NWf	49

Section 32

Felix DUNLAVEY	Washtenaw	MI	July 6,1831	Ep/SEf	79
Patrick GALLAGHER	Washtenaw	MI	Dec. 5,1832	Wp/SEf	72
	Livingston	MI	Jan. 20,1837	NEf$\frac{1}{4}$	63
Mathew C O'BRIEN	Washtenaw	MI	Nov. 21,1835	Wp/NWf	88
	Livingston	MI	Aug. 7,1837	Ep/NWf	72
Felix DONLEVY &					
William EDMINISTER	Washtenaw	MI	Nov. 21,1835	SE/SWf	69
Palmer FORCE	Washtenaw	MI	Dec. 12,1835	NW/SWf	64

Section 33

Patrick GALLAGHER	Washtenaw	MI	Sept. 13,1832	W$\frac{1}{2}$/SW	80
			Oct. 25,1836	Wp/NWd	56
James GALLAGHER	Washtenaw	MI	Sept. 13,1832	E$\frac{1}{2}$/SW	80
			Oct. 26,1836	SE/NW	40
Cornelius MORROW	Washtenaw	MI	Mar. 16,1833	NW/SE	40
			Jan. 23,1835	W$\frac{1}{2}$/NEf	71
John RYAN	Livingston	MI	Nov. 10,1834	Ep/NEf	79
Patrick CONNOR	Wayne	MI	Aug. 1,1835	E$\frac{1}{2}$/SE	80
			Oct. 25,1836	SW/SE	40
Cornelius O'MARA	Livingston	MI	Apr. 5,1836	NE/NWf	35

Hamburg township

Section 34
Stodard W TWITCHELL	Madison	NY	May 20,1833	N½/NE		80
	Livingston	MI	Dec. 18,1835	SW/NW		40
Abner BUTTERFIELD	Madison	NY	May 28,1833	SE/NE		40
Willis HALE	Madison	NY	May 28,1833	W½/SE & SW¼		240
Daniel LARKIN	Washtenaw	MI	Sept. 4,1835	NW/NW		40
Jacob VAN DEWALKER	Washtenaw	MI	Feb. 6,1836	E½/SE		80
Levi KNIGHT	Livingston	MI	June 4,1836	SE/NW		40
Daniel SULLIVAN	Wayne	MI	Oct. 26,1836	SW/NW		40
Calvin SWIFT	Cayuga	NY	Dec. 9,1836	NE/NW		40

Section 35
Heman LAKE	Washtenaw	Mi	Oct. 28,1831	E½/SE		80
Abner BUTTERFIELD	Madison	NY	May 28,1833	NW¼ & NE/SW		200
Cornelius OLSAVER	Madison	NY	June 15,1833	SW/SE		40
Hiram MASON	Livingston	MI	May 23,1834	SW/NE		40
William H TWITCHELL	New Haven	CN	Sept. 30,1834	NW/SE		40
George W CASE	Onondaga	NY	May 13,1836	E½/NE		80
John A BOTHWELL	Washtenaw	MI	Sept. 19,1836	SE/SW		40
Samuel VANDERFORD	Washtenaw	MI	Sept. 19,1836	SW/SW		40
Elizabeth HALL	Livingston	MI	Dec. 19,1836	NW/NE		40
Richard E BUTLER	Livingston	MI	Aug. 1,1837	NW/SW		40

Section 36
Cornelius W MILLER	Stueben	NY	Oct. 7,1831	E½/SE		80
Heman LAKE	Washtenaw	MI	Oct. 28,1831	W½/SW		80
Augusta HALL	Yates	NY	Oct. 3,1832	E½/NW		80
Jesse HALL	Washtenaw	MI	June 6,1833	N½/NE		80
Phellman Handy HILL	Madison	NY	Oct. 23,1833	W½/NW		80
Thomas J RICE	Washtenaw	MI	Jan. 5,1836	SE/NE		40
	Livingston	MI	June 13,1838	NW/SE		40
Samuel GARDNER	Ashtabula	OH	June 24,1836	E½/SW & SW/SE	120
Hiram G BEACH			(June 13,1893)	SW/NE		40

NAME	COUNTY & STATE		DATE	LAND	ACRES
Section 1					
Horace W VAUGHN	Oakland	MI	Mar. 25,1836	E½/SW	80
William BARNET	Monroe	NY	Apr. 1,1836	SW/SW	40
Joseph B CRAFT	Livingston	NY	May 5,1836	NEf¼ & NE/SE	177
			May 13,1836	SE/SE	40
George CURTISS	Livingston	NY	May 9,1836	NWf¼	130
Joel BANFIELD	Tompkins	NY	June 9,1836	NW/SW	40
Richard R BUSH	Tompkins	NY	June 9,1836	W½/SW	80
Section 2					
Walty SMITH	Livingston	NY	Nov. 5,1835	E½/SW	80
Ralph FOWLER	Livingston	NY	Nov. 5,1835	W½/SW	80
Calvin HANDY	Tompkins	NY	Mar. 25,1836	SE¼ & Sp/NE	240
Frank MOORE &					
Lacarias CHANDLER	Wayne	MI	June 4,1836	NWf¼	124
Charles P BUSH	Tompkins	NY	June 9,1836	Np/NE	46
Section 3					
Ralph FOWLER	Livingston	NY	Nov. 5,1835	E½/SE	80
Charles P BUTLER	(New York city)		Apr. 2,1836	NEf¼ & NWf¼	
				SW¼ & W½/SE	490
Section 4					
John B FOWLER	Livingston	NY	Apr. 18,1836	NWf¼	124
Henry W DELEVAN	Saratoga	NY	Sept. 23,1836	SE¼ & SW¼	320
Nicholas GRUMBACH	Wayne	MI	Apr. 25,1838	Sp/NE	80
Phineas SILSBY	Wayne	MI	Aug. 7,1838	Np/NEf	45
Section 5					
Cornelius ISREAL	Wayne	MI	July 15,1836	W½/SE & E½/SW	
				& SW/SW	200
John W EDMONDS	Columbia	NY	Oct. 25,1836	E½/SE & Sp/NE	160
Gustave DeNEVEN	Genessee	NY	Nov. 5,1836	NWf¼ & NW/SW	166
			Apr. 13,1838	Np/NEf	45

Handy township

Section 6

Henry W DELEVEN	Saratoga	NY	Sept. 23,1836	SE¼	160
Ebenezer McCORMICK	Genessee	NY	Nov. 5,1836	Sp/NE	80
Gustave DeNEVEN	Genessee	NY	Apr. 14,1838	Np/NEf	49
George E ADAMS			Dec. 13,1853	NWf¼	97
John THOMAS			Dec. 13,1853	SWf¼	114

Section 7

Polly SANDERS	Washtenaw	MI	Nov. 28,1835	NW/NE	40
John B FOWLER	Livingston	NY	Apr. 18,1836	E½/NE	80
Nathan JENKS	Ontario	NY	June 14,1836	E½/SE	80
John W EDMONDS	Columbia	NY	Nov. 4,1836	NWf¼	112
Mathew STRAIGHT	Wayne	MI	Jan. 24,1837	W½/SE & SW/NE	120
George W SEE	Livingston	MI	Apr. 15,1853	SWf¼	109

Section 8

John B FOWLER	Livingston	NY	Apr. 18,1836	W½/NW	80
Flavius J B CRANE	Livingston	MI	Apr. 23,1836	E½/SE	80
Nathan JENKS	Ontario	NY	June 14,1836	SW¼	160
William C BLACKWOOD	Seneca	NY	July 13,1836	E½/NE	80
Samuel BLACKWOOD	Oakland	MI	July 13,1836	W½/NE	80
George W ISREAL	Wayne	MI	July 15,1836	E½/NW	80
Samuel BRIANT	Wayne	MI	Jan. 24,1837	W½/SE	80

Section 9

Peter A COWDREY	(New York city)		Oct. 23,1853	SE¼	160
George McINTOSH	Oakland	MI	Mar. 26,1838	W½/SW	80
Joseph LAURENCE	(New London,CN)		May 2,1838	E½/SW	80
Russell FORSYTHE	Albany	NY	Oct. 24,1838	NE¼ & NW¼	320

Section 10

Ralph FOWLER	Livingston	NY	Aug. 24,1835	SE¼ & E½/SW & E½/NE	320
Peter A COWDREY	(New York city)		Oct. 23,1836	W½/SW	80
Henry W DELAVAN	Saratoga	NY	Sept. 23,1836	NW¼	160
Amos ADAMS	Livingston	MI	Dec. 28,1836	W½/NE	80

Handy township

Section 11

C Nelson SANFORD	Washtenaw	MI	Apr. 25,1834	SW¼	160
Ralph FOWLER	Livingston	NY	Aug. 28,1835	W½/NE	80
Harvey METCALF	Livingston	NY	Nov. 28,1835	SE¼	160
Charles P BUSH	Tompkins	NY	Mar. 26,1836	E½/NW	80
			Apr. 1,1836	W½/NE	80
Loren TAINTER	Livingston	NY	May 7,1836	E½/NE	80

Section 12

Flavius J B CRANE	Livingston	MI	Nov. 27,1835	SW¼	160
Francis FIELD	Livingston	MI	Jan. 11,1836	SW/SE	40
William J HAMILTON	Cauga	NY	Apr. 25,1836	NW/SE	40
Mary TAINTER	Livingston	NY	May 7,1836	W½/NW	80
Joel BANFIELD	Tompkins	NY	June 3,1836	E½/NW	80
*James E HAND	Livingston	MI	Sept. 23,1836	E½/SE	80
Stephen AVERY	Livingston	NY	Dec. 8,1836	W½/NE	80
Charles L HARRISON	Livingston	NY		E½/NE	80

Section 13

James M HITCHINGS	Monroe	NY	June 10,1836	NW/SW	40
Amos CHAFFEE	Wayne	MI	July 15,1836	SW¼	160
Morris TOMPKINS	(New York city)		Sept. 24,1836	E½/NW	80
Daniel O'CONNER	Columbia	NY	Oct. 25,1836	SE¼	160
Wells BROCKWAY	Ontario	NY	Oct. 27,1836	NE¼	160
Victory CURTIS & Almon WHIPPLE	Livingston	MI	Dec. 27,1837	SW/NW	40

Section 14

Sanford BRITTON	Wayne	MI	Apr. 25,1836	W½/NW	80
Peleg OATMAN	Orleans	NY	May 17,1836	SW¼	160
James M HITCHINGS	Monroe	NY	June 10,1836	E½/NW & W½/NE W½/SE & NE/NE	280
Victory CURTIS & Almon WHIPPLE	Livingston	MI	Dec. 27,1837	SE/NE	40

Section 15

Ralph FOWLER	Livingston	NY	Aug. 27,183_	NE¼ & E½/NW	240
Nathaniel DORR	Norfolk	MA	Aug. 28,183_	SE¼ & SW¼	320
Nathan JENKS	Ontario	NY	June 14,183_	W½/NW	80

*(known as James HEAD)

70

Handy township

Section 16(school section)

W H MILLER		Oct. 5,1852	NE/NE	40
FOWLER & POWER		July 26,1854	NW/NE	40
James HANLEY		Dec. 10,1852	SE/NE	40
R E ADAMS		Nov. 23,1853	SW/NE	40
M W FRADENBURGH		Dec. 23,1853	NE/NW	40
J T SPRAGUE		Dec. 23,1853	NW/NW	40
Charles WHITNEY		1870	$N\frac{1}{2}/S\frac{1}{2}/NW$	40
John M RUGGLES		1870	$S\frac{1}{2}/S\frac{1}{2}/NW$	40
James CASTILLON		Dec. 11,1852	NE/SE	40
D W ADAMS		Nov. 23,1853	SE/SE	40
David DUNN		Oct. 9,1866	NW/SE	40
P H BARBER		Oct. 9,1866	SW/SE	40
Jonathan FOX		Oct. 9,1866	NE/SW	40
N COFFEY		July 31,1854	SE/SW	40
Edwin SCHOOLEY		Mar. 7,1854	NW/SW	40
Belden LYMAN		Mar. 7,1854	SW/SW	40

Section 17

Charles PLACE	(New York city)		Dec. 4,1835	$W\frac{1}{2}/NW$	80
Henry BARBER	Washtenaw	MI	June 6,1836	$W\frac{1}{2}/SW$	80
John &					
James MULLHOLAND	Washtenaw	MI	July 1,1836	$E\frac{1}{2}/SW$	80
David A McFARLAN	Wayne	MI	Apr. 4,1837	$E\frac{1}{2}/NW$	80
			Apr. 5,1837	$W\frac{1}{2}/NE$ & $W\frac{1}{2}/SE$	160
John M RUGGLES	Livingston	MI	Sept. 23,1857	$E\frac{1}{2}/SE$	80
Daniel S LEE	Livingston	MI	Jan. 2,1854	$E\frac{1}{2}/NE$	80
E KNICKENBOCKER	Livingston	MI	Aug. 3,1854	$E\frac{1}{2}/SE$	80

Section 18

Charles PLACE	(New York city)		Dec. 4,1835	$E\frac{1}{2}/NE$	80
Benjamin P VEALY	Wayne	MI	June 14,1836	$W\frac{1}{2}/NE$	80
Alanson KNICKERBOCKER	Wayne	MI	June 17,1836	$S\frac{1}{2}/SE$	80
Hannah KNICKERBOCKER	Wayne	MI	June 18,1836	$N\frac{1}{2}/SE$	80
George M RICH	Wayne	MI	Feb. 8,1837	$SWf\frac{1}{4}$	105
Almira COLLINS	Livingston	MI	Apr. 14,1849	$S\frac{1}{2}/NWf$	53
Martin COFFEY	Livingston	MI	Nov. 22,1854	$N\frac{1}{2}/NWf$	53

Handy township

Section 19

Name	County	State	Date	Description	Acres
Alanson KNICKERBOCKER	Wayne	MI	June 17,1836	E½/NE	80
Ebenezer J PENNIMAN	Wayne	MI	June 17,1836	E½/SE	80
Garial DEAN	Jackson	MI	June 25,1836	W½/SE & W½/NE	160
Hannah KNICKERBOCKER	Livingston	MI	Jan. 9,1837	S½/NWf & N½/SWf	102
Mary MEECH	Livingston	MI	Mar. 1,1837	N½/NWf	51
Timothy LYON	Wayne	MI	Mar. 1,1837	S½/SWf	50

Section 20

Name	County	State	Date	Description	Acres
Leonard PARKER	Genessee	NY	May 23,1836	E½/SE	80
Charles JANNINGS	Genessee	NY	May 23,1836	W½/SE	80
James McGREGOR & John A McGRAW	(Boston, MA)		May 24,1836	E½/SW	80
Alanson KNICKERBOCKER	Wayne	MI	June 17,1836	NW¼	160
Ebenezer J PENNIMAN	Wayne	MI	June 17,1836	W½/SW	80
Charles STRONG	Livingston	NY	Aug. 3,1836	NW/NE & E½/NE	120
Timothy LYON	Wayne	MI	Mar. 1,1837	SW/NE	40

Section 21

Name	County	State	Date	Description	Acres
James McGREGOR & John A McGRAW	(Bostob,MA)		May 23,1836	NE¼	160
			May 24,1836	SW¼	160
			June 4,1836	E½/NW	80
Clark C BOUTWELL	Wayne	MI	May 23,1836	SE¼	160
Nelson COFFEE	Livingston	MI	Aug. 3,1854	W½/NW	80

Section 22

Name	County	State	Date	Description	Acres
Hosea B THORP	Chataque	NY	May 19,1836	W½/NW	80
James WILLIAMS	Wayne	MI	May 30,1836	W½/SW	80
Abram BOCKHOVEN	Morris	NY	June 9,1836	NE¼ & SE¼ & E½/NW & E½/SW	480

Section 23

Name	County	State	Date	Description	Acres
John COSART	Livingston	MI	July 14,1836	E½/SE	80
Spalding M CASE	Wayne	MI	Aug. 1,1836	SW¼	160
Hosea L STRONG	Wayne	MI	Oct. 25,1836	NW/NW	40
			Jan. 21,1837	SW/NW	40
Russell FORSYTH	Albany	NY	Oct. 26,1836	E½/NW	80
Samuel KILPATRICK	Washtenaw	MI	Oct. 27,1836	NE¼	160
William GUTHRIE	Washtenaw	MI	July 24,1838	W½/SE	80

Handy township

Section 24

Name	County	State	Date	Description	Acres
John OWEN &					
Marshall CHAPIN	Wayne	MI	July 14,1836	SW¼	160
Thomas O'CONNER	Wayne	MI	Oct. 25,1836	NW¼	160
John McKINNEY	Livingston	NY	Oct. 25,1836	SE¼	160
Samuel KILPATRICK	Washtenaw	MI	Oct. 27,1836	NE¼	160

Section 25

Name	County	State	Date	Description	Acres
Elijah CRANE	Wayne	MI	July 14,1836	SW¼ & W½/NW	240
Rufas Ames LEONARD		NY	Dec. 20,1837	E½/NE	80
George W HANMER	Tompkins	NY	Mar. 16,1837	W½/NE	80
Charles P BUSH	Ingham	MI	Nov. 17,1854	E½/NW & SE¼	240

Section 26

Name	County	State	Date	Description	Acres
Seth BELKNAP	Genessee	NY	June 6,1836	SW/NE & NE/SW	80
George B DEGRAF	Cayuga	NY	June 13,1836	W½/SW	80
Elijah CRANE	Wayne	MI	July 14,1836	E½/NE	80
John COSART	Livingston	MI	July 14,1836	SE¼	160
Jason W POWERS	Madison	NY	Aug. 1,1836	W½/NW	80
David PHELPS	(New York city)		Sept. 24,1836	E½/NW	80
Russell DISBROW	Genessee	NY	June 1,1837	NW/NE & SE/SW	80

Section 27

Name	County	State	Date	Description	Acres
Milo M STOCKWELL	Cayuga	NY	May 19,1836	W½/SW	80
Jeremiah DEGRAFF	Cayuga	NY	June 13,1836	E½/SE	80
Hiram H HANSON	Seneca	NY	Aug. 1,1836	NE¼	160
Charles ANDREWS	Wayne	MI	Mar. 16,1837	W½/NW	80
Isreal S SPENCER	Madison	NY	Feb. 15,1838	W½/SE	80
Mathew KNOWLES	Wayne	MI	June 22,1839	E½/SW	80
Leonard MORSE	Washtenaw	MI	Aug. 27,1847	NE/NW	40
Leonard NOBLE	Livingston	MI	Feb. 5,1858	SE/NW	40

Section 28

Name	County	State	Date	Description	Acres
Alanson CHURCH	Genessee	NY	May 23,1836	N½/SW	80
Clark C BOUTWELL	Wayne	NY	May 23,1836	NE¼	160
Andrew KING	Orange	NY	June 1,1836	SE¼	160
Jesse NORTON	Genessee	NY	July 2,1836	SW¼ & S½/SW	240

Handy township

Section 29

Orson CHURCH	Genessee	NY	May 23,1836	NE$\frac{1}{4}$	160
James McGREGOR & John A McGRAW	(Boston,MA)		May 24,1836	E$\frac{1}{2}$/NW	80
Lewis WASTFALL	Wayne	MI	June 27,1836	W$\frac{1}{2}$/SW	80
James S KIMBERLY	(New York city)		July 16,1836	E$\frac{1}{2}$/SE	80
Samuel PORTER	Oakland	MI	Mar. 16,1837	W$\frac{1}{2}$/SE & E$\frac{1}{2}$/SW	160
Richard PARISH	Wayne	MI	June 25,1836	W$\frac{1}{2}$/NW	80

Section 30

Lewis WESTFALL	Wayne	MI	June 27,1836	E$\frac{1}{2}$/SE	80
John WHALEY	Washtenaw	MI	June 30,1836	SW/SE	40
Richard PARISH	Wayne	MI	June 25,1836	E$\frac{1}{2}$/NE	80
David A McFARLAN	Wayne	MI	Mar. 18,1837	NWf$\frac{1}{4}$	99
Losson GORDON	Wayne	MI	Mar. 28,1837	SWf$\frac{1}{4}$	96
Alexander GRANT	Wayne	MI	Apr. 24,1838	NW/SE	40
Flavius J B CRANE	Livingston	MI	June 27,1836	W$\frac{1}{2}$/NE	80

Section 31

Flavius J B CRANE	Livingston	MI	June 27,1836	S$\frac{1}{2}$/SE	80
Lewis WESTFALL	Wayne	MI	June 27,1836	W$\frac{1}{2}$/NE & N$\frac{1}{2}$/SE	160
John ORR	Washtenaw	MI	June 23,1836	E$\frac{1}{2}$/NE	80
William REUN	Livingston	MI		NWf$\frac{1}{4}$	

Section 32

John B BONTA	Montgomery	NY	June 23,1836	W$\frac{1}{2}$/NW & NE/NW	120
Roswell SHERTLUFF	Windsor	VT	June 29,1836	SW$\frac{1}{4}$	160
Orestus H WRIGHT	Addison	VT	July 1,1836	W$\frac{1}{2}$/NE & SE/NW	120
			July 9,1836	E$\frac{1}{2}$/SE	80
Flavius J B CRANE	Livingston	MI	July 5,1836	E$\frac{1}{2}$/NE & W$\frac{1}{2}$/SE	160

Section 33

Dennis CONRAD	Oakland	MI	May 21,1836	NE/NE	40
Lewis W DECKER	Ontario	NY	May 31,1836	E$\frac{1}{2}$/SE	80
Joseph BLANCHARD & Willard BLANCHARD	Onondaga	NY	June 1,1836	S$\frac{1}{2}$/SW	80
Adolphus BRIGAM	Wayne	MI	June 1,1836	W$\frac{1}{2}$/SE	80
William MARTIN	Wayne	MI	June 1,1836	W$\frac{1}{2}$/NE & E$\frac{1}{2}$/NW	160
Orestus H WRIGHT	Addison	VT	July 9,1836	NW/SW	40
James S KIMBERLY	(New York city)		July 16,1836	NE/SW	40
Nathaniel ANDREWS	Oakland	MI	Mar. 16,1837	SE/NE	40
Joseph S SCOFFIELD	Oakland	MI	Mar. 16,1837	W$\frac{1}{2}$/NW	80

Handy township

Section 34
Dennis CONRAD	Oakland	MI	May 19,1836	$W\frac{1}{2}$/NW	80
Silas MUNSELL	Wayne	MI	May 30,1836	$SE\frac{1}{4}$ & $SW\frac{1}{4}$	320
Joel CHOATE	Genessee	NY	July 2,1836	$NE\frac{1}{4}$	160
Joseph S STOCKFIELD	Oakland	MI	Mar. 16,1837	$E\frac{1}{2}$/NW	80

Section 35
Joel H PRESCOTT	Ontario	NY	Mar. 25,1836	$W\frac{1}{2}$/SW	80
Benjamin SMITH	Wayne	NY	Mar. 25,1836	$E\frac{1}{2}$/SW	80
Reuben S DURFEE	Wayne	MI	Mar. 25,1836	$SE\frac{1}{4}$	160
Luther HAMMON	Ontario	NY	May 30,1836	$NW\frac{1}{4}$	160
Joseph MORROW	Ontario	NY	May 30,1836	$NE\frac{1}{4}$	160

Section 36
Dana SHAW	Orleans	NY	Apr. 9,1836	$E\frac{1}{2}$/SE & $E\frac{1}{2}$/NE	160
John A BUCKLAND	Orleans	NY	Apr. 9,1836	$W\frac{1}{2}$/SW	80
Daniel P BIGLOW	Orleans	NY	Apr. 9,1836	$E\frac{1}{2}$/SW	80
Samuel HILL	Orleans	NY	Apr. 9,1836	$W\frac{1}{2}$/SE	80
Francis MITTLEBERGER	Oakland	MI	June 11,1836	$W\frac{1}{2}$/NE	80
Aaron LAWRENCE	Washtenaw	MI	July 17,1836	$E\frac{1}{2}$/NW	80
James S KIMBERLY	(New York city)		July 15,1836	$W\frac{1}{2}$/NW	80

HARTLAND township-FIRST Land Owners

NAME	COUNTY & STATE		DATE	LAND	ACRES
Section 1					
William THOMPSON	Seneca	NY	Apr. 12,1836	NWf¼	200
Amos F ALBRIGHT	Oakland	MI	June 22,1836	E½/SW	80
Hiram R SCOLLARD	Oakland	MI	June 22,1836	W½/SW	80
Ledyard FLINT	Allegeny	NY	June 22,1836	SE¼	160
			Dec. 12,1836	NEf¼	205
Section 2					
William H TOWNSEND	(New York city)		Oct. 1,1835	NWf¼	198
William THOMPSON	Seneca	NY	Apr. 12,1836	NEf¼	195
Thomas EMERSON	Wayne	MI	May 17,1836	SE¼ & SW¼	320
Section 3					
John J BLACKMER	Monroe	NY	Apr. 21,1836	Np/NWf	118
Van Rensellaer &					
Henry HAWKINS	Genessee	NY	June 27,1836	W½/SW	80
Levi ANDRUS	Madison	NY	July 14,1836	SE¼	160
Josiah C WHALEN	Livingston	MI	Oct. 25,1836	Np/NEf	117
Jacob WESTERVELT	Wayne	MI	Oct. 26,1836	SW/NW	40
Sumner E DARROW	Madison	NY	Oct. 27,1836	Sp/NE	80
Alanson OLDS	Oakland	MI	Jan. 9,1837	E½/SW	80
Samuel COWLES	Wayne	MI	Apr. 28,1837	SE/NW	40
Section 4					
James WEBBER	Monroe	NY	Oct. 16,1835	W½/SW & SE/SW	120
Major CURTIS	Oakland	MI	Jan. 11,1836	Np/NWf &	
				SW/NWf	156
Franklin CURTIS	Oakland	MI	Mar. 22,1836	SE/NW	40
Austin WAKEMAN	Oakland	MI	Mar. 29,1836	Np/NEf	117
Van Rensellaer &					
Henry HAWKINS	Genessee	NY	June 27,1836	E½/SE	80
Calvin BUSSEY	Livingston	MI	Sept. 21,1836	W½/SE	80
Thomas BUSSEY	Livingston	MI	Sept. 23,1836	NE/SW	40
Jacob WESTERVELT	Wayne	MI	Oct. 26,1836	Sp/NE	80

Hartland township

Section 5

Isaac PARSHALL	Tioga	NY	Sept. 21,1835	W½/SW & NW/NWf & SW/NWf	179
Ezra GLEASON	Niagara	NY	Oct. 2,1835	E½/SE	80
John J RICE	Monroe	NY	Nov. 23,1835	W½/SE	80
Major CURTIS	Oakland	MI	Dec. 28,1835	NEf¼	197
David CURTIS	Oakland	MI	Mar. 17,1836	SE/NW	40

Section 6

James MAPLEBECK	Wayne	MI	June 27,1834	SW/SWf & SE/SWf	79
Samuel MAPES	Washtenaw	MI	Dec. 12,1835	SE/SE	40
William CHAPMAN	Washtenaw	MI	Apr. 6,1835	NE/NEf	59
Calvin BUSSEY	Washtenaw	MI	June 9, ?	SW/SE	40
Elisha GLEASON	Livingston	MI	May 22,1836	NE/SW	40
Russell MORTON	Washtenaw	MI	Jan. 11,1836	NW/NWf	56
Henry W ROBERTS	Livingston	MI	June 30,1836	NW/NE & SW.NEf & SW/SWf	139
Elijah GLEASON	Livingston	MI	Sept. 20,1836	NE/NWf & SE/NWf	96
Abel HYDE	Livingston	NY	Oct. 24,1836	N½/SE	80
John WHALEN	Livingston	MI	Oct. 24,1836	SW/NW	40
Abner ROBERTS	Livingston	MI	Nov. 14,1836	SE/NE	40

Section 7

Alvah TENNY & Rufas TENNY	Monroe	NY	Oct. 30,1832	SWf¼ & NW/SE	197
John T BROWN	Monroe	NY	Feb. 12,1835	NWf¼	157
			Aug. 19,1835	W½/NE & SE/NE	120
Abby MAPES	Washtenaw	MI	June 15,1835	NE/NE	40
Asa PARSHALL	Tioga	NY	Sept. 21,1835	E½/SE	80
Samuel BIDDLEMAN	Tioga	NY	Sept. 21,1835	SW/SE	40

Hartland township

Section 8

James MAPLEBECK	Wayne	MI	Nov. 15,1837	SW/SE	40
Gary GRISWOLD	Livingston	MI	May 10,1837	SE/NW	40
Benjamin TOWNLEY	Livingston	MI	Dec. 28,1836	SE/NW	40
			June 13,1836	NW/SW	40
Abram DEAN	Livingston	MI	Dec. 12,1836	SE/SE	40
Samuel MAPES	Washtenaw	MI	Dec. 12,1834	NW/NW	40
Abby MAPES	Livingston	MI	Oct. 6,1835	SE/SW	40
Nehemiah LAMB	Oakland	MI	Nov. 13,1835	E$\frac{1}{2}$/NE	80
			Dec. 14,1835	W$\frac{1}{2}$/NE	80
William GANNON	Wayne	MI	July 12,1836	SW/SW	40
Daniel GRISWOLD	Livingston	MI	July 15,1836	SW/NW	40
John VANDERHOOP	Wayne	MI	Oct. 26,1836	NE/SE	40
Almon DEAN	Livingston	MI	Nov. 16,1836	NW/SE	40
Dennis WHALEN	Livingston	MI	Nov. 18,1836	NE/SW	40

Section 9

James S WEBBER	Monroe	NY	Oct. 11,1835	W$\frac{1}{2}$/NW	80
Trumen NICHOLS	Oakland	MI	Nov. 21,1835	E$\frac{1}{2}$/NW & NW/NE	120
Cyrus JACKSON	Wayne	NY	June 15,1836	SE$\frac{1}{4}$ & SW$\frac{1}{4}$	320
Calvin BUSSEY	Livingston	MI	Sept. 21,1836	E$\frac{1}{2}$/NE	80
Thomas BUSSEY	Washtenaw	MI	Dec. 5,1836	SW/NE	40

Section 10

James CHAMBERS	Livingston	MI	May 24,1836	SE/SE	40
Cyrus JACKSON	Wayne	NY	June 15,1836	SW$\frac{1}{4}$ & W$\frac{1}{2}$/SE	240
Seth J SMITH	Oakland	MI	June 23,1836	N$\frac{1}{2}$/NW	80
John HOPKINSON	Cayuga	OH	Sept. 20,1836	W$\frac{1}{2}$/NE	80
Zepariah SHAW	Livingston	MI	Sept. 20,1836	SE/NE	40
Peter HARTMAN	Ontario	NY	Sept. 21,1836	S$\frac{1}{2}$/NW	80
Smith IRISH	Wayne	MI	Nov. 15,1836	NE/SE	40
Dennis WHALEN	Livingston	MI	Nov. 18,1836	NE/NE	40

Hartland township

Section 11

Name	County	State	Date	Description	Acres
John WHALEN	Wayne	MI	Nov. 3,1836	NW/NE	40
Freelove ADAMS	Oakland	MI	Apr. 27,1836	NW/SW	40
James CHAMBERS	Livingston	MI	May 24,1836	SW/SW	40
Samuel HOSFORD	Wayne	NY	June 1,1836	SW/NW	40
Samuel L HALE	Cayuga	OH	June 13,1836	E½/SW	80
Joseph B ENOS	Orleans	NY	June 15,1836	E½/NE & SW/NE	120
Josiah C WHALEN	Livingston	MI	June 28,1836	NE/SE	40
Royal BAKER	Monroe	NY	July 6,1836	SE/SE	40
Hugh S SNIDEKER	Ontario	NY	Sept. 23,1836	E½/NW & NW/NW	120
Josiah HALE	Cayahoga	OH	Oct. 28,1836	SW/SE	40

Section 12

Name	County	State	Date	Description	Acres
Abram C TAGGERT	Monroe	NY	May 24,1836	NW/NW	40
Ledyard FLINT	Allegeny	NY	June 22,1836	NE¼	160
			June 23,1836	E½/NW	80
Van Rensellaer & Henry HAWKINS	Genessee	NY	June 27,1836	W½/SW	80
Hugh S SNIDEKER	Ontario	NY	Sept. 23,1836	SE¼ & E½/SW	240
John WHALEN	Livingston	MI	Oct. 24,1836	SW/NW	40

Section 13

Name	County	State	Date	Description	Acres
Dennis WHALEN	Livingston	MI	July 12,1834	SW/NW	40
Jeptha COBURN	Oakland	MI	May 27,1836	NW/NW	40
Hubbard BULLARD	Livingston	MI	June 27,1836	SW/SW	40
Hugh J SNIDAKER	Ontario	NY	Sept. 23,1836	E½/NW & W½/NE & NE/NE	200
Adolphus CAREY Jr.	Livingston	MI	Oct. 24,1836	W½/SE & E½/SW	160
James WHALEN	Livingston	MI	Oct. 24,1836	NW/SW	40
Noah COWLES	Wayne	MI	Apr. 28,1837	NE/SE	40
John C RUSSELL	Livingston	MI	Dec. 6,1838	SE/SE	40

Section 14

Name	County	State	Date	Description	Acres
John WILLIAMS	Monroe	NY	June 28,1834	E½/SE	80
Aaron PHELPS	Monroe	NY	July 12,1834	W½/SE	80
Dennis WHALEN	Livingston	MI	July 12,1834	E½/NE	80
Eli LEE	Monroe	NY	July 17,1835	W½/NE	80
George HUNTLEY	Livingston	MI	July 17,1835	SE/SW	40
Thomas HALL	Cayuga	OH	May 17,1836	W½/NW & NE/SW	120
Elisha B HALE	Cayuga	OH	May 17,1836	E½/NW	80
*Moses SAGERT	Genessee	NY	June 27,1836	W½/SW	80

*(listed in history book as TAGGERT)

79

Hartland township

Section 15

Name	County	State	Date	Description	Acres
Aaron PHELPS	Monroe	NY	July 12,1834	E½/SW	80
Orman HOLMES	Monroe	NY	Sept. 2,1835	W½/SE	80
Chancey W PIERCE	Deleware	NY	Oct. 5,1835	W½/SW	80
Thomas HALL	Cayuga	OH	May 17,1836	W½/NW	80
James SNOW	Wayne	NY	June 15,1836	E½/NE	80
Cyrus JACKSON	Wayne	NY	June 15,1836	W½/NE & E½/NW	160
George HASTINGS	Wayne	MI	Oct. 25,1836	SE/SE	40
Adolphus CAREY Jr.	Livingston	MI	Dec. 6,1836	NE/SE	40

Section 16(school section)

Name	Date	Description	Acres
A F ALBRIGHT	Oct. 11,1837	N½/SW & NW/SE	120
ALLBRIGHT & FLINT	Aug. 1,1839	SW/NW	40
J FLINT	Aug. 1,1839	SE/NW & SW/SE & S½/SW	160
Lucy STEVENS	Sept. 26,1843	SW/NE	40
H GLEASON	Nov. 28,1843	SE/NE	40
J D CROUSE	Sept. 9,1845	NW/NE	40
	Sept. 16,1845	NE/NW	40
	Oct. 21,1845	NE/NE	40
	May 19,1847	NW/NE	40
Lucy NORTON	Mar. 21,1848	NE/SE	40
H H MIDDAH	July 12,1850	SE/SE	40

Section 17

Name	County	State	Date	Description	Acres
John BROPHY & Ellen BROPHY	Wayne	MI	Mar. 23,1835	W½/SE & W½/NE	160
James BROPHY	Wayne	MI	Mar. 23,1835	E½/NE & E½/SE	160
John CULLEN	Wayne	MI	Dec. 10,1835	E½/NW & E½/SW	160
Thomas MACKEY	Wayne	MI	Dec. 22,1835	W½/NW	80
Thomas SULLIVAN	Wayne	MI	Jan. 9,1836	SW/SW	40
Thomas KELLEY	Livingston	MI	Sept. 23,1836	NW/SW	40

Hartland township

Section 18

Thomas TYRELL	Wayne	MI	Mar. 21,1835	NW¼	157
	Livingston	MI	Aug. 1,1835	N½/SWf	79
John JORDAN	Livingston	MI	Aug. 1,1835	W½/NE	80
			Sept. 23,1836	NE/SE	40
Thomas KELLY	Wayne	MI	Dec. 11,1835	NW/SE	40
Thomas SULLIVAN	Wayne	MI	Jan. 9,1836	SE/SE	40
John CULLEN	Livingston	MI	Jan. 9,1836	SW/SE	40
William GANNON	Wayne	MI	Jan. 21,1836	E½/NE	80
Barnard O'CAVANAUGH	Livingston	MI	May 18,1837	SE/SWf	40
James GANNON	Livingston	MI	May 18,1837	SW/SWf	39

Section 19

Benjamin WAIT	(New York city)		Oct. 13,1835	Ep/SW	80
Catherine PECOARD	Wayne	MI	Jan. 29,1836	NE/NE	40
James McDONNELL	Wayne	MI	Mar. 11,1836	NW/SWf	39
Elihu HAINES	Livingston	NY	Mar. 26,1836	W½/SE & NE/SE	120
George LEMON	Allegeny	NY	June 21,1836	W½/NE & SE/NE	120
Isaac L PLATT	(New York city)		Aug. 3,1836	SE/SE	40
Joseph B WEEDEN	(New York city)		Sept. 24,1836	NWf¼	157
Hugh McKEEVER	Genessee	NY	Aug. 27,1838	SW/SWf	39

Section 20

David F HESS	Orleans	NY	Oct. 12,1835	SE/SE	40
Holsey BIDWELL	Cayuga	OH	May 27,1836	SW¼ & NW/SE	200
Joseph HARD	Orleans	OH	June 11,1836	NE/SE	40
Thomas CONLON	Livingston	MI	June 13,1836	SW/SE	40
George LEMON	Allegeny	NY	June 21,1836	W½/NW	80
Dennis O'REARDON	Monroe	MI	Nov. 17,1836	NE/NE	40
Patrick CROSBY	Shiawassee	MI	Aug. 16,1837	SE/NE	40
Hugh McKEEVER	Genessee	NY	Aug. 27,1838	SE/NW & SW/NE	80
John CULLENS	Livingston	MI	July 12,1854	NE/NW	40

Hartland township

Section 21

Norman BRAINARD	Oakland	MI	June 1,1835	E½/NE & NW/NE	120
			Dec. 23,1835	SW/NE	40
	Livingston	MI	Oct. 26,1836	NE/SE	40
David F HESS	Orleans	NY	Oct. 12,1835	SW/SW	40
Solomon FOSTER	Erie	NY	July 5,1836	NW/SE	40
Solomon DUILLARD	Schenectady	NY	Aug. 6,1836	NWf¼ & E½/SW	240
Russel D HESS	Orleans	NY	Sept. 21,1836	SW/SE	40
Relecta HASTINGS	Wayne	MI	Apr. 28,1837	SE/SE	40
Patrick KELLEY	Livingston	MI	Sept. 19,1837	NW/SW	40

Section 22

John G HORTON	Ontario	NY	May 27,1835	W½/NE & NE/NW	120
Chancy W PIERCE	Deleware	NY	Oct. 5,1835	W½/NW	80
Lavius TENNY	Livingston	MI	Mar. 3,1836	E½/NE	80
	Oakland	MI	Sept. 24,1836	NE/SE	40
*Corwell LANNING	Washtenaw	MI	Mar. 22,1836	W½/SW	80
			May 27,1836	E½/SW	80
Russel D HESS	Orleans	NY	Sept. 21,1836	SE/NW	40
Laura HUBBELL	Livingston	MI	Nov. 29,1836	SE/SE	40

Section 23

John WILLIAMS	Monroe	NY	June 28,1834	E½/NE	80
George HUNTLEY	Monroe	NY	June 28,1834	W½/NE	80
George BULKLEY	Monroe	NY	June 28,1834	NE/SW	40
Aaron PHELPS	Monroe	NY	July 5,1834	SE¼	160
Rufas TENNY	Oakland	MI	Dec. 22,1835	SE/NW	40
Eunice TENNY	Oakland	MI	Jan. 20,1836	NW/SW	40
John B SMITH	Livingston	NY	May 9,1836	SE/SW	40
Bliss CHARLES	Genessee	NY	June 28,1836	NE/NW	40
Cornelius T CHARLES	Genessee	NY	June 28,1836	W½/NW	80
John HOPKINSON	Cayuga	OH	Sept. 20,1836	W½/SE	80
Laura HUBBELL	Livingston	MI	Dec. 2,1836	SW/SW	40

*(Listed as Charles LANSING in history book)

Hartland township

Section 24

Erastus J SMITH	Monroe	NY	Sept. 6,1833	E½/SW	80
	Livingston	MI	June 13,1835	E½/SE	80
George BURNET	Livingston	MI	Apr. 25,1834	SW/SW	40
John WILLIAMS	Monroe	MI	Oct. 21,1834	SW/NW	40
	Livingston	MI	Feb. 5,1835	SE/NW	40
Harriet SMITH	Oakland	MI	June 25,1835	SW/SE	40
Crocker HASTINGS	Livingston	MI	Oct. 29,1835	SE/NE	40
Josiah T CLARK	Oakland	MI	Nov. 10,1835	SW/NE	40
Noah P MORSE	Oakland	MI	Sept. 24,1836	NW/SE	40
Samuel T ARMSTRONG	Livingston	MI	Oct. 25,1836	N½/NW	80
Adolphus CAREY	Livingston	MI	Oct. 24,1836	NW/NE	40
B B KERCHIVAL	Wayne	MI	Oct. 29,1836	NW/SW	40
John C RUSSEL	Livingston	MI	Dec. 6,1838	NE/NE	40

Section 25

Charles SMITH	Washtenaw	MI	Apr. 12,1833	SW¼	160
Lavius TENNY	Oakland	MI	May 9,1833	E½/NE	80
Eli LEE	Monroe	NY	May 24,1833	W½/NE & NW/SE	120
Erastus SMITH	Monroe	NY	Sept. 6,1833	E½/NW & NW/NW	120
William KINNEY	Monroe	NY	Oct. 20,1833	E½/SE	80
Elias ARMSTRONG	Monroe	NY	June 18,1835	SW/SE	40
John C MORSE	Oakland	MI	Nov. 2,1836	SW/NW	40

Section 26

John GLINES	Livingston	MI	July 12,1834	NE/NE	40
			Nov. 29,1836	SE/NE	40
Aaron PHELPS	Oakland	MI	Mar. 13,1835	NW/NE	40
Eber ADAMS	Monroe	NY	July 15,1835	W½/SE & E½/SW	160
Adonaron HUBBELL	Livingston	MI	Nov. 20,1835	NE/NW	40
			May 31,1836	SE/NW	40
			Oct. 25,1836	NW/SW	40
Jeptha COBURN	Oakland	MI	Feb. 6,1836	SW/NE	40
Charles SMITH	Livingston	MI	Feb. 10,1836	NE/SE	40
Erastus J SMITH	Livingston	MI	May 27,1836	W½/NW	80
William KINNEY	Livingston	MI	Sept. 23,1836	SE/SE	40

Hartland township

Section 27

Abner HYDE	Oakland	MI	Jan. 30,1836	SW/NE	40
Noah P MORSE	Oakland	MI	May 5,1836	SE/NW	40
Charles B PHILLIPS	Monroe	NY	May 5,1836	E½/SW	80
Levi MAXFIELD	Cayuga	OH	May 20,1836	NE/SE	40
Isaac Y BRANT		NY	Aug. 2,1836	W½/NW & NE/NW	120
George CORNELL	Livingston	MI	Sept. 23,1836	E½/NE	80
John GLINES	Livingston	MI	Oct. 25,1836	SE/SE	40
			Oct. 16,1855	NW/SE	40
Benjamin BREVOORT	Livingston	MI	Oct. 29,1836	SW/SE	40
James HANDY	Livingston	MI	Nov. 30,1854	NW/NE	40
Lorenzo L ARMSTRONG	Livingston	MI	Jan. 31,1856	SW/SW	40
James GRUBB	Livingston	MI	Jan. 13,1860	NW/SW	40

Section 28

David F HESS	Orleans	NY	Oct. 12,1835	E½/NW	80
*Isaac H S HULBERT	Orleans	NY	Oct. 12,1835	W½/NW	80
Elisha MUDGE	Erie	NY	July 16,1836	N½/SW	80
Isaac F BRANT		NY	Aug. 2,1836	W½/SE & SW/SW	120
Laura M HESS	Orleans	NY	Sept. 21,1836	NW/NE	40
Medah FERRY	Livingston	MI	Jan. 23,1838	SW/NE	40
John B SMITH	Livingston	MI	June 25,1838	NE/SE	40
Laura LEWIS	Orleans	NY	Aug. 24,1838	SE/SW	40
Samuel MAPES	Livingston	MI	Nov. 15,1852	NE/NE	40
John H HANDY	Livingston	MI	Dec. 15,1854	SE/NE	40
Hazard A POTTER	Ontario	NY	May 31,1853	SE/SE	40

Section 29

Isaac H S HULBERT	Orleans	NY	Oct. 12,1835	E½/NE	80
Michael McDONNELL	Newport	RI	May 16,1836	W½/NW	80
Stephen C HATHAWAY	Washtenaw	MI	May 30,1836	W½/SW	80
Thomas CONLON	Livingston	Mi	June 13,1836	NW/NE	40
William J COCHRANE		NY	Aug. 2,1836	SE¼ & E½/NW	
				& E½/SW	320
Julia A HESS	Livingston	MI	Feb. 9,1839	SW/NE	40

*(Listed as HURLBERT in history book)

84

Hartland township

Section 30

Name	Residence		Date	Description	Acres
Abijah ROGERS Jr.	Oakland	MI	May 2,1836	SW/NWf	39
Michael McDONNELL	Newport	RI	May 2,1836	NE¼	160
James GLEASON	Monroe	NY	May 26,1836	Ep/NW	80
Mary McGUIRE	Wayne	MI	May 16,1836	NW/NWf	39
Ira C HATHAWAY	Washtenaw	MI	May 30,1836	SE¼	160
Silas HATHAWAY	Washtenaw	MI	May 30,1836	Wp/SWf & NE/SWf	119
William N HOYT	Livingston	MI	Sept. 20,1836	SE/SW	40

Section 31

Name	Residence		Date	Description	Acres
Robert B RUGGLES	(New York city)		Aug. 1,1835	SWf¼	165
Benjamin TANNER	(New York city)		Apr. 20,1836	SE¼	160
Henry S LISK	Ontario	NY	May 31,1836	Ep/NW & NW/NE	120
Patrick MULLEN	Wayne	MI	June 2,1836	SW/NE	40
Charles BARTLEY	Wayne	MI	Aug. 4,1836	SW/NE	40
William A CLARK	(New York city)		Sept. 21,1836	W½/NWf	81

Section 32

Name	Residence		Date	Description	Acres
Charles ROBINSON	Livingston	MI	July 16,1834	W½/SE	80
Joseph ROBINSON	Livingston	NY	June 3,1835	NE/SE	40
Henry S LISK	Ontario	NY	May 31,1836	W½/NW	80
Samuel KILPATRICK	Washtenaw	MI	May 31,1836	E½/NW	80
Abram M TOPPING	(New York city)		Aug. 3,1836	SW¼	160
Isaac L PLATT	(New York city)		Aug. 3,1836	NE¼	160
Benjamin BLAIN	Livingston	MI	Nov. 15,1854	SE/SE	40

Section 33

Name	Residence		Date	Description	Acres
Benjamin TANNER	(New York city)		Apr. 20,1836	E½/SW & NW/SW	120
Elijah MARSH	Livingston	NY	June 24,1836	E½/NW	80
Isaac F BRANT		NY	Aug. 2,1836	W½/NE	80
Betsey MARSH	Livingston	MI	Oct. 24,1836	NW/NW	40
Isreal ARMS	Livingston	MI	Feb. 23,1837	NE/NE	40
Hiram H WARNER	Livingston	MI	Oct. 3,1837	SE/SE	40
Samuel CRIPPEN	Livingston	MI	May 23,1838	NW/SE	40
*Morris WHITEHEAD	Livingston	MI	Feb. 24,1846	SW/NW	40
John J HANDY	Livingston	MI	Feb. 15,1853	SE/NE	40
Michael WALSH	Livingston	MI	Aug. 20,1853	SW/SE	40
Franklin WALSH	Livingston	MI	Mar. 31,1858	NE/NE	40
Robert SLOAN	Livingston	MI	Mar. 4,1854	SW/SW	40

*(Listed as WHITEHOUT in history book)

Hartland township

Section 34

Name	County	State	Date	Description	Acres
Heirome GOODSPEED	Washtenaw	MI	July 2,1835	E$\frac{1}{2}$/SE	80
Joseph YOUNG	Oakland	MI	May 30,1836	SW$\frac{1}{4}$	160
William H JOHNSTON	Washtenaw	MI	June 4,1836	E$\frac{1}{2}$/NW	80
Chancey CHILDS	Wayne	MI	Sept. 20,1836	W$\frac{1}{2}$/NW & W$\frac{1}{2}$/NE	160
Benjamin BREVOORT	Livingston	MI	Dec. 6,1836	NE/NE	40
Isaac COLLINS	Livingston	MI	Sept. 29,1838	SE/NE	40
Lorenzo M ARMSTRONG	Livingston	MI	Dec. 14,1853	NW/SE	40
Henry T ROSS	Livingston	MI	DEc. 1,1854	SW/SE	40

Section 35

Name	County	State	Date	Description	Acres
Benjamin WOOD	Washtenaw	MI	Dec. 6,1833	NE/NE	40
Corwell LANNING	Washtenaw	MI	Mar. 21,1835	NW/SE & SW/NE	80
Ibrook TOWER	Washtenaw	MI	May 21,1835	NW/SW	40
Jesse TENNY & Rufas TENNY	Oakland	MI	July 15,1835	E$\frac{1}{2}$/NW & NW/NE	120
Charles SMITH	Livingston	MI	Nov. 5,1835	SW/NW	40
John B SMITH	Livingston	MI	Dec. 10,1835	NW/NW	40
*Frederick W GOODENOW	Livingston	MI	Dec. 22,1835	SE/NE	40
William KINNEY	Livingston	MI	Sept. 23,1836	NE/SE	40
Solomon COOPER	Livingston	MI	Nov. 9,1837	SW/SW	40
Wells FARR	Livingston	MI	Jan. 19,1838	SE/SE	40
Keyes CHILD	Livingston	MI	June 26,1838	SW/SE	40
Emeline HEWITT	Livingston	MI	Jan. 18,1839	E$\frac{1}{2}$/SW	80

Section 36

Name	County	State	Date	Description	Acres
Alvah TENNY	Monroe	NY	Oct. 30,1832	E$\frac{1}{2}$/NE	80
Jesse TENNY	Oakland	MI	Apr. 11,1833	W$\frac{1}{2}$/NE	80
John C MORSE	Oakland	MI	May 15,1833	NE/SE	40
Erastus J SMITH	Monroe	NY	Sept. 6,1833	NW/SE	40
John WOOD	Washtenaw	MI	Dec. 6,1833	E$\frac{1}{2}$/NW	80
Benjamin WOOD Sr.	Washtenaw	MI	Dec. 6,1833	NW/NW	40
John COSART	Oakland	MI	Oct. 24,1835	E$\frac{1}{2}$/SW & SW/SE	120
	Livingston	MI	Nov. 5,1836	SE/SE	40
William KINNEY	Livingston	MI	Sept. 23,1836	SW/NW	40
			Nov. 1,1836	NW/SW	40
Henry T ROSS	Livingston	MI	Dec. 1,1854	SW/SW	40

*(Known as Fred GOODMAN in history book)

NAME	COUNTY & STATE		DATE	LAND	ACRES

Section 1
Silas TITUS &

Bickford P HUCHINGSON	Wayne	MI	Feb. 18,1836	SE$\frac{1}{4}$ & NEf$\frac{1}{4}$	324
Edward PECK	Genessee	NY	May 23,1836	W$\frac{1}{2}$/SW	80
Joseph HEATH	Monroe	NY	June 9,1836	NWf$\frac{1}{4}$	156
Daniel BOUTELL	Onondaga	NY	Nov. 14,1836	E$\frac{1}{2}$/SW	80

Section 2

William W SHUTES	Oakland	MI	Oct. 19,1835	Sp/NW	80
Ezra FRISBEE	Montgomery	NY	Oct. 19,1835	Np/NWf	69
William S GREGORY	Wayne	MI	May 23,1836	Sp/NE	80
Patrick TOBIN	Livingston	MI	May 28,1836	SW$\frac{1}{4}$	160
Horace HEATH &					
Appollas SMITH	(U.S.)		June 10,1836	Np/NEf	72
Harvey S BRADLEY	Niagara	NY	Oct. 22,1838	E$\frac{1}{2}$/SE	80
Joseph BRADLEY	Wayne	MI	Nov. 2,1838	NW/SE	40
Maria BRADLEY	Wayne	MI	Feb. 5,1839	SW/SE	40

Section 3

John SANFORD	Oakland	MI	July 8,1834	NEf$\frac{1}{4}$	141
	Livingston	MI	June 8,1836	Np/NEf	64
William CARPENTER	Niagara	NY	May 21,1836	W$\frac{1}{2}$/SW	80
Ebenezer WARREN	Livingston	NY	May 21,1836	W$\frac{1}{2}$/SE & E$\frac{1}{2}$/SW	160
Henry W RANDALL	Niagara	NY	May 21,1836	E$\frac{1}{2}$/SE	80
David HYDE	Livingston	MI	Sept. 16,1846	SW/NE	40
			Feb. 23,1848	SE/NE	40

Section 4

Samuel M SPENCER	Livingston	NY	May 7,1836	W$\frac{1}{2}$/SW	80
Garret S LAKE	Livingston	NY	May 28,1836	SW/SE	40
Mark HEALY &					
B B KERCHIVAL	(U.S.)		May 28,1836	E$\frac{1}{2}$/SW & E$\frac{1}{2}$/SE	
				& NW/SE	200
Purdy WILLIAMS	(New York city)		June 15,1836	W$\frac{1}{2}$/NWf	67
William HYDE	Livingston	NY	Nov. 17,1854	E$\frac{1}{2}$/NEf	69
Almon WHIPPLE	Livingston	NY	Nov. 23,1854	E$\frac{1}{2}$/NWf &	
				W$\frac{1}{2}$/NEf	136

Howell township

Section 5

Name	Location	State	Date	Description	Acres
Nathan CHIDESTER	Genessee	NY	May 4,1836	NEf¼	130
William SLATER	Livingston	NY	May 5,1836	NWf¼ & NE/SW	
				& W½/SW	247
			May 13,1836	SE/SW	40
Samuel M SPENCER	Livingston	NY	May 7,1836	E½/SE	80
John W PIERCE	Wayne	MI	June 24,1836	W½/SE	80

Section 6

Name	Location	State	Date	Description	Acres
Joseph B CRAFT	Livingston	NY	May 5,1836	NWf¼ & NEf¼	134
Justus BOYD	Livingston	NY	May 5,1836	E½/SE & NW/SE	
				& NEf¼	247
Charles P BUSH	Tompkins	NY	June 9,1836	Np/SWf	82
William HORTON	(New York city)		June 15,1836	S½/SWf &	
				Sw/SE	122

Section 7

Name	Location	State	Date	Description	Acres
Joseph PORTER	Washtenaw	MI	July 21,1834	Wp/SW	81
John BENNETT	Washtenaw	MI	July 14,1835	Nwf¼	163
Jeremiah GREENFIELD	Cayuga	NY	Oct. 10,1835	Ep/SW & SW/SE	120
Nathan CHIDESTER	Genessee	NY	May 4,1836	E½/NE	80
Stephen S BULLOCK	Wayne	MI	June 14,1836	E½/SE & N½/NE	160
Garret S LAKE	Livingston	MI	Apr. 13,1837	NW/SE	40

Section 8

Name	Location	State	Date	Description	Acres
William H TOWNSEND	(New York city)		Oct. 1,1836	SE¼	160
William C BLACKWOOD	Seneca	NY	May 6,1836	NW¼	160
Mark HEALY &					
BB KERCHIVAL &					
Ramsey McHENRY &					
F D F SMITH	(U.S.)		May 14, 1836	NE¼	160
HEALY & KERCHIVAL	(U.S.)		May 28,1836	SW¼	160

Section 9

Name	Location	State	Date	Description	Acres
Isaac R STOWE	Ontario	NY	Oct. 16,1835	W½/SW	80
William SPAFFORD	Genessee	NY	May 20,1836	W½/NW	80
Lester K GOULD	Genessee	NY	May 20,1836	E½/NW & E½/SW	160
Garret S LAKE	Livingston	NY	May 28,1836	NE¼	160
Edward C DOWSER	Livingston	NY	June 27,1836	W½/SE	80
William BLOODWORTH	Washtenaw	MI	Jan. 9,1837	E½/SE	80

Howell township

Section 10

Harry W PHILLIPS	Niagara	NY	May 21,1836	SE$\frac{1}{4}$ & SW$\frac{1}{4}$	320
William CARPENTER	Niagara	NY	May 21,1836	NE$\frac{1}{4}$ & NW$\frac{1}{4}$	320

Section 11

Moses THOMPSON	Herkimer	NY	Sept. 3,1835	E$\frac{1}{2}$/SE	80
Anthony SHAW	Saratoga	NY	May 21,1836	NW$\frac{1}{4}$	160
Patrick TOBIN	Livingston	MI	May 28,1836	SW$\frac{1}{4}$	160
Aaron SICKELS				SE/NE	40
John SICKELS			May 8,1838	NE/NE	40
Odell J SMITH	Livingston	MI	Aug. 4,1838	SW/NE & NW/SE	80
Charles S FURGUSON			July 5,1853	SW/SE	40
Levi D SMITH	Livingston	MI	Nov. 1,1855	NW/NE	40

Section 12

Moses THOMPSON	Herkimer	NY	Sept. 3,1835	W$\frac{1}{2}$/SW	80
Ezra J MUNDY	Livingston	MI	Apr. 30,1836	SW/SE	40
John F SICKEL	Wayne	NY	May 18,1836	NE$\frac{1}{4}$ & NW$\frac{1}{4}$ & E$\frac{1}{2}$/SW & E$\frac{1}{2}$/SE & NW/SE	520

Section 13

George W TEEPLE	Stueben	NY	July 7,1835	SW/SW	40
Ezra J MUNDY	Livingston	MI	Apr. 30,1836	W$\frac{1}{2}$/NE & E$\frac{1}{2}$/NW	160
Elisha THOMPSON	Livingston	MI	May 27,1836	NE/NE	40
Lewis THOMPSON	Livingston	MI	May 27,1836	E$\frac{1}{2}$/SW & NW/SW	120
Patrick TOBIN	Livingston	MI	May 28,1836	W$\frac{1}{2}$/NW	80
Levi HOTCHKISS	Livingston	MI	July 28,1836	SE$\frac{1}{4}$ & SE/NE	200

Section 14

George W TEEPLE	Stueben	NY	July 1,1835	SE/SE	40
Orrin H HARDING	Niagara	NY	Sept. 28,1835	SW$\frac{1}{4}$	160
Elijah GASTON	Livingston	MI	May 2,1836	W$\frac{1}{2}$/NW	80
Edward PECK	Genessee	NY	May 23,1836	W$\frac{1}{2}$/NE	80
William S GREGORY	Wayne	MI	May 23,1836	E$\frac{1}{2}$/NE & NE/SE	120
Patrick TOBIN	Livingston	MI	May 28,1836	E$\frac{1}{2}$/NW	80
Victory CURTISS	Livingston	MI	Sept. 24,1836	W$\frac{1}{2}$/SE	80

Howell township

Section 15

Orrin H HARDING	Niagara	NY	Sept. 28,1835	$E\frac{1}{2}$/SE	80
Mortimer B MARTIN	Wayne	MI	Feb. 15,1836	$NW\frac{1}{4}$	160
George CURTIS	Livingston	MI	May 2,1836	$E\frac{1}{2}$/NE	80
John CURTIS	Livingston	MI	May 2,1836	$W\frac{1}{2}$/NE	80
Ramsey McHENRY &					
O F SMITH &					
Mark HEALY &					
B B KERCHIVAL	(U. S.)		May 24,1836	$SW\frac{1}{4}$	160
Benjamin J SPRING	Livingston	MI	June 24,1836	$W\frac{1}{2}$/SE	80

Section 16 (school section)

Mary JONES	Jan. 21,1848	SE/SE	40
J LeGRANGE	Apr. 17,1848	NW/SE	40
A LeGRANGE	June 14,1848	SW/SW	40
William MORE	June 12,1849	NE/SE	40
	Jan. 19,1853	SW/NE	40
Anson LeGRANGE	Mar. 11,1851	SE/SW	40
O P BRAYTON	Apr. 30,1851	SE/NE	40
Charles O REED	June 28,1851	$N\frac{1}{2}$/SW	80
John LeGRANGE	Aug. 16,1851	SE/NW	40
C A DORRANCE	Oct. 8,1853	NW/NW	40
J McDANIELS	Oct. 14,1853	NW/NE	40
E MARR	Oct. 17,1853	SW/NW	40
Robert McLEAN	Oct. 20,1853	NE/NW	40
J WHIPPLE	Aug. 7,1854	NE/NE	40
Henry PELL	Nov. 19,1867	SW/SE	40

Section 17

Chilson SANFORD	Washtenaw	MI	Apr. 25,1834	$E\frac{1}{2}$/SW	80
Whitely WOODWORTH	Washtenaw	MI	Oct. 27,1834	SW/SW	40
Samuel WADDELL	Oakland	MI	July 14,1835	$E\frac{1}{2}$/SE	80
Clement STEVENS	Oakland	MI	Sept. 29,1835	SW/SE	40
William H TOWNSEND	(New York city)		Oct. 1, 1835	$NE\frac{1}{4}$	160
Flavius J B CRANE	Livingston	MI	Nov. 27,1835	NW/SW	40
Abram A VAN NEST	Washtenaw	MI	Mar. 16,1836	$NW\frac{1}{4}$	160
Henry LAKE	Livingston	MI	June 17,1836	NW/SE	40

Howell township

Section 18

James HISCOCK	Washtenaw	MI	Dec. 18,1834	E½/SE	80
Alfred A DWIGHT	Wayne	MI	July 17,1835	W½/SE	80
Silas TITUS &					
Bickford P HUCHINSON	Wayne	MI	July 17,1835	E½/NW	80
Morgan LYON	Chenango	NY	Sept. 28,1835	NE¼	160
Edwin HUBBARD	Washtenaw	MI	Oct. 14,1835	E½/SW	80
Harvey HUBBARD	Washtenaw	MI	Oct. 14,1835	W½/NW	80
Ebenezer DEMMON	Livingston	MI	Jan. 25,1837	Wp/SWf	77

Section 19

Clement STEBINS	Oakland	MI	Sept. 29,1835	E½/NE	80
Mark HEALY &					
B B KERCHIVAL	(U.S.)		May 28,1836	SE¼ & SWf¼ & NWf¼ & W½/NE	548

Section 20

Chilson SANFORD	Washtenaw	MI	Apr. 25,1834	NW¼	160
Sterry LYON	Washtenaw	MI	July 21,1834	E½/NE	80
Nancy GREGORY	Washtenaw	MI	June 20,1835	W½/NE	80
Charles S GREGORY	Washtenaw	MI	June 20,1835	W½/SE & SE/SE	120
Alfred A DWIGHT &					
Buckford P HUCHINSON	Wayne	MI	July 17,1835	NE/SE	40
Flavius J B CRANE	Livingston	MI	Nov. 27,1835	SW¼	160

Section 21

Elisha H SMITH	Ontario	NY	Nov. 6,1834	W½/SW	80
Villeroy E SMITH	Ontario	NY	May 22,1835	W½/NW	80
John W SMITH	Ontario	NY	May 22,1835	SE/SW	40
	Livingston	MI	Oct. 12,1837	NW/NE	40
Robert PIXLEY	Livingston	MI	Oct.15,1835	E½/NE & SW/NE	120
Isaac R STOWE	Livingston	MI	Oct. 16, 1835	SE¼	160
Jarvis W CARR	Ontario	NY	Oct. 16,1835	E½/NW	80
Josiah SNOW &					
George W H FISK	Wayne	MI	Feb. 8,1836	NE/SW	40

Howell township

Section 22

Name	County	State	Date	Description	Acres
Dennis HOGAN	Washtenaw	MI	May 23,1835	SW¼	160
Paul D CORNELL &					
Alonzo CORNELL	Rensellaer	NY	July 11,1835	W½/NW & NE/NW	120
Peter BREWER	Niagara	NY	Sept. 9,1835	SE/SE	40
Daniel CASE	Livingston	MI	Mar. 10,1836	NE/SE & SE/NE	80
			Apr. 4,1836	NE/NE	40
Luther B WILLARD	Wayne	MI	Apr. 23,1836	W½/NE	80
			Aug. 6,1836	SE/NW	40
Paul STOWELL	Genessee	NY	Mar. 9,1837	W½/SE	80

Section 23

Name	County	State	Date	Description	Acres
Silas TITUS &					
Beckford P HUCHINSON	Wayne	MI	July 17,1835	E½/SE	80
Moses THOMPSON	Herkimer	NY	Aug. 18,1835	E½/NE	80
Sally JOHNSON	Livingston	MI	Aug. 18,1835	SE/SW	40
David WADHAMS	Madison	NY	Sept. 3,1835	SW/SE	40
Peter BREWER	Niagara	NY	Sept. 9,1835	W½/SW	80
Justin DURFEE	Monroe	NY	Oct. 26,1835	W½/NW	80
James SAGE	Livingston	MI	May 9,1836	SE/NW	40
Patrick HEFFERMAN	Wayne	MI	May 28,1836	NW/SE & NE/SW	80
Agnes WOOD	Niagara	NY	June 2,1836	NE/NW	40
Victory CURTIS	Livingston	MI	Sept. 24,1836	W½/NE	80

Section 24

Name	County	State	Date	Description	Acres
George W TEEPLE	Stueben	NY	July 7,1835	W½/NW	80
Alfred A DWIGHT	Wayne	MI	July 17,1835	W½/SW	80
Samuel RIDDLE Jr.	Washtenaw	MI	Apr. 26,1836	E½/NW & W½/NE	160
William PACHARD	Wayne	MI	May 16,1836	E½/SW	80
William J PEASE	(NEW YORK city)		Nov. 16,1836	E½/NE	80
Alvin L CRITTENDON	Livingston	MI	Dec. 14,1836	N½/SE	80
Aaron SAUNDERS	Livingston	MI	June 11,1846	SE/SE	40
			Oct. 17, 1849	SW/SE	40

Section 25

Name	County	State	Date	Description	Acres
Checkley S PALMER	Genessee	NY	Oct. 7,1833	W½/NW	80
Moses THOMPSON	Herkimer	NY	May 15,1834	W½/SE	80
			July 10,1835	E½/SW	80
			Sept. 3,1835	W½/SW	80
	Livingston	MI	July 9,1849	NW/NE & SE/SE	80
Robert R ROWLAND	Wayne	NY	May 30,1835	S½/NW	80
Elizabeth THOMPSON	Oakland	MI	July 10,1835	SW/NE & NE/SE	80
Edward THOMPSON	Livingston	MI	May 27,1836	SE/NE	40
Joseph R THOMPSON	Oakland	MI	May 31,1839	NE/NE	40

92

Howell township

Section 26

Name	County	State	Date	Description	Acres
Itha J WEST	Niagara	NY	Sept. 9,1835	W½/NW	80
William McCREERY	Washtenaw	MI	Dec. 2,1834	E½/SW	80
Thomas WEST	Niagara	NY	July 17,1835	W½/SE	80
Alfred A DWIGHT &					
Bickford P HUCHINSON	Wayne	MI	July 17,1835	E½/NE	80
Jonathan AUSTIN	Herkimer	NY	Aug. 8,1835	SW/SW	40
Moses THOMPSON	Livingston	MI	Aug. 18,1835	E½/SE	80
Clarissa JOHNSON	Livingston	MI	Aug. 18,1835	E½/NW	80
David WADHAM	Madison	NY	Sept. 3,1835	W½/NE	80
John HAZE	Oakland	MI	Feb. 13,1838	NW/SW	40

Section 27

Name	County	State	Date	Description	Acres
Ormon COE	Genessee	NY	May 20,1833	E½/SW	80
Henry S LARNED	Livingston	MI	June 15,1835	SW/NW	40
			July 21,1835	NW/NW	40
Alfred A DWIGHT &					
Bickford P HUCHINSON	Wayne	MI	July 17,1835	W½/SW	80
George W PENNOCK	(Upper Canada)		Aug. 3,1835	W½/SE	80
Itha J WEST	Niagara	NY	Sept. 9,1835	NE/NE	40
Jonathan AUSTIN	Livingston	MI	Oct. 28,1835	E½/SE	80
Harvey METCALF	Livingston	MI	June 4,1836	W½/NE & E½/NW	160
John HAZE	Oakland	MI	Sept. 16,1837	SE/NE	40

Section 28

Name	County	State	Date	Description	Acres
Francis MOORE	Ontario	NY	Nov. 6,1834	SW¼	160
John W SMITH	Ontario	NY	May 22,1835	NE/NW	40
Isreal POWERS	Ontario	NY	June 8,1835	W½/NE	80
B L POWERS	Yates	NY	June 8,1835	E½/NE	80
Jacob LEROY	Genessee	NY	Aug. 11,1835	SE¼	160
Flavius J B CRANE	Livingston	MI	Jan. 13,1836	W½/NW & SE/NW	120

Section 29

Name	County	State	Date	Description	Acres
Eliphalet LEWIS	Washtenaw	MI	July 14,1835	E½/NE & NW/NE	120
Mark HEALY &					
B B KERCHIVAL	(U. S.)		May 28,1836	NW¼ & SW¼ & SE¼ & SW/NE	520

Section 30

Name	County	State	Date	Description	Acres
Mark HEALY &					
B B KERCHIVAL	(U.S.)		May 28,1836	Frac. section	621

Howell township

Section 31
Mark HEALY & B B KERCHIVAL	(U.S.)		May 28,1836	frac. section 6	12

Section 32
Rial LAKE	(Philedelphia)		Aug. 12,1835	SE¼	160
Mark HEALY & B B KERCHIVAL	(U.S.)		May 28,1836	NE¼ & NW¼ & SW¼	480

Section 33
Jacob LEROY	Genessee	NY	Aug. 11,1835	E½/NE	80
Rial LAKE	(Philedelphia)		Aug. 12,1835	W½/SW	80
Leonard COLLAR	Orleans	NY	Oct. 26,1835	W½/NE	80
Edward S GREGORY	Washtenaw	MI	Apr. 26,1836	E½/SW	80
Mark HEALY & B B KERCHIVAL	(U.S.)		May 28,1836	NW¼	160

Section 34
Moses THOMPSON	Herkimer	NY	May 9,1834	NE¼ & E½/NW & NE/SW	280
Morris THOMPSON	Herkimer	NY	May 15,1834	NW/SE	40
Brown BRISTOL	Genessee	NY	July 4,1835	E½/SE	80
Hesiekia CARPENTER & Socrates W CARPENTER	Genessee	NY	Aug. 11,1835	W½/NW	80
Edward GREGORY	Washtenaw	MI	May 24,1836	SW/SW	40
Joseph S CRISPEL	Livingston	MI	June 12,1840	SE/SW	40
Rice TYLER	Livingston	MI	July 10,1852	SW/SE	40
E G ALMY	Livingston	MI	Jan. 9,1854	NW/SW	40

Section 35
C C TROWBRIDGE	(Detroit)		June 26,1833	E½/SE	80
John D PINKNEY	Dutchess	NY	Dec. 3,1833	E½/NE	80
George T SAGE	Washtenaw	MI	Dec. 3,1833	W½/NW & W½/NE E½/SW & W½/SE	320
Benjamin BABBIT	Livingston	MI	July 8,1834	W½/SW	80

Section 36
John EAMAN	Jackson	MI	Oct. 11,1833	W½/SE	80
John D PINKNEY	Dutchess	NY	Dec. 3,1833	E½/SE & SW¼ & NW¼	280
Moses THOMPSON	Herkimer	NY	May 15,1834	E½/NW	80
	Oakland	MI	Aug. 5,1834	W½/NE	80
	Livingston	MI	May 26,1836	E½/NE	80
William ROOD	Montgomery	NY	Oct. 3,1835	NW/NW	40

NAME	COUNTY & STATE		DATE	LAND	ACRES
Section 1					
Horace HEATH	Wayne	MI	June 10,1836	W½/SW	80
Hiram P SPENCER	Columbia	NY	July 2,1836	NWf¼	203
Guy C LEE	Livingston	MI	July 11,1836	W½/SE	80
William M OLCOTT	Madison	NY	Nov. 17,1838	E½/SW	80
Roger GLENEN	Washtenaw	MI	Nov. 18,1837	Ep/NP/NEf	61
			Dec. 20,1837	SW/NE	40
John O'HARA	Washtenaw	MI	Feb. 13,1838	NW/NEf &	
				SE/NEf	101
Henry H NORTON	Livingston	MI	Sept. 6,1853	NE/SE	40
			Dec. 13,1853	SE/SE	40
Section 2					
Sterling ARMSTRONG	(New York city)		May 20,1836	SW¼	160
Hiram P SPENCER	Columbia	NY	July 2,1836	NEf¼ & E½/SE	284
Silas B MUNSELL	Washtenaw	MI	Nov. 4,1836	Sp/NW	80
George W LEE	Livingston	MI	June 15,1837	Wp/SE	80
Sarah Lucinda KILBORN	Livingston	MI	Apr. 22,1854	NE/NWf	63
George W CLARK	Livingston	MI	Sept. 6,1855	NW/NWf	63
Section 3					
William P SPAFFORD	Genessee	NY	May 19,1836	SW¼	160
William H REDFIELD	Ontario	NY	May 30,1836	NW/NWf	61
Lewis W DECKER	Ontario	NY	May 31,1836	Sp/NWf &	
				Ne/NWf	141
Andrew KING	Orange	NY	June 1,1836	SE¼	160
Erasmus D KEYS	(New York city)		July 15,1836	NEf¼	206
Section 4					
William H REDFIELD	Ontario	NY	May 30,1836	NE/NEf	61
Joseph &					
William BLANCHARD	Onondaga	NY	June 1,1836	Np/NWf	126
Lucius H EMERY	Erie	NY	June 11,1836	NE/SE	40
Josiah LOREE	Stueben	NY	Aug. 1,1836	NW/NEf &	
				SW.NEf	141
			Aug. 3,1836	NW/SE & NE/SW	80
Seth HART	Monroe	NY	Sept. 23,1836	W½/SW	80
Samuel H DODGE	Seneca	NY	Nov. 16,1836	Sp/NW	80
Cornelius BONTER	Livingston	MI	Apr. 4,1839	SE/SE	40
Nathan KNOWLES	Wayne	MI	June 22,1839	SE/SW	40
Joseph B COLE	Livingston	MI	Aug. 13,1839	SW/SE	40

Iosco township

Section 5

John H NORTHROUP	Onieda	NY	June 13,1836	SE¼ & E½/SW	240
Amos P GRIDLEY	Onieda	NY	June 14,1836	Sp/NEf & SE/NW	120
William PEASE	(New York city)		Nov. 16,1836	Np/NEf	129
Asa C TUTTLE	Oakland	MI	Jan. 24,1837	W½/SW	80
Alexander RICHMOND	Washtenaw	MI	Dec. 9,1837	SE/NWf	65
Henry WOODEN	Livingston	MI	June 28,1848	SW/NW	40
Merrill COLBY	Wayne	MI	July 31,1853	NW/NWf	65

Section 6

Patrick CONNER	Livingston	MI	Sept. 21,1836	W½/SE & SWf¼	175
Michael MULVENY	Washtenaw	MI	Nov. 1,1836	Np/NWf	87
William FAULK	Washtenaw	MI	Nov. 22,1836	Sp/NWf	49
Jonathan O HATHAWAY	Oakland	MI	Aug. 31,1837	E½/SE	80
John COLBY	Livingston	MI	Nov. 8,1853	NE/NEf	67
Michael FLINN	Livingston	MI	June 19,1854	NW/NEf & SW/NE	107
James LINDSEY	Livingston	MI	Aug. 21,1855	SE/NE	40

Section 7

Samuel H DODGE	Seneca	NY	Nov. 16,1836	W½/SE	80
B B KERCHIVAL	Wayne	MI	Nov. 26,1836	NE¼	160
Emery BEAL	Livingston	MI	Jan. 11,1837	E½/SE	80
John FOSTER	Washtenaw	MI	Jan. 19,1837	Sp/NWf	46
Jacob GROVER	Wayne	MI	July 9,1836	SWf¼	89
Dotha BARNUM	Livingston	MI	July 17,1838	N½/NWf	46

Section 8

Elbert PARKER	Livingston	MI	Oct. 29,1835	SE¼	160
Samuel RANNEY	Franklin	MA	Nov. 5,1835	NE¼	160
William RANNEY	Franklin	MA	Nov. 5,1835	NE/NW	40
James ABBOTT	Monroe	NY	Sept. 23,1836	SW¼	160
Peter CHASE	Oakland	MI	Sept. 14,1836	SE/NW & W½/NW	120

Iosco township

Section 9

William KIRKLAND	Wayne	MI	Jan. 1,1836	$E\frac{1}{2}$/SE	80
Seth SPENCER	Onondaga	NY	May 19,1836	$W\frac{1}{2}$/SW & SW/NW	120
Theodore H DRAKE	Ontario	NY	May 23,1836	$W\frac{1}{2}$/NE	80
Samuel CARPENTER	Allegeny	NY	Sept. 21.1836	$W\frac{1}{2}$/SE & $E\frac{1}{2}$/SW	160
*Moses KEYES	Seneca	NY	Nov. 16,1838	$E\frac{1}{2}$/NW & NW/NW	120
John I SMITH	Washtenaw	MI	Jan. 12,1838	SE/NE	40
Jonah POYER Jr.	Livingston	MI	Oct. 10,1844	NE/NE	40

Section 10

William KIRKLAND	Wayne	MI	Jan. 1,1836	$SW\frac{1}{4}$	160
Henry BROWER	Genessee	NY	May 20,1836	$W\frac{1}{2}$/NW	80
Sterling ARMSTRONG	(New York city)		May 20,1836	$NE\frac{1}{4}$	160
Enoch TERHUNE	Washtenaw	MI	May 31,1836	$SE\frac{1}{4}$	160
Henry M WOOD	Washtenaw	MI	Nov. 5,1836	$E\frac{1}{2}$/NW	80

Section 11

John WOOD	Washtenaw	MI	Nov. 24,1835	$SW\frac{1}{4}$ & $W\frac{1}{2}$/NW & SE/NW	280
John W HILTON	Oswego	NY	May 13,1836	$E\frac{1}{2}$/NE & NW/NE	120
George SEWELL	Niagara	NY	May 28,1836	SE/SE	40
Henry M WOOD	Washtenaw	MI	Nov. 5,1836	$W\frac{1}{2}$/SE	80
Isaac S TUTTLE	Oakland	MI	Oct. 30,1839	NE/SE	40
Thomas SCHOONHOVEN	Livingston	MI	June 23,1842	NE/NW	40
Martha Ann WOOD	Livingston	MI	May 7,1845	SW/NE	40

Section 12

Alonzo PLATT	Washtenaw	MI	Aug. 12,1835	$E\frac{1}{2}$/SE	80
John H LECOUNT	Wayne	MI	Mar. 25,1836	$S\frac{1}{2}$/NE	80
Wallace GOODWIN	Ontario	NY	Apr. 5,1836	$W\frac{1}{2}$/SE	80
Richard STORMS	Livingston	MI	July 15,1836	NW/NW	40
William M OLCOTT	Madison	NY	Nov. 17,1836	NW/NE	40
Thomas B HOYT	Livingston	MI	Mar. 22,1837	SW/NW	40
Abel W WALKER	Washtenaw	MI	May 30,1837	NE/NE	40
James H WOOD	Ontario	NY	Sept. 4,1838	$E\frac{1}{2}$/NW	80
Philetus STARK	Livingston	MI	Sept. 30,1852	NW/SW	40
Cornelius Y ROSS	Livingston	MI	Feb. 15,1853	NE/SW	40
William GORTON	Livingston	MI	Dec. 17,1853	SW/SW	40
Elisha F BEACH				SE/SW	40

*(mispelled? KIES in tract)

Iosco township

Section 13

Name	County	State	Date	Description	Acres
Lyman E BEACH	Erie	NY	Apr. 23,1836	E½/SE	80
William DAVIS	Erie	NY	Apr. 23,1836	E½/NE	80
Samuel COOLY	Genessee	NY	May 24,1836	NE/NW	40
William VANNOCKER	Genessee	NY	May 24,1836	NW/NE	40
Joseph H GORTON	Washtenaw	MI	Nov. 14,1836	E½/SW	80
Hiram WARD	Washtenaw	MI	Nov. 18,1836	W½/SE	80
			Nov. 29,1836	SW/SW	40
James M HIMES	Washtenaw	MI	May 28,1838	SE/NW & SW/NE	80
William HIMES	Washtneaw	MI	May 28,1838	NW/SW	40
William GORTON	Washtenaw	MI	DEc. 17,1853	W½/NW	80

Section 14

Name	County	State	Date	Description	Acres
William MILLER	Washtenaw	MI	May 23,1836	N½/SW	80
Joseph MARRIOT	Monroe	NY	May 28,1836	NW¼ & W½/NE	240
George SEWELL	Niagara	NY	May 28,1836	E½/NE	80
Joseph HUBBARD	Orleans	NY	May 30,1836	E½/SE & SW/SE	120
Silas MUNSELL	Wayne	MI	May 30,1836	S½/SW	80
Joseph LOREE	Livingston	MI	June 30,1837	NW/SE	40

Section 15

Name	County	State	Date	Description	Acres
Jeramiah NICHOLS	Oakland	MI	Feb. 15,1836	E½/SW	80
			May 12,1836	SW/SE	40
George W McINTOSH	Oakland	MI	Feb. 15,1836	NE/NW & W½/NW	120
Andrew LYTLE	Washtenaw	MI	May 23,1836	NE¼	160
Levi W MUNSELL	Wayne	NY	June 6,1836	SE/SE	40
John J TRAVER	Schenectady	NY	June 13,1836	N½/SE	80
Amos P GRIDLEY	Onieda	NY	June 14,1836	SE/NW	40
Adolphus COBURN	Albany	NY	Aug. 6,1836	W½/SW	80

Iosco township

Section 16 (school section)

F LOCKWOOD			Nov. 11,1846	NE/NE	40
J ACKER			Oct. 28,1847	NW/NE	40
J R GOODRICH			Nov. 16,1853	SW/NE	40
W H SIMONS			Oct. 6,1847	NE/NW	40
R SIMONS			Oct. 6,1847	NW/NW	40
R ACKER			Oct. 19,1847	SW/NW	40
Walter WRIGHT			Feb. 10,1848	SE/NW	40
J S A WRIGHT			May 6,1846	N½/SE	80
			Oct. 19,1847	SE/NE	40
John W WRIGHT			Apr. 24,1854	SE/SE	40
S and N TRACY			Nov. 11,1846	SW/SE	40
			May 9,1846	SE/SW	40
R and J ACKER			May 6,1846	W½/SW	80
P L WILHELM			Feb. 17,1847	SW/SW	40

Section 17

Robert J BARRY	Washtenaw	MI	Nov. 2,1835	NE¼ & E½/NW	240
			May 13,1836	W½/NW	80
Henry M WOOD	Washtenaw	MI	Mar. 12,1836	E½/SW & SW/SE	120
			Aug. 3,1836	NW/SE	40
Peter B WILHELM	Washtenaw	MI	May 27,1836	E½/SE	80
Hiram DEWEY	Stueben	NY	June 27,1836	W½/SW	80

Section 18

John A KEMP	Livingston	NY	July 9,1836	SWf¼	81
Jacob GROVER	Wayne	MI	July 9,1836	NWf¼	85
Emery BEAL	Washtenaw	MI	Sept. 21,1836	NE/SE	120
John B STIMPSON	Washtenaw	MI	Jan. 11,1837	W½/NE	80
Joseph N VOORHEIS	Oakland	MI	Jan. 24,1837	E½/NE	80
Enoch SMITH	Ingham	MI	Oct. 25,1843	SE/SE	40

Section 19

Richard M GUGGINS	Livingston	MI	May 30,1836	SWf¼ & W½/SE	
				& E½/SE	236
Robert L TAYLOR	(New York city)		June 13,1836	NWf¼	78
David H RICHARDSON	Ontario	NY	Sept. 21,1836	W½/NE	80
Richard PRICE	Livingston	MI	Dec. 19,1853	E½/NE	80

Iosco township

Section 20

Grace FASQUELLE & J Louis F B FASQUELLE	Livingston	MI	May 2,1836	NE/NE & W½/NE & E½/NW	200
Richard M GUGGINS	Livingston	MI	June 13,1836	SE¼	160
Orilla GUGGINS	Livingston	MI	June 18,1836	SE/NE	40
Hiram DEWEY	Stueben	NY	June 27,1836	SW¼	160
Leonard BARTON	Franklin	MA	Oct. 4,1837	NW/NW	40
Francis CRAWFORD	Wayne	MI	Jan. 11,1855	SW/NW	40

Section 21

Grace FASQUELLE	Livingston	MI	May 2,1836	NW/NW	40
Richard GUGGINS	Livingston	MI	May 13,1836	W½/SW	80
Luther HARVIE	Addison	VT	May 28,1836	SW/SE	40
Orilla GUGGINS	Livingston	MI	May 30,1836	SW/NW	40
			June 18,1836	NW/SE	40
Hiram DEWEY	Stueben	NY	June 27,1836	W½/NE & E½/NW	160
Marvin CALDWELL	Washtenaw	MI	Sept. 21,1836	SE/SE	40
Emery BEAL	Washtenaw	MI	Sept. 21,1836	E½/SW	80
Moses KIES	SENECA	NY	Nov. 16,1836	NE/SE & E½/NE	120

Section 22

John LOREE	Livingston	MI	Feb. 29,1836	E½/SW	80
Joseph LOREE	Livingston	MI	Mar. 21,1836	W½/SE	80
Rueben RHODES	Wayne	MI	May 20,1836	E½/NE	80
William R SPAFFORD	Genessee	NY	June 20,1836	E½/SE	80
Steven SHERWOOD	Orleans	NY	June 30,1836	NW¼	160
Chauncey EGGLESTON	Genessee	NY	July 3,1836	NW/SW	40
Jesse TUXBURY	Wayne	MI	July 4,1836	W½/NE	80
Marvin CALDWELL	Washtenaw	MI	Sept. 21,1836	SW/SW	40

Section 23

James MILLER	Stueben	NY	May 21,1836	W½/SW	80
Joseph LOREE	Stueben	NY	May 23,1836	E½/SW	80
Nathan FIELD	Genessee	NY	May 30,1836	NW¼ & SE ¼ & W½/NW	400
James B BARNARD	Orleans	NY	May 30,1836	E½/SW	80

Iosco township

Section 24

Name	County	State	Date	Description	Acres
Daniel PERSON	Erie	PA	Apr. 23,1836	NE¼	160
Abijah P BACKUS	Erie	PA	May 14,1836	S½/SE	80
Lorenzo BACKUS	Erie	PA	May 14,1836	NE/SE	40
Columbus MORGAN	(Heberon?)	NY	Nov. 14,1836	E½/NW	80
David ROGERS	Ingham	MI	Feb. 23,1837	E½/SW	80
Robert ROBINSON	Wayne	MI	Nov. 30,1836	NW/SE	40
Lauson JUDSON	Livingston	MI	Oct. 30,1837	W½/NW & NW/SW	120
William J JEWETT	Livingston	MI	Oct. 29,1845	SW/SW	40

Section 25

Name	County	State	Date	Description	Acres
Amos H BREED	Cayuga	NY	May 13,1836	SE¼ & E½/SW & SW/NE & SE/NW	320
Warren SEELY	Cayuga	NY	May 13,1836	SE/NE	40
James R PARDEE	Monroe	NY	May 18,1836	N½/NE & W½/NW & NE/NW	200
E COLEMAN			Dec. 13,1853	W½/SW	80

Section 26

Name	County	State	Date	Description	Acres
Erastus HALLOWAY	Wayne	NY	May 20,1836	W½/NW & NE/NW	120
Seth G WILSON	Addison	VT	May 28,1836	W½/SW	80
Peter J KUHN	Washtenaw	MI	Oct. 27,1836	W½/NE & SE/NW	120
Alfred DENNIS	Livingston	MI	Dec. 16,1836	E½/SW	80
Enoch WEBSTER	Stueben	NY	May 4,1837	W½/SE	80
State of Michigan				E½/NE & E½/SE	160

Section 27

Name	County	State	Date	Description	Acres
Seth G WILSON	Addison	VT	May 28,1836	E½/SE	80
Luther HAVEN	Addison	VT	May 28,1836	NW¼	160
Elsley W FULLER	Onondaga	NY	June 6,1836	W½/NE	80
Jabez PAUL	Onondaga	NY	June 6,1836	SW¼ & W½/SE	240
Josiah P FULLER	Courtland	NY	June 6,1836	E½/NE	80

Section 28

Name	County	State	Date	Description	Acres
Luther HAVEN	Addison	NY	May 28,1836	E½/NE	80
William S CASKEY	Washtenaw	MI	June 11,1836	E½/SE	80
Bastion WILLIAMS	Washtenaw	MI	July 11,1836	W½/SE	80
Marvin CALDWELL	Washtenaw	MI	Sept. 21,1836	W½/NW	80
Adeline HAVILAND	Washtenaw	MI	Jan. 11,1837	W½/SW	80
Harrison P & John R GOODRICH	Livingston	MI	Oct. 5,1847	E½/NW & W½/NE	160
Joseph S POST	Livingston	MI	Feb. 3,1854	SE/SW & NE/SE	80

101

Iosco township

Section 29

Seth SPENCER	Onondaga	NY	May 19,1836	NE¼ & SE¼	320
James WRIGHT	Onondaga	NY	May 19,1836	NW¼ & SW¼	320

Section 30

Richard M GUGGINS	Livingston	MI	May 30,1836	NWf¼	73
Nathan JONES	Livingston	MI	Mar. 1,1837	NW/NE	40
Ard OSBORN	Washtenaw	MI	Apr. 1,1846	SE ¼ & SWf¼ & S½/NE	311
James WRIGHT	Livingston		Apr. 1,1846	NE/NE	40

Section 31

Ard OSBORN	Washtenaw	MI	May 19,1836	NWf¼	51
John COOL	Livingston	MI	June 7,1837	NE¼	160
Samuel CASE	Livingston	MI	July 3,1837	N½/SWf	33
David DUTTON	Livingston	MI	July 15,1844	SW/SE	40
			June 3,1847	SE/SW	40
Elizabeth Ann DYER	Livingston	MI	Dec. 14,1853	S½/SWf	33
Joseph S DYER	Livingston	MI	Dec. 14,1853	NW/SE	40
John J DYER	Livingston	MI	Dec. 14,1853	NE/SE	40

Section 32

Phillip DYER	Livingston	MI	June 7,1836	SW¼ & E½/NW & W½/NE	320
David VAN SICKEL	Washtenaw	MI	June 20,1836	SE¼	160
Marvin CALDWELL	Washtenaw	MI	Sept. 21,1836	E½/NE	80
David H RICHARDSON	Ontario	NY	Sept. 21,1836	W½/NW	80

Section 33

Joseph P JEWETT	Washtenaw	MI		S½/SW	80
Putnam SMITH	Washtenaw	MI		NE/NE	40
Marvin CALDWELL	Washtenaw	MI		W½/NW	80
Emery BEAL	Washtenaw	MI		E½/NW & NW/SW	120
B B KERCHIVAL	Wayne	MI		W½/SE	40
David A McFARLAN	Wayne	MI		NE/SW	40
L D PRESTON				W½/NE	80
W H CHAPMAN	Ingham	MI		SE/SE	40
William S CASKEY	Livingston	MI		SE/NE	40
Harvey B LATSON				NE/SE	40

Iosco township

Section 34

Name	County	State	Date	Description	Acres
Alfred DENNIS	Addison	VT	May 28,1836	$E\frac{1}{2}$/NE	80
Martin SPRAGUE	Erie	NY	July 12,1836	$NW\frac{1}{4}$	160
Frederick BOLLES	Washtenaw	MI	Oct. 27,1836	$W\frac{1}{2}$/NE	80
Patrick FARLEY	Livingston	MI	Oct. 8,1837	$W\frac{1}{2}$/SW	80
David DENIO	Livingston	MI	Jan. 3,1838	$E\frac{1}{2}$/SW	80

Section 35

Name	County	State	Date	Description	Acres
Anna SOUTHERLAND	Washtenaw	MI	June 8,1836	$W\frac{1}{2}$/SE	80
George REEVES	Washtenaw	MI	June 8,1836	$E\frac{1}{2}$/SW	80
Ambrose CRANE	Genessee	NY	June 23,1836	$E\frac{1}{2}$/NW	80
			June 30,1836	Nw/NE	40
Alvin MANN	Genessee	NY	Sept. 21,1836	SW/NE & SE/SE	80
Frederick BOLLES	Washtenaw	MI	Oct. 27,1836	$W\frac{1}{2}$/SW	80
Thomas W HARFORD	Livingston	MI	Jan. 6,1853	$W\frac{1}{2}$/SW	80
Andrew LOVE	Livingston	MI	Mar. 3,1854	NE/SE	40
Hiram BACKUS	Livingston	MI	Jan. 13,1855	NE/NE	40
James T WILLIAMS	Livingston	MI	Jan. 13,1855	SE/NE	40

Section 36

Name	County	State	Date	Description	Acres
*J Louis F B FASQUELLE	Livingston	MI	May 2,1836	SE/NE	40
Simeon BACKUS	Erie	NY	May 14,1836	$N\frac{1}{2}$/NE	80
Hiram WARD	Washtenaw	MI	Nov. 29,1836	NE/NW	40
Olive WARD	Washtenaw	MI	Jan. 6,1837	SW/NE	40
Moses FULLER	Livingston	MI	Mar. 23,1837	SE/SE	40
			Jan. 31,1839	SW/SE	40
Benjamin NICHOLS	Columbia	NY	June 17,1836	NE/SE	40
John CONNOR	Livingston	MI	Mar. 8,1849	SE/NW	40
Samuel G SOUTHERLAND	Washtenaw	MI	Dec. 15,1848	NW/SE	40
Charles BAILEY	Oakland	MI	Dec. 15,1853	$W\frac{1}{2}$/NW	80
Eli ANNIS			Feb. 15,1865	NE/SW	40
M C BARTON			Feb. 12,1867	SE/SW	40
State of Michigan				$W\frac{1}{2}$/SW	80

*(Jean Louis Francois Benoit Fasquelle, 7th Prof. at
University of Michigan, Language department)

MARION township-FIRST Land Owners

NAME	COUNTY	STATE	DATE	LAND	ACRES
Section 1					
John D PINCKNEY	Duchess	NY	Dec. 3,1833	Np/NEf	135
Ira A BLOSSOM &					
Elijah D EFNER	Erie	NY	Sept. 2,1835	Np/NW	147
John FRAZER	(New York city)		Oct. 26,1835	Sp/NE	80
Flavius J B CRANE	Livingston	MI	Nov. 27,1835	W$\frac{1}{2}$/SW & Sp/NW	160
Herman HARRINGTON	Oakland	MI	Mar. 14,1836	E$\frac{1}{2}$/SE	80
William C SHAFT	Washtenaw	MI	June 9,1836	E$\frac{1}{2}$/SW	80
Henry A NAGLEE	Wayne	MI	June 29,1836	Sp/NW	80
Fred CAREY	Lenawee	MI	July 14,1836	W$\frac{1}{2}$/SE	80
Section 2					
Jonathan EASTERBROOK	Cataraga	NY	May 14,1834	SE/SW	40
Sardis DAVIS	Cataraga	NY	Sept. 15,1834	NW/NWf	38
Samuel HUBBARD	Livingston	NY	May 13,1835	W$\frac{1}{2}$/SE	80
	Livingston	MI	Aug. 25,1835	NE/SW	40
James T ALLEN &					
David GODFREY	Washtenaw	MI	May 26,1835	NEf$\frac{1}{4}$	232
David W WETMORE	(New York city)		June 30,1835	Sp/NE/NWf	156
George W JEWITT	Washtenaw	MI	Oct. 9,1835	E$\frac{1}{2}$/SE & W$\frac{1}{2}$/SW	160
Ira A BLOSSOM &					
Elijah D EFNER	Erie	NY	Sept. 2,1835	SW/NWf	38
Section 3					
Jonathan AUSTIN	Livingston	MI	July 5,1834	NE/NEf	35
James HISCOCK	Washtenaw	MI	Dec. 18,1834	W$\frac{1}{2}$/SE & E$\frac{1}{2}$/SW	160
George W JEWETT	Washtenaw	MI	Oct. 9,1835	E$\frac{1}{2}$/SE	80
Isaac R STOWE	Ontario	NY	Oct. 21,1835	S$\frac{1}{2}$/Np/NEf	77
Townsend DREW	Stueben	NY	May 20,1836	NWf$\frac{1}{4}$ & W$\frac{1}{2}$/SW	315
Robert F RANDALL	Washtenaw	MI	Jan. 9,1837	NW/NEf	38
James A HICKS &					
Samuel T BUELL	Wayne	MI	Mar. 16,1837	NW/NWf & Sp/NE118	

Marion township

Section 4
Rial LAKE	(Philadelphia)		Aug. 12,1835	Np/NWf	152
			Aug. 4,1836	Sp/NW	80
John D RIDDLE &					
Rueben MOORE	Washtenaw	MI	Oct. 29,1835	Np/NEf	154
Townsend DREW	Livingston	MI	May 9,1837	S½/NE	80
Joseph COLLIER	Washtenaw	MI	May 20,1837	W½/SE	80
			Mar. 2,1837	NE/NE	40
Luke HEMINGWAY	(New York city)		Mar. 27,1837	SW¼	160
John BENNETT	Livingston	MI	Oct. 1,1851	SE/SE	40

Section 5
Alexander BOYDEN	Washtenaw	MI	July 17,1835	NE/SW & Sp/NW	120
	Livingston	MI	Apr. 19,1837	SW/SW	40
Rial LAKE	(Philadelphia)		Aug. 4,1836	SE/ME	40
	(New York city)		June 15,1837	SE/NE	40
Francis J PREVOOST	Washtenaw	MI	July 17,1835	NW/SW	40
John BALLARD	Wayne	MI	July 25,1835	Np/NE	150
Charles A BOGART	Ontario	NY	Sept. 30,1835	SE/SW	120
Mary Ann PREVOOST	Livingston	MI	Jan. 2,1836	SW/NE	40
James HADDEN	Livingston	MI	May 25,1837	NE/NE	40
Benjamin SMITH	Livingston	MI	June 29,1836	Sp/Np/NWf	73
Gaines DAYTON	Wayne	MI	Mar. 21,1837	Np/NWf	73

Section 6
Francis J PREVOOST	Washtenaw	MI	July 17,1835	SE¼	160
			July 25,1835	E½/SW	80
Gains DAYTON	Wayne	MI	Mar. 2,1837	Sp/NE	80
Thomas Schoonhoven	Washtenaw	MI	Mar. 20,1837	SW/SWf	42
James HADDEN	Washtenaw	MI	May 25,1837	W½/NWf	71
Rial LAKE	(Philedelphia)		June 15,1837	E½/Np/NEf	71
			June 28,1837	Wp/Np/NEf	72
	Livingston	MI	Apr. 6,1838	NE/Np/NEf	36
Samuel P JEWETT	Washtenaw	MI	Jan. 3,1838	Sp/NWf	81
George W KEELER	Livingston	MI	Mar. 15,1855	SE/Np/NEf	36
H H NORTON	Livingston	MI	Dec. 13,1853	NW/SWf	42

Marion township

Section 7

John BALLARD	Wayne	MI	July 17,1835	NE¼	160
Pierpont L SMITH	Washtenaw	MI	Aug. 7,1835	Ep/NWf &	
				SW/NWf	123
			Dec. 5,1835	SW/SE	40
Alonzo PLATT	Washtenaw	MI	Aug. 12,1835	Wp/SWf	87
Stoddard SMITH	Washtenaw	MI	Sept. 16,1835	E½/SW	80
Louis F B FASQUELLE	Washtenaw	MI	Oct. 9,1835	NW/SEf	40
Guy C LEE	Madison	NY	Apr. 18,1836	NE/SE	40
Lynn E BLACK	Erie	PA	Apr. 23,1836	SE/SE	40
Cornelius POTTER	Livingston	MI	Apr. 28,1836	NW/NWf	43

Section 8

Charle A BOGART	Ontario	NY	Sept. 30,1835	NW/NE	40
James T BASHFORD	Wayne	MI	Mar. 25,1836	E½/SE	80
Guy C LEE	Madison	NY	Apr. 18,1836	W½/NW & NW/SW	120
George W LEE	Livingston	MI	July 11,1836	SE/NW	40
Lyman E BEACH	Erie	NY	Apr. 23,1836	W½/SE & SW/SW	120
Thomas L HANCOCK	Washtenaw	MI	June 8,1836	SE/SW	40
Isreal S SPENCER	Madison	NY	Sept. 24,1836	E½/NE	80
Rial LAKE	Livingston	MI	Mar. 28,1836	SW/NE & NE/NW	80
Richard DAY	Washtenaw	MI	Oct. 30,1852	NE/SW	40

Section 9

James COLLINS	Genessee	NY	Sept. 23,1833	W½/SW	80
Rial LAKE	Livingston	MI	Nov. 28,1836	W½/NW	80
Conrad WOOL	Livingston	MI	Nov. 26,1836	SE/NE	40
B B KERCHIVAL	Wayne	MI	Dec. 26,1836	SE¼ & E½/SW	240
George CORSELUS	Wayne	MI	Dec. 26,1836	W½/NE & E½/NW	160
Ezra F OLDS	Livingston	MI	June 25,1837	NE/NE	40

Section 10

Pierce MORSE	Genessee	MI	Oct. 23,1835	W½/NE	80
Samuel LYON	Stueben	NY	May 20,1836	E½/NW & SE/SW	120
			July 7,1836	NE/SE	40
William GIBB	New Haven	CN	June 3,1836	E½/NE	80
Roswin KINGSLEY	Monroe	NY	July 6,1836	W½/SE	80
Conrad WOOL	Livingston	MI	Oct. 27,1836	W½/NW	80
Jonathan SEELEY	Wayne	MI	Nov. 15,1836	W½/SW	80
Edward ESTEYS	Wayne	MI	May 12,1837	NE/SW	40
Zebelon M DREW	Livingston	MI	Oct. 8,1838	SE/SE	40

Marion township

Section 11

Isreal BRANCH	Washtenaw	MI	July 10,1835	SE¼	160
			Nov. 27,1835	NE/SW	40
John D RIDDLE &					
Rueben MOORE	Washtenaw	MI	Oct. 29,1835	NE¼	160
Isreal BENNET 2cd	Washtenaw	MI	Nov. 23,1835	SE/SW	40
Charles MOSLEY	Washtenaw	MI	Nov. 27,1835	W½/SW & W½/NW	160
Elisha A AVERY &					
Charles ELDREDGE	Wayne	MI	Jan. 11,1837	E½/NW	80

Section 12

John M BROWN	Ontario	NY	July 16,1835	W½/SW	80
John P THORNTON	Wayne	MI	Nov. 14,1835	SW/NW	40
Adna SAWYER	Yates	NY	June 4,1836	NE¼	160
Giles CHURCH	Monroe	NY	June 13,1836	E½/NW	80
Enoch WEBSTER	Stueben	NY	June 22,1836	W½/NE & E½/SW	160
Edward G WILBER	Columbia	NY	June 23,1836	E½/SE	80
Verry GOLDTHWAIT	Washtenaw	MI	Mar. 10,1851	NW/NW	40

Section 13

John M BROWN	Ontario	NY	July 16,1835	NW¼	160
Dwight HAWK	Oakland	MI	Mar. 17,1836	NE¼	160
William J WEBSTER	Stueben	NY	June 22,1836	W½/SE & E½/SW	160
	Livingston	MI	Oct. 30,1837	SW/SW	40
Edward G WILBER	Columbia	NY	June 23,1836	E½/SE	80
William C DECKER	Livingston	MI	Apr. 15,1853	NW/SW	40

Section 14

John M BROWN	Ontario	NY	July 16,1835	NE/NE	40
Walter R SEYMOUR	Wayne	MI	Nov. 14,1835	NW/SW & NE/SW	80
Aaron SEYMOUR	Wayne	MI	Jan. 20,1836	SE/SW	40
John P THORNTON	Wayne	MI	Nov. 14,1835	W½/NE & E½/NW	160
Edgar M GALLOWAY	Wayne	MI	Mar. 14,1836	W½/SE	80
William CLAY	Wayne	MI	June 16,1836	E½/SE	80
Edward ESTES	Washtenaw	MI	June 18,1836	SW/NW	40
Zebelon M DREW	Livingston	MI	Jan. 9,1837	NW/NW	40
Joseph SAXTON	Washtenaw	MI	Sept. 25,1837	NW/SW	40
Parley H STEPHENS	Livingston	MI	Oct. 15,1846	SE/NE	40

Marion township

Section 15

Hiram WING &					
John L WING	Washtenaw	MI	Oct. 26,1835	E$\frac{1}{2}$/SW & W$\frac{1}{2}$/SE	160
Josiah DOTY	Monroe	NY	Nov. 19,1835	W$\frac{1}{2}$/NE & E$\frac{1}{2}$/NW	160
William KIRKLAND	Wayne	MI	Jan. 1,1836	W$\frac{1}{2}$/NW & W$\frac{1}{2}$/SW	160
Jeramiah KENT	Washtenaw	MI	May 31,1836	E$\frac{1}{2}$/NE	80
Kenneth DAVIDSON	Washtenaw	MI	June 7,1836	E$\frac{1}{2}$/SE	80

Section 16 (school section)

M S HAVEN	Sept. 16,1841	NE/NW & N$\frac{1}{2}$/SE/SW	60
S W COFFEY	Oct. 24,1845	SE/NE	40
Lyman CLARK	Mar. 14,1849	W$\frac{1}{2}$/NW	80
Nelson COFFEY	May 8,1849	NE/SE	40
J N BASHFORD	Sept. 26,1849	NW/NE	40
C COLEMAN	Oct. 9,1850	NW/SW	40
H C MALLORY	July 22,1851	SE/SE	40
William HUNTINGTON	Dec. 20,1854	NE/NE & SW/NE	80
A T ALLRIGHT	Mar. 8,1855	SE/SW	40
Pierce ELWELL	Nov. 11,1856	SW/SW	40
James HARGER	Nov. 29,1858	SW/SE & NW/SW	80
Chester GOODRICH	Nov. 29,1858	S$\frac{1}{2}$/SE/NW	20

Section 17

Seth C DARWIN	Livingston	NY	Oct. 27,1835	SE$\frac{1}{4}$ & E$\frac{1}{2}$/NE	240
Lyman E BEACH	Erie	PA	Apr. 23,1836	E$\frac{1}{2}$/NW	80
Nelson A SMITH	Erie	PA	June 20,1836	W$\frac{1}{2}$/NE	80
Ashwell W PRIOR	Madison	NY	Jan. 14,1837	W$\frac{1}{2}$/NW	80
Waters CLARK	Madison	NY	June 1,1837	S$\frac{1}{2}$/SW	80
Lyman CLARK	Livingston	MI	Mar. 2,1849	NE/SW	40
			Sept. 1,1868	NW/SW	40

Section 18

Jeptha JEWETT	Wayne	MI	Oct. 2,1835	Ep/NW	80
Alvin S McDONALD	Niagara	NY	Oct. 14,1835	E$\frac{1}{2}$/NE	80
Hiram FISK	Niagara	NY	Oct. 14,1835	W$\frac{1}{2}$/NE	80
Lincy RASH &					
George RASH	Washtenaw	MI	Dec. 29,1835	Ep/SW & W$\frac{1}{2}$/SE	160
George RASH	Washtenaw	MI	Apr. 15,1836	Wp/SWf	87
William DAVIS	Erie	PA	Apr. 23,1836	Wp/NWf	87
Robert MUNNS	Livingston	MI	Dec. 28,1838	SE/SE	40
John Andrew EZEL	Livingston	MI	Dec. 4,1847	NE/SE	40

Marion township

Section 19

Name	County	State	Date	Description	Acres
Sylvester ROUNDS	Wayne	MI	Jan. 14,1836	NWf$\frac{1}{4}$	166
Robert MUNNS	Wayne	MI	Feb. 8,1836	NE/SW	40
Hiram P BAKER	Monroe	NY	May 18,1836	Wp/SW	84
Joseph N WALKER	Allegheny	NY	May 23,1836	SE$\frac{1}{4}$ & SE/SW & E$\frac{1}{2}$/NE & SW/NE	320
William HIMES	Washtenaw	MI	July 12,1838	NW/NE	40

Section 20

Name	County	State	Date	Description	Acres
Seth G DAVIDSON	Livingston	MI	May 23,1836	NE$\frac{1}{4}$	160
Joseph WALKER	Allegheny	NY	May 23,1836	W$\frac{1}{2}$/SW & SW/NW	120
Robert MUNNS	Livingston	MI	May 23,1836	NW/NW	40
George MITCHELL	Madison	NY	June 1,1836	E$\frac{1}{2}$/SW	80
Hiram MITCHELL	Livingston	MI	June 1,1836	SE/NW & SE/NW	80
Spencer MITCHELL	Madison	NY	June 1,1836	W$\frac{1}{2}$/SE	80
George BATES	(Plymouth,MI)		June 18,1836	E$\frac{1}{2}$/SE	80

Section 21

Name	County	State	Date	Description	Acres
Seth C DARWIN	Livingston	MI	Oct. 21,1835	NW$\frac{1}{4}$	160
Hiram WING	Washtenaw	MI	Mar. 8,1836	NE/NE	40
Samuel CLARK	Wayne	NY	May 18,1836	SE$\frac{1}{4}$	160
Henry VAN GUSON	Washtenaw	NI	May 31,1836	SE/SW	40
George BATES	(Plymouth,MI)		June 18,1836	SW/SW	40
Henry H SMITH	Genessee	NY	June 3,1836	W$\frac{1}{2}$/NE & SE/NE	120
			May 16,1837	NE/SW	40
David T WOOD	Livingston	MI	Apr. 15,1847	NW/SW	40

Section 22

Name	County	State	Date	Description	Acres
George RASH	Washtenaw	MI	Dec. 29,1835	N$\frac{1}{2}$/NW	80
John L WING	Washtenaw	MI	Nov. 8,1836	NW/NE	40
William R MARSHALL	Washtenaw	MI	May 6,1836	S$\frac{1}{2}$/NW	80
Charles VAN WINKLE	Allegheny	NY	June 6,1836	SE/SW	80
Ezra N FAIRCHILD	Macomb	MI	June 24,1836	W$\frac{1}{2}$/SW	80
Joseph H STEELE	Wayne	MI	June 24,1836	NE/SW	40
James BAVIN	(England)		June 25,1836	SE$\frac{1}{4}$ & E$\frac{1}{2}$/NE$\frac{1}{4}$ & SW/NE	280

Marion township

Section 23

George W MOORE	Ontario	NY	Oct. 22,1835	E½/NE	80
Edgar M GALLOWAY	Wayne	NY	Mar. 14,1836	E½/NW & NW/NW	120
Morris K HENRY	Wayne	MI	June 16,1836	W½/SE	80
Jason BUTTERFIELD	Otsego	NY	June 11,1836	SW¼	160
Jenks CHASE	Ontario	NY	June 11,1836	E½/SE	80
James BAVIN	(England)		June 24,1836	SW/NW	40
John C BULL	Wayne	MI	July 11,1836	W½/NE	80

Section 24

Timothy R BENNETT	Livingston	MI	July 24,1835	E½/SW	80
Justus E BROWN	Columbia	NY	Oct. 22,1835	NW¼	160
Horace GRIFFETH	Stueben	NY	May 26,1836	SW/SE	40
			June 22,1836	W½/NE	80
Eastman GRIFFETH	Livingston	MI	June 8,1836	E½/NE	80
Catherine GRIFFETH	Livingston	MI	Nov. 3,1836	NW/SE	40
Jenks CHASE	Ontario	NY	June 18,1836	W½/SW	80
William L TOMPKINS	Livingston	MI	Dec. 29,1836	SE/SE	40
Jacob D GALE	Livingston	MI	Aug. 24,1846	NE/SE	40

Section 25

James SLOAN	Washtenaw	MI	June 17,1836	W½/SW	80
Jenks CHASE	Ontario	NY	June 18,1836	W½/NW	80
Christopher HOAGLAND	Livingston	MI	Nov. 3,1836	SE/NE	40
Jacob FISHBECK	Livingston	MI	Jan. 20,1837	NE/SE	40
Levi FISHBECK	Livingston	MI	Jan. 20,1837	W½/SE	80
Adam RUBBINS	Livingston	MI	July 16,1837	SE/SE	40
James D GALE	Livingston	MI	June 9,1847	NE/NE	40
Richard D BENTLEY	Livingston	MI	Dec. 3,1853	SW/NE	40
			Feb. 8,1854	NW/NE	40

Section 26

Rueben BENNETT	Livingston	MI	May 21,1836	W½/SE	80
Eastman GRIFFETH	Stueben	NY	May 21,1836	SW¼	160
James SLOAN	Washtenaw	MI	June 17,1836	E½/SE	80
Jenks CHASE	Ontario	NY	June 18,1836	E½/NE	80
Verry GOLDTHWAIT	Washtenaw	MI	Mar. 10,1837	W½/NE	80

Marion township

Section 27

William FORSHEE	Cayuga	NY	May 25,1836	SWf¼	133
C HOAGLAND &					
E GRIFFETH	Stueben	NY	May 26,1836	NEf¼	159
John HOLDEN	Providence	RI	May 30,1836	SEf	130
Charles VAN WINKLE	Allegheny	NY	June 6,1836	Ep/NEf	70
Stephen Thomas PROBETT	Livingston	MI	June 10,1836	W½/NW	80

Section 28

Ezra N FAIRCHILD	Genessee	NY	May 23,1836	NE¼	160
Stephen T PROBETT	Livingston	MI	June 10,1836	SE¼	160
			June 19,1836	SWf¼	90
Joseph H STEELE	Wayne	MI	June 24,1836	Wp/NWf	79
			June 28,1836	Ep/NW	80

Section 29

Silas RAYMOND	Erie	NY	June 13,1836	E½/NW	80
Edwin Mark CUST	(England)		June 20,1836	SW¼ & SEf¼	283
Elijah F BURT	Windham	VT	June 15,1837	SW/NW	40
Joseph H STEELE	Wayne	MI	Aug. 16,1837	NEf¼	115
Eri COLEMAN	Livingston	MI	Sept. 3,1849	NW/NW	40

Section 30

Jesse SCHAFFER	Washtenaw	MI	June 13,1836	E½/NE	80
Steven AVERILL	Erie	PA	Apr. 23,1836	SE¼	160
Henry BOWER	Genessee	NY	May 13,1836	Wp/SWf	85
Lewis PARDEE	Monroe	NY	May 18,1836	Ep/SW & Ep/NW	
				& NW/NE	200
Benjamin HILL	Wayne	MI	Apr. 11,1837	SW/NE	40
Rial LAKE	(Philadelphia)		June 15,1837	SW/NE	40

Section 31

Thomas HASKINS	Washtenaw	MI	June 17,1836	NE¼	160
Benjamin NICHOLS	Columbia	NY	June 17,1836	NWf¼	162
Caleb RICE	Yates	NY	Sept. 23,1836	SWf¼	154
Jeramiah D SAMSON	Wayne	MI	Aug. 10,1837	W½/SE	80
Ira ANNIS	Livingston	MI	Nov. 30,1852	SE/SE	40

Marion township

Section 32

John S FARRAND	Cayuga	NY	May 30,1836	SW/NE	40
Lemeul BRYANT	Washtenaw	MI	May 31,1836	SE/SW	40
William WING	Russell	NY	May 31,1836	SE$\frac{1}{4}$ & E$\frac{1}{2}$/NE	240
Thomas HASKINS	Washtenaw	MI	Sept. 21,1836	W$\frac{1}{2}$/NW	80
Horace H SMITH	Washtenaw	MI	Nov. 29,1836	E$\frac{1}{2}$/NW	80
William LOVE	Livingston	MI	May, 1837	SW/SW & NE/SW	80
Elizabeth BASING	Livingston	MI	July 15,1844	NW/NE	40

Section 33

George P JEFFRIES	Washtenaw	MI	May 31,1836	SE/SE	40
Aaron YOUNGLOVE	Washtenaw	MI	June 1,1836	W$\frac{1}{2}$/SE	80
			June 4,1836	NE$\frac{1}{4}$	160
Russell PALMER	Washtenaw	MI	June 17,1836	NE/SE	40
Henry G LOVE	(England)		June 25,1836	NW$\frac{1}{4}$ & SW$\frac{1}{4}$	320

Section 34

George CORSELUS	Wayne	MI	Mar. 14,1836	E$\frac{1}{2}$/SW	80
William FORSHEE	Cayuga	NY	May 25,1836	NW$\frac{1}{4}$	160
John HOLDEN	Providence	RI	May 30,1836	Wp/NE	80
George JEFFRIES	Washtenaw	MI	May 31,1836	W$\frac{1}{2}$/SW	80
Aaron YOUNGLOVE	Washtenaw	MI	June 1,1836	SEf$\frac{1}{4}$	109
Randall HOLDEN	Providence	RI	June 8,1836	Ep/NEf	87

Section 35

Miles CHUBB	Livingston	MI	Dec. 14,1835	SE$\frac{1}{4}$ & Sp/NWf	254
Ephriam C HENDEE	Livingston	NY	June 9,1836	NE$\frac{1}{4}$	160
John HOLDEN	Providence	RI	June 9,1836	SWf$\frac{1}{4}$	114
Randall HOLDEN	Providence	RI	June 28,1836	Np/NW	80

Section 36

Miles CHUBB	Livingston	MI	Dec. 14,1835	W$\frac{1}{2}$/SW	80
Ephriam C HENDEE	Livingston	NY	June 9,1836	NW$\frac{1}{4}$	160
James TATE	Washtenaw	MI	Dec. 14,1836	E$\frac{1}{2}$/NE & E$\frac{1}{2}$/SE	160
Lewis AUSTIN	Wayne	MI	Jan. 18,1837	W$\frac{1}{2}$/NE	80
			Jan. 14,1837	NW/SE	40
Thomas MORRISSEY	Washtenaw	MI	Apr. 26,1837	SW/SE & E$\frac{1}{2}$/SW	120

OCEOLA township—FIRST Land Owners

NAME	COUNTY & STATE		DATE	LAND	ACRES
Section 1					
Isreal PARSHALL	Livingston	MI	June 26,1835	S½/SE	80
Guy N ROBERTS	Livingston	MI	Dec. 2,1835	SW¼	160
Russell MORTON	Washtenaw	MI	Jan. 11,1836	NE/NEf	58
Ezekial PAGE	Washtenaw	MI	Mar. 19,1836	N½/SE	80
John VAN TUHL	Yates	NY	May 21,1836	NWf¼	196
Thomas VAN TUHL	Yates	NY	Oct. 25,1836	Wp/NEf	98
Henry TRIPP	Livingston	NY	July 14,1837	SE/NE	40
Section 2					
Samuel GRISWOLD	Livingston	MI	Oct. 29,1835	W½/SE & E½/SW	160
John STEEVENS	Livingston	MI	Oct. 29,1835	SE/SE	40
			Oct. 25,1836	Np/NEf	114
Jacob SNELL	Tioga	NY	May 11,1836	W½/SW & Sp/NW	160
Peter MARTIN	Yates	NY	May 21,1836	NE/SE & SE/NE	80
Thomas VAN TUHL	Livingston	MI	Sept. 21,1836	SW/NE	40
John A VAN CAMP	Livingston	MI	Nov. 26,1836	Np/NWf	110
Section 3					
Daniel W LEROY	Montgomery	NY	Jan. 1,1836	E½/SW & SW/SW	120
Joseph MERRELL	Genessee	NY	Apr. 18,1836	Np/NWf &	
				SW/NWf	144
			Apr. 19,1836	SE/NW	40
Jacob SNELL	Tioga	NY	May 11,1836	E½/SE	80
Jacob LONG	Wayne	MI	June 3,1836	NW/NEf	53
Rodney C BOUTWELL	(Hillsborough,NY)		June 16,1836	W½/SE & Sp/NE	160
Isreal C PARSHALL	Livingston	MI	Dec. 26,1836	NW/SW	40
B B KERCHIVAL	Wayne	MI	Dec. 27,1836	NE/NEf	53
Section 4					
William PAGE	Washtenaw	MI	Mar. 29,1836	W½/SW & Sp/NW	200
			Mar. 30.1836	E½/SW	80
Samuel WHITE	Oakland	MI	Apr. 7,1836	SE¼	160
Garrett MARTIN	Yates	NY	May 27,1836	NEf¼ &	
				Np/NWf	276

113

Oceola township

Section 5

Name	County	State	Date	Description	Acres
William PAGE	Washtenaw	MI	Mar. 29,1836	E½/SE & Sp/NE	160
			Apr. 4,1836	Np/NEf & W½/SE	172
Allen C HODGES	Oakland	MI	May 9,1836	SW/SW	40
John B FRANKLIN	Monroe	NY	May 9,1836	E½/SW & SE/NW	120
Cornelius NEISSE	Orange	NY	June 20,1836	SW/NWf & NW/SW	168

Section 6

Name	County	State	Date	Description	Acres
William J HAMILTON	Cayuga	NY	Apr. 25,1836	SWf¼	158
Roswell BARNES	Madison	NY	June 1,1836	NWf¼	165
Conrad MOORE	Orange	NY	June 20,1836	E½/SE	80
William B EAGER	Orange	NY	June 20,1836	NEf¼ & W½/SE	246

Section 7

Name	County	State	Date	Description	Acres
John W DURFEE	Wayne	NY	May 11,1836	NWf¼ & SWf¼	315
Charles VAN KUERAN	(New York city)		June 20,1836	SE¼	160
William B EAGER	Orange	NY	June 20,1836	E½/NE & SW/NE	120
John CURRAN	Livingston	MI	Nov. 16,1848	NW/NE	40

Section 8

Name	County	State	Date	Description	Acres
Asa PARKER	Oakland	MI	Nov. 4,1835	E½/NE	80
Thomas K PARSHALL	Livingston	MI	Dec. 10,1835	W½/NE & E½/NW	160
John M COE	Oakland	MI	Apr. 15,1836	NE/SE	40
Isaac MUNSON	Otsego	NY	Apr. 26,1836	W½/NW	80
William W JOHNSON	Wayne	MI	May 6,1836	W½/SW & SE/SW	120
			Dec. 27,1836	NE/SW	40
Robert EDWARDS	Wayne	MI	May 6,1836	SE/SE	40
			May 9,1836	NW/SE	40
Moses BEIDLEMAN	Livingston	MI	May 9,1837	SW/SE	40

Section 9

Name	County	State	Date	Description	Acres
Joseph WHITAKER	Livingston	MI	Dec. 11,1835	W½/NW	80
Norman SPELLAN	Oakland	MI	Dec. 23,1835	W½/SE & SW/NE	120
Jabez MEAD	Oakland	MI	Dec. 23,1835	E½/SW	80
			Jan. 13,1836	SE/NW	40
Joseph WILLIS	Oneida	NY	Jan. 25,1836	E½/SE	80
Samuel WHITE	Oakland	MI	Apr. 7,1836	E½/NE & NW/NE	120
John M COE	Oakland	MI	Apr. 15,1836	NW/SW	40
Robert EDWARDS	Wayne	MI	May 6,1836	SW/SW	40
			May 9,1836	NE/NW	40

Oceola township

Section 10

Name	County	State	Date	Description	Acres
Henry S CHAPLIN	Oakland	MI	Nov. 2,1835	SW/SE	40
Benjamin ELDRED	Courtland	NY	Nov. 6,1835	SE/SE	40
Daniel W LEROY	Montgomery	NY	Jan. 1,1836	NW¼	160
	Oakland	MI	June 11,1836	SW¼	160
William PEABODY	Monroe	NY	May 28,1836	NE¼	160
Asa PARSHALL	Chemung	NY	June 11,1836	NE/SE	40
John CRANE	Erie	NY	June 27,1836	NW/SE	40

Section 11

Name	County	State	Date	Description	Acres
Joseph S GIBBS	Niagara	NY	Jan. 20,1836	SW/SW	40
Patrick TOBIN	Livingston	MI	May 28,1836	E½/SE	80
Ann GRISWOLD	Livingston	MI	June 11,1836	NW/NE & NE/NW	80
Samuel GRISWOLD	Livingston	MI	June 11,1836	E½/NE & SW/NE SE/NW & NE/SW	200
Asa PARSHALL	Chemung	NY	June 11,1836	W½/NW & NW/SW	120
John P BUSH	Ontario	NY	June 13,1836	W½/SE	80
Valentine H KETCHUM	(New York city)		July 7,1836	SE/SW	40

Section 12

Name	County	State	Date	Description	Acres
George PETERS	Washtenaw	MI	Dec. 12,1834	E½/NE	80
John T BROWN	Monroe	NY	Jan. 24,1835	SE¼	160
			Feb. 12,1835	SW¼	160
Benjamin GRISWOLD	Livingston	MI	Dec. 10,1835	Nw/NW	40
Ira KNIGHT	Seneca	NY	Apr. 6,1836	W½/NE & E½/NW	160
Elisha GRISWOLD	Livingston	MI	July 15,1836	SW/NW	40

Section 13

Name	County	State	Date	Description	Acres
William E REDDING	Rensellaer	NY	Nov. 5,1832	NW/NE & NE/NW	80
Charles K GRAVES	St. Clair	MI	Aug. 6,1834	E½/NE	80
	Livingston	MI	June 6,1835	SW/NW	40
Thomas K PARSHALL	Livingston	MI	May 28,1835	SE/NW	40
			Aug. 26,1835	SW/NE	40
Archibald NELSON	Oakland	MI	Oct. 19,1835	SW/SW	40
Jonathan NELSON	Oakland	MI	Nov. 7,1835	NW/SW	40
Guy N ROBERTS	Livingston	MI	Dec. 2,1835	NW/NW	40
William P SHANNON	Genessee	NY	June 11,1835	E½/SE	80
Nathan JENKS	Ontario	NY	June 14,1836	W½/SE	80
Nehemiah BOUTWELL	(Hillsborough,NY)		June 16,1836	E½/SW	80

Oceola township

Section 14

Name	Location	State	Date	Description	Acres
Hardy H GRAVES	Livingston	MI	Aug. 1,1835	SE/NE	40
Hosea ROOT	Lenewee	MI	Sept. 9,1835	E½/SW & W½/SE SW/SE & SE/NW	240
Archibald NELSON	Oakland	MI	Oct. 12,1835	NE/SE	40
			Oct. 19,1835	SE/SE	40
Benjamin ELDRED	Courtland	NY	Nov. 6,1835	W½/NW	80
Russell BLOOD	Washtenaw	MI	Sept. 20,1836	W½/SW	80
Norman SPELLAN	Livingston	MI	Oct. 26,1836	NE/NE	40
Harvey H NEFF	Livingston	MI	Dec. 8,1836	NW/NE	40
Caroline AUSTIN	Livingston	MI	Dec. 10,1836	NE/NW	40

Section 15

Name	Location	State	Date	Description	Acres
Polly FULLER	Oakland	MI	Nov. 2,1835	W½/NE	80
Benjamin ELDRED	Courtland	NY	Nov. 6,1835	E½/NE	80
Jonas G POTTER	Franklin	MA	June 15,1836	NW¼	160
Francis MITTLEBERGEN	Ashtabula	OH	June 15,1836	SE¼	160
George W SUTTON	Oakland	MI	July 7,1837	NE/SW	40
Grandus THOMPSON	Oakland	MI	Jan. 15,1839	SW/SW	40
David BLOOD	Monroe	NY	May 16,1839	SE/SW	40
John L LEWIS	Erie	NY	Sept. 16,1851	NW/SW	40

Section 16 (school section)

Name	Date	Description	Acres
J H FERGUSON	Oct. 4,1848	NE/NW	40
William HOLMES	Apr. 2,1850	NE/NE	40
	Dec. 29,1856	NE/SE	40
H McKEWEN	Oct. 22,1850	NW/SW	40
R A FURGESON	Mar. 6,1850	NW/NE	40
B FEELEY	Apr. 3,1851	SW/NW	40
S C CRITTENDEN	May 4,1853	E½/SW & SW/SW	120
W P HOLMES	Sept. 16,1853	SE/NW	40
Robert HOLMES	Sept. 19,1853	SW/NE	40
Isaac HAYWOOD	Oct. 5,1853	NW/NW	40
J B SEE	Nov. 15,1853	SE/NE	40
F McDONOUGH	May 9,1854	SW/SE	40
P McKINNEY	Aug. 22,1854	SE/SE	40
Francis McDONOUGH JR.	Oct. 30,1862	SW/SE	40

Section 17

Name	Location	State	Date	Description	Acres
William BARBER	Orange	NY	May 13,1836	W½/SE	80
John F LAWSON	(New York city)		May 17,1836	NW¼ & SW¼	320
Friend BURT	Genessee	NY	June 13,1836	NE¼	160
Charles VAN KEUREN	(New York city)		June 20,1836	E½/SE	80

116

Oceola township

Section 18

Stephen J MILLER	Bennington	VT	May 12,1836	SE¼	160
Volney HINMAN	Orleans	NY	May 14,1836	SWf¼	158
Ezra J MUNDY	Livingston	MI	May 24,1836	NW/NWf	38
Charles VAN KEUREN	(New York city)		June 20,1836	NE¼	160
John CRANE	Erie	NY	June 27,1836	Ep/NWf &	
				SW/NWf	118

Section 19

Flavius J B CRANE	Livingston	MI	Apr. 18,1836	SWf¼	159
			June 11,1836	E½/SE	80
Jonas M WHEELER	Ontario	NY	Apr. 18,1836	W½/SE & NE¼	240
Volney HINMAN	Orleans	NY	May 16,1836	NWf¼	158

Section 20

+Charles PINCKEY	Washtenaw	MI	Dec. 24,1835	S½/SE	80
Samuel H WEST	Wayne	NY	Dec. 24,1835	E½/SW	80
James HUGHSON	Oakland	MI	Mar. 24,1836	E½/NE & NW/NE	120
Thomas M HOWELL	Ontario	NY	Apr. 18,1836	NW¼	160
			July 5,1836	W½/SW	80
Gabriel DEAN	Wayne	MI	June 9,1836	N½/SE	80
Geo. Washington WALKER	Livingston	MI	Oct. 12,1837	SW/NE	40

Section 21

Obed DURFEE	Oakland	MI	Mar. 29,1836	W½/NW	80
Anson NELSON	Oakland	MI	Apr. 12,1836	E½/NW	80
Amasa B NELSON	Ontario	NY	Apr. 20,1836	W½/NE	80
Andrew RIDDLE	Livingston	MI	May 28,1838	SE¼	160
Pomeroy EASTON	Rutland	VT	June 4,1836	E½/NE	80
John K BUEL	Monroe	NY	June 14,1836	SW¼	160

Section 22

Joseph H RUMSEY	Washtenaw	MI	Nov. 16,1835	SW¼	160
James G RUMSEY &					
Jesse B RUMSEY	Washtenaw	MI	Nov. 16,1835	SE¼	160
*Artemus S HANDY	Livingston	MI	June 21,1836	SE/NE	40
			Nov. 1,1836	SW/NE	40
Amos B ROOT	Rutland	VT	June 4,1836	W½/NW & SE/NW	120
George W ARMSTONG	Livingston	MI	Nov. 26,1851	NE/NE	40
Barnard JUDGE	Livingston	MI	Nov. 27,1854	NE/NW & NW/NE	80

*(Handy is HARDY in the history book)
+(Pinckney in the history book)

Oceola township

Section 23

Orvil MURDOCK	Monroe	NY	Oct. 13,1835	NE/NE	40
John P SPRINGTEEN	Monroe	NY	Oct. 22,1835	SE¼ & W½/NE	
				& SE/NE	280
William H JOHNSON	Washtenaw	MI	Oct. 31,1835	S½/NW	80
Ephriam HARDY	Washtenaw	MI	Nov. 22,1835	SW¼	160
Artemas S HARDY	Livingston	MI	June 2,1836	N½/NW	80

Section 24

Orvil MURDOCK	Monroe	NY	Oct. 13,1835	NW/NW	40
Peter Y BROWNING	Monroe	NY	Mar. 29,1836	W½/SW	80
			Apr. 9,1836	E½/NW	80
Charles McDONNELL	Wayne	MI	May 18,1836	NE/SE	40
Edmond A BRUSH	Wayne	MI	May 25,1836	SE/SE	40
William P SHANNON	Genessee	NY	June 11,1836	NE/NE	40
Nathan JENKS	Ontario	NY	June 14,1836	W½/NE & SE/NE	120
William A CLARK	(New York city)		Sept. 21,1836	W½/SE & E½/SW	160
Sarah MURDOCK	Livingston	MI	Dec. 10,1836	SW/NW	40

Section 25

Rueben MOORE	Washtenaw	MI	Oct. 27,1835	SE¼	160
Peter Y BROWNING	Monroe	NY	Mar. 29,1836	W½/NW	80
Orramond B WOOD	Genessee	NY	Apr. 9,1836	NE/NE	40
Clark C BOUTWELL	(Hillsborough,NY)		June 16,1836	W½/SW	80
Flavius J B CRANE	Livingston	MI	July 5,1836	E½/NW & W½/NE	160
Charles A WALLACE	Washtenaw	MI	July 13,1836	E½/SW	80
Horace R HUDSON	(New York city)		Sept. 24,1836	SE/NE	40

Section 26

Peter Y BROWNING	Monroe	NY	Mar. 29,1836	E½/NE & N½/NW	160
Harvey RHODES	Washtenaw	MI	June 1,1836	W½/SE	80
Pomeroy EASTON	Rutland	VT	June 4,1836	E½/SW	80
Clark C BOUTWELL	(Hillsborough,NY)		June 16,1836	E½/SE	80
Conner BERGEN	Livingston	MI	Nov. 24,1836	W½/SW	80
Jesse B RUMSEY	Livingston	MI	Dec. 9,1836	W½/NE	80
Robert CHAMBERS	Monroe	NY	May 21,1836	S½/NW	80

Section 27

Ellis LUTHER	Washtenaw	MI	Nov. 9,1835	W½/SW	80
Joel B RUMSEY	Washtenaw	MI	Nov. 16,1835	NW¼ & W½/NE	240
Liberty JUDD	Genessee	NY	June 15,1836	SE¼ & E½/SW	
				& E½/NE	320

Oceola township

Section 28
Philister JESSUP	Washtenaw	MI	Nov. 9,1835	W½/SE	80
Joseph A PINCKNEY	Washtenaw	MI	Nov. 9,1835	SW¼	160
Ellis LUTHER	Washtenaw	MI	Nov. 9,1835	SE/SE	40
Milan GLOVER	Washtenaw	MI	Dec. 1,1835	NW¼	160
Joseph H RUMSEY	Washtenaw	MI	Jan. 11,1836	NE/NE	40
Andrew RIDDEL	Livingston	MI	May 28,1836	W½/NE	80
Artemas S HANDY	Livingston	MI	June 2,1836	SE/NE	40
Joel B RUMSEY	Livingston	MI	June 8,1836	NE/SE	40

Section 29
Henson WALKER	Washtenaw	MI	Nov. 9,1835	E½/SE	80
Milan GLOVER	Washtenaw	MI	Dec. 1,1835	E½/NE	80
Gardiner MASON	Washtenaw	MI	Apr. 13,1836	NW/NW	40
Jonas M WHEELER	Ontario	NY	May 20,1836	W½/SW	80
William C RUMSEY	Livingston	MI	Aug. 1,1836	E½/NW	80
Emily L RUMSEY	Livingston	MI	Aug. 1,1836	SW/NW	40
Solomon SAUNDERS	Livingston	MI	Nov. 14,1836	W½/NE	80
James A HICKS & Samuel T BUEL	Wayne	MI	Mar. 16,1837	W½/SE & E½/SW	160

Section 30
Addison LACKOR	Washtenaw	MI	Aug. 7,1835	S½/NW	80
Rensellaer LACKOR	Washtenaw	MI	Aug. 7,1835	N½/SW	80
Moses THOMPSON	Herkimer	NY	Sept. 5,1835	SE/SW	40
Mary THOMPSON	Herkimer	NY	Sept. 5,1835	SW/SE	40
Gardner MASON	Washtenaw	MI	Apr. 13,1836	NE/NE	40
Jonas M WHEELER	Ontario	NY	May 20,1836	E½/SE	80
William C RUMSEY	Livingston	MI	Aug. 1,1836	W½/NE	80
Emily L RUMSEY	Livingston	MI	Aug. 1,1836	SE/NE	40
Charles A JEFFRIES	Washtenaw	MI	Nov. 21,1836	NE/NW	40
John LOWE	Wayne	MI	Mar. 8,1837	SW/SWf	40
Nahum P THAYER	Wayne	MI	Feb. 1,1849	NW/NW	40

Oceola township

Section 31

Rufas NICOLS	Washtenaw	MI	May 14,1835	SW/NE	40
John FRASER	(New York city)		July 2,1835	Wp/SWf	86
Jacob S SORTER	Stueben	NY	July 10,1835	$W\frac{1}{2}$/SE	80
Paul D CORNELL &					
Alonzo CORNELL	Rensellaer	NY	July 11,1835	$E\frac{1}{2}$/SE & $E\frac{1}{2}$/NE	
				$E\frac{1}{2}$/NW & NW/NE	200
Alexander FRASER	Livingston	MI	Oct. 26,1835	SW/NWf	41
Joseph H STEELE	Wayne	MI	July 5,1836	Ep/SW	80
Van Rensellaer HAWKINS					
& Henry HAWKINS	Genessee	NY	July 5,1836	NW/NWf	41
Morris THOMPSON	Livingston	MI	Feb. 28,1848	NW/NWf	41

Section 32

John WALKER	Washtenaw	MI	Nov. 9,1835	NE/NE	40
Joseph H STEELE	Wayne	MI	July 5,1836	$SW\frac{1}{4}$	160
Jacob W MOORE	Wayne	MI	July 7,1836	$W\frac{1}{2}$/NW	80
William TALMAN	Ontario	NY	July 11,1836	$W\frac{1}{2}$/NE & $E\frac{1}{2}$/NW	160
Philester JESSUP	Livingston	MI	Jan. 17,1837	$E\frac{1}{2}$/SE & SW/SE	120
Orson ELLIOT	Wayne	MI	June 8,1837	SE/NE	40
Samuel COLBURN	Oneida	NY	May 15,1839	NW/SE	40

Section 33

John WALKER	Washtenaw	MI	Nov. 9,1835	NW/NW	40
Ephriam HANDY	Washtenaw	MI	Nov. 23,1835	$E\frac{1}{2}$/SE	80
Benjamin EARL	Washtenaw	NI	Feb. 16,1836	SW/SE	40
Noah BRIGGS	Washtenaw	MI	Mar. 15,1836	NE/SE	40
Joseph WHITAKER	Washtenaw	MI	Mar. 31,1836	SE/NE	40
John W RUEN	Wayne	MI	June 1,1836	$W\frac{1}{2}$/NE & NW/SE	120
John FRENCH	Wayne	MI	June 1,1836	$E\frac{1}{2}$/NW	80
Robert WHITACRE	Washtenaw	MI	July 8,1836	SW/NW	40
Riley EARL	Washtenaw	MI	July 13,1836	$E\frac{1}{2}$/SW	80
Philester JESSUP	Livingston	MI	Oct. 29,1836	$W\frac{1}{2}$/SW	80

Oceola township

Section 34
Ellis LUTHER	Washtenaw	MI	Nov. 9,1835	NW/NW	40
Ephriam HANDY	Washtenaw	MI	Nov. 23,1835	SW/SW	40
William H PHILLIPS	Washtenaw	MI	Mar. 8,1836	E½/NE	40
Noah BRIGGS	Washtenaw	MI	Mar. 15,1836	E½/NW & SW/NW	120
	Livingston	MI	Jan. 3,1854	NW/NE	40
Joseph WHITACRE	Washtenaw	MI	Mar. 31,1836	NW/SW	40
Conner BERGEN	Livingston	MI	Nov. 24,1836	E½/SE	80
Alanson WILCOX	Oakland	MI	June 24,1837	SE/SW	40
William H KIMBALL	Niagara	NY	Aug. 21,1837	W½/SE	80
Washington JACKSON	Wayne	MI	Sept. 4,1837	SW/NE	40
William BARBOUR	Livingston	MI	Nov. 24,1854	NE/SW	40

Section 35
*John STOWE	Ontario	NY	May 7,1836	NE¼	160
John THUIRVAHTER	Wayne	MI	June 7,1836	W½/SE	80
Martin GEORGE	Wayne	MI	June 7,1836	E½/SE	80
Flavius J B CRANE	Livingston	MI	Aug. 3,1836	SW¼	160
Conner BERGEN	Livingston	MI	Nov. 24,1836	W½/NW	80
Edward NICHOLS	Livingston	MI	Nov. 28,1836	E½/NW	80

Section 36
Erastus KELLOGG	Washtenaw	MI	Feb. 17,1836	SW¼ & W½/NW	240
+ Gustave BAETCKE	Wayne	MI	July 2,1836	E½/SE	80
Solomon GUE	Orleans	NY	July 9,1836	NE¼ & E½/NW	240
Samuel HARNED	(New York city)		Sept. 24,1836	W½/SE	80

*(listed as John Stone in history book)

+(mispelled Bachche in tract)

121

NAME	COUNTY & STATE		DATE	LAND	ACRES
Section 1					
Major CHUBB	Washtenaw	MI	Dec. 14,1835	Np/NWf &	
				NW/SW & SE/SW	134
Barry BUTLER	Wayne	MI	July 8,1836	E½/SE	80
Thomas CRAWFORD	Onondaga	NY	July 8,1836	SW/SW	40
John NORTON	Wayne	MI	Sept. 21,1836	W½/SE	80
Elijah BENNETT	Livingston	MI	Dec. 26,1836	NE/SW	40
Ira CHUBB	Livingston	MI	Oct. 11,1837	SW/NE	40
Lewis BUTLER	Livingston	MI	Sept. 28,1838	E½/NEf	72
Henry A NAGLE	Wayne	MI	June 29,1836	Sp/NW	80
John H WATSON	Livingston	MI	Dec. 2,1847	NW/NEf	32
Section 2					
Major CHUBB	Washtenaw	MI	Dec. 14,1835	NEf¼	128
Thomas L JEWITT	Orleans	NY	June 18,1836	NWf¼	128
James M SOVERHILL	Ontario	NY	June 29,1836	SE¼	160
Thomas CRAWFORD	Onondaga	NY	June 29,1836	E½/SW	80
Nathan N POND	Washtenaw	MI	Apr. 23,1838	W½/SW	80
Section 3					
George CORSELUS	Washtenaw	MI	Aug. 14,1835	Np/NW & SW/NW	90
Benjamin EAMAN	Washtenaw	MI	Dec. 5,1835	SW/SW	40
James KINGSLEY	Washtenaw	MI	Mar. 5,1836	E½/SW	80
Aaron YOUNGLOVE	Washtenaw	MI	June 1,1836	Np/NEf	49
Joseph PIXLEY	Seneca	NY	July 11,1836	SE¼	160
James W STANSBURY	Wayne	MI	Aug. 2,1836	NW/SW	40
Horace ANDERSON	Stueben	NY	Mar. 10,1838	Sp/NE	80
Philander MONROE	Livingston	MI	Nov. 26,1855	SE/NW	40
Section 4					
Thomas MARTIN	Wayne	MI	Oct. 1,1835	W½/SE & SE/SE	120
Thomas WELLER	Washtenaw	MI	Dec. 12,1835	SE/SW	40
William KIRKLAND	Wayne	MI	Jan. 1,1836	W½/SW	80
John S FARRAND	Cayuga	NY	May 30,1836	NWf¼	132
Aaron YOUNGLOVE	Washtenaw	MI	June 1,1836	Np/NEf	51
Thomas CRAWFORD	Onondaga	NY	June 29,1836	NE/SW	40
Henry A NAGLE	Wayne	MI	June 29,1836	Sp/NE	80
William W STANSBURY	Wayne	MI	Aug. 2,1836	NE/SE	40

122

Putnam township

Section 5
Hiram WELLER	Washtenaw	MI	Dec. 12,1835	W½/SE & SE/SE	120
John G PETERSON	Washtenaw	MI	May 16,1836	Np/NEf	53
Lemuel BRYANT	Washtenaw	MI	May 16,1836	NWf¼ & Sp/NEf	215
John D HUGHES	Livingston	MI	Dec. 23,1840	NE/SE	40
+Moses FULLER	Washtenaw	MI	(May 5,1837)	SW¼	160

Section 6
Freeman R BURDEN	Washtenaw	MI	Sept. 21,1836	SE¼ & SE/SW	200
			Oct. 5,1837	SE/NE	40
Erastus BLANCHARD	Washtenaw	MI	Oct. 29,1836	NWf¼	134
Caleb LYNDEN	Washtenaw	MI	Nov. 14,1836	Wp/SWf	73
Patrick KELLY	Wayne	MI	June 19,1838	NE/SW	40
William BOYLE	Livingston	MI	Oct. 30,1852	SW/NE	40
Fredrick WILLIAMS	Livingston	MI	July 23,1853	Np/NEf	58

Section 7
Cassius SWIFT	Ontario	NY	Oct. 12,1835	W½/SE & W½/NE & Ep/NW	240
James GRIEVE	Ontario	NY	Oct. 12,1835	SW¼	160
Sylvanius P GERMAIN	Albany	NY	Mar. 4,1836	E½/SE	80
John CAMERON	Erie	NY	Sept. 23,1836	E½/NE & Wp/NWf	156

Section 8
Freeman WEBB	Genessee	NY	Nov. 27,1835	SW/SE	40
Benjamin ANNIS	Washtenaw	MI	Nov. 27,1835	W½/SW & SE/SW & SE/SE	160
Daniel BURGESS	Livingston	MI	Dec. 12,1835	NE/NW & NW/NE	80
*William KIRKLAND	Wayne	MI	Jan. 1,1836	E½/NE	80
Richard M BAGLEY	Ontario	NY	June 8,1836	N½/SE & NE/SW	120
Antha WELLER	Livingston	MI	Nov. 17,1836	SW/NE & SE/NW	80
Rueben ROBIE	Stueben	NY	Dec. 6,1836	W½/NW	80

*(founder of Village of Pinckney)

+(patent date)

Putnam township

Section 9

Name	County	State	Date	Description	Acres
Hiram WELLER	Washtenaw	MI	Dec. 12,1835	NW/NE	40
William KIRKLAND	Wayne	MI	Jan. 1,1836	W½/NW	80
Richard M BAGLEY	Ontario	NY	June 8,1836	W½/SW	80
Patrick MONKS	Wayne	MI	Aug. 4,1836	SE/SE	40
			Apr. 1,1837	W½/SE	80
Rueben ROBIE	Stueben	NY	Dec. 6,1836	E½/NW	80
Cassius SWIFT	Livingston	MI	Dec. 6,1836	E½/SW	80
William MOORE	Wayne	MI	Apr. 1,1837	NE/SE	40
Furnam G ROSE	Livingston	MI	Feb. 14,1838	NE/NE	40
Freeman WEBB	Livingston	MI	Nov. 13,1838	SW/NE	40

Section 10

Name	County	State	Date	Description	Acres
Henry G BUSH	Washtenaw	MI	Aug. 2,1836	NW¼	160
Major BENTLEY	Washtenaw	MI	Sept. 24,1836	E½/SW	80
	Livingston	MI	Oct. 27,1836	NW/SE	40
Ezekial PAGE	Washtenaw	MI	Feb. 14,1837	W½/SW & SE/SE	120
Thomas GAWLEY	Livingston	MI	Mar. 19,1849	NW/NE	40
James SPEER	Livingston	MI	Mar. 19,1849	SW/NE	40
David WHITE	Livingston	MI	Nov. 18,1854	NE/SE	40
William A HALL	Livingston	MI	Jan. 21,1867	SW/SE	40

Section 11

Name	County	State	Date	Description	Acres
Samuel NASH	Niagara	NY	Jan. 18,1836	SE¼	160
Major BENTLEY	Livingston	MI	Oct. 27,1836	W½/SW	80
Samuel S FITCH	Wayne	MI	Nov. 26,1836	E½/SW	80
			June 5,1838	W½/NW	80
William O'HARA	Washtenaw	MI	Jan. 26,1837	E½/NE	80
Joel S MEAD	Monroe	NY	May 28,1838	NE/NW	40
Jesse D HAUSE	Livingston	MI	Sept. 6,1838	SW/NE	40
William S WAIT	Livingston	MI	Jan. 31,1848	NW/NE	40
			Aug. 23,1853	SE/NW	40

Section 12

Name	County	State	Date	Description	Acres
Ralph SWARTHOUT	Livingston	NY	Aug. 1,1836	NW¼ & SE¼ & E½/NE	400
	Livingston	MI	Apr. 14,1837	SW/NE	40
Silas HODGKINS	Wayne	MI	Nov. 2,1836	W½/SW	80
B B KERCHIVAL	Wayne	MI	Feb. 4,1837	E½/SW	40
Samuel S FITCH	Livingston	MI	Feb. 23,1839	NW/NE	40

Putnam township

Section 13

Joseph KIRKLAND	Oneida	NY	June 7,1836	SW$\frac{1}{4}$ & W$\frac{1}{2}$/SE	240
Joseph ABEL	Washtenaw	MI	June 13,1836	E$\frac{1}{2}$/SE	80
Robert DUNLAP	Oswego	NY	Sept. 23,1836	W$\frac{1}{2}$/NW	80
Samuel S FITCH	Wayne	MI	Mar. 10,1837	W$\frac{1}{2}$/NE & E$\frac{1}{2}$/NW	160
			Mar. 14,1837	E$\frac{1}{2}$/NE	80

Section 14

Ira A WHITE	Stueben	NY	July 1,1836	NE$\frac{1}{4}$	160
Henry G BUSH	Washtenaw	MI	Aug. 2,1836	S$\frac{1}{2}$/SW	80
Joseph KIRKLAND	Oneida	NY	Sept. 24,1836	W$\frac{1}{2}$/SE	80
John DUNN	Washtenaw	MI	Jan. 26,1837	NW$\frac{1}{4}$	160
George B MARTIN	Wayne	MI	Mar. 2,1837	E$\frac{1}{2}$/SE	80
William MOORE	Wayne	MI	Apr. 1,1837	N$\frac{1}{2}$/SW	80

Section 15

Linus ARNOLD	Washtenaw	MI	June 29,1835	SW/SW	40
Evelina ARNOLD	Washtenaw	MI	Dec. 19,1835	NW/NW	40
Nelson BARBER	Livingston	MI	May 26,1836	NE/SE & SE/NE	80
Nelson JENKINS	Washtenaw	MI	June 1,1836	E$\frac{1}{2}$/SW & NW/SW	120
Luke HEMINGWAY	(New York city)		Jan. 27,1837	W$\frac{1}{2}$/NE & NE/NE	120
Christopher MONKS	Wayne	MI	Feb. 10,1837	W$\frac{1}{2}$/SE	80
James BURKE	Wayne	MI	Apr. 1,1837	SE/SE	40
			Nov. 1,1837	SE/NW	40
Joseph KIRKLAND	Oneida	NY	Oct. 27,1840	SW/NW	40
*David HYANIAN	Livingston	MI	Dec. 2,1854	NE/NW	40

Section 16 (school section)

H H STURNS		Aug. 1,1839	NE/NE	40
F WEBB Jr.		Oct. 7,1847	N$\frac{1}{2}$/NW/NE	20
		Mar. 25,1848	S$\frac{1}{2}$/NW/NE	20
		Apr. 1,1850	SW/NE & SE/SW	80
		May 28,1844	NW/NW	40
		Oct. 7,1847	NE/NW	40
J S NASH		Sept. 16,1841	SE/NE	40
F G ROSE		May 28,1844	SW/NW	40
J BROOKS		Aug. 1,1839	NE/SE	40
W H STEVENS		Aug. 1,1839	SE/SE	40
William KIRKLAND		Aug. 1,1839	W$\frac{1}{2}$/SE & E$\frac{1}{2}$/SW	160
C BRITAIN		Aug. 1,1839	W$\frac{1}{2}$/SW	80

*(called Hyaman in history book)

Putnam township

Section 17

Abner BRUEN	Washtenaw	MI	Mar. 3,1835	E½/SW	80
Leander FOSTER	Washtenaw	MI	Mar. 21,1835	W½/SW	80
Samuel M C HINCHEY	Monroe	NY	May 20,1835	E½/SE	80
John S HINCHEY	Monroe	NY	May 20,1835	W½/SE	80
Silas PERRY	Washtenaw	MI	Oct. 27,1835	E½/NW	80
William HUGHSON	Washtenaw	MI	Oct. 27,1835	W½/NW	80
Freeman WEBB	Genessee	NY	Nov. 27,1835	NW/NE	40
William KIRKLAND	Wayne	MI	Jan. 1,1836	E½/NE & SW/NE	120

Section 18

Alfred HARTSHORN	Wayne	MI	Nov. 1,1834	SE¼	160
Leander FOSTER	Washtenaw	MI	Mar. 30,1835	Wp/SWf & NE/SW	125
James H WOODS	Ontario	NY	Aug. 15,1835	Wp/NWf	83
Sanford MARBLE	Livingston	MI	Oct. 3,1835	S½/NE	80
Benjamin EAMAN	Washtenaw	MI	Nov. 9,1835	N½/NE	80
William KIRKLAND	Wayne	MI	Jan. 1,1836	Ep/NW & SE/SW	120

Section 19

James G PETERSON	Washtenaw	MI	July 8,1836	Ep/SW	80
Alexander STEPHENS	Washtenaw	MI	Sept. 21,1836	NW/SE	40
Bennet SEWELL	Washtenaw	MI	Sept. 21,1836	SW/NE	40
			Oct. 24,1836	NW/NE & SW/SE	80
James GRIEVE	Livingston	MI	Sept. 23,1836	Ep/NW	80
Otto S BIGNELL	Washtenaw	MI	Nov. 22,1836	Wp/SWf	88
John FLINN	Wayne	MI	Jan. 23,1837	Wp/NWf & E½/NE	167
John PATTERSON	Livingston	MI	May 11,1852	NE/SE	40
Gideon WEBB	Livingston	MI	Nov. 22,1854	SE/SE	40

Section 20

John S HINCHEY	Monroe	NY	May 20,1835	E½/NE	80
Charles M MOSES	Washtenaw	MI	Oct. 20,1835	NW/NW	40
Abner BRUEN	Washtenaw	MI	Jan. 30,1836	NE/NW	40
Warren ROGERS	Washtenaw	MI	Oct. 27,1836	SE/SE	40
Michael McFADDEN	Wayne	MI	Jan. 9,1837	NE/SE	40
Moses BABCOCK	Washtenaw	MI	Jan. 18,1837	W½/SE	80
John FLINN	Wayne	MI	Jan. 23,1837	S½/NW	80
Chester F PARSONS	Cayuga	NY	Feb. 9,1837	W½/NE	80
Henry GARDINER	Livingston	MI	Mar. 14,1849	SE/SW	40
Thomas C WEBB	Livingston	MI	Dec. 14,1853	SW/SW & NW/SW & NE/SW	120

Putnam township

Section 21

William WHITE &					
James S NASH	Washtenaw	MI	June 23,1834	$E\frac{1}{2}$/NE	80
Alvan A HOLCOMB	Litchfield	CN	May 14,1835	$W\frac{1}{2}$/NE	80
	Washtenaw	MI	Aug. 20,1835	NW/SE	40
Samuel M C HINCHEY	Monroe	NY	May 20,1835	$W\frac{1}{2}$/NW	80
Anson B CHIPMAN	Washtenaw	MI	July 1,1835	NE/NW	40
Joel BROOKS	Livingston	MI	Apr. 1,1836	NE/SE	40
Robert DUNLAP	Oswego	NY	Aug. 2,1836	SE/SE & SE/NW	80
Warren ROGERS	Washtenaw	MI	Oct. 27,1836	SW/SW	40
Michael McFADDEN	Wayne	MI	Jan. 9,1837	$E\frac{1}{2}$/SW & NW/SW	120
Nelson JENKINS	Livingston	MI	Jan. 11,1837	SW/SE	40

Section 22

Sanford MARBLE	Washtenaw	MI	July 16,1834	$E\frac{1}{2}$/SE	80
John O'BRIEN	Litchfield	CN	Aug. 19,1834	$W\frac{1}{2}$/SE & $E\frac{1}{2}$/SW	160
Joel BROOKS	Washtenaw	MI	Oct. 6,1834	SW/NW	40
John SYKES	Washtenaw	MI	May 14,1835	SE/NW & SW/NE	80
Linus ARNOLD	Washtenaw	MI	June 29,1835	NW/NW	40
William KIRKLAND	Wayne	MI	Feb. 17,1836	$E\frac{1}{2}$/NE	80
William WHITE	Livingston	MI	Mar. 26,1836	$W\frac{1}{2}$/SW	80
Samuel KILPATRICK	Washtenaw	MI	May 31,1836	NW/NE & NE/NW	80

Section 23

Solomon PETERSON		MI	May 13,1828	$W\frac{1}{2}$/SE & $E\frac{1}{2}$/SW	160
Benjamin WELLER	Washtenaw	MI	June 19,1834	SW/SW	40
Jefferson J M NEWCOMB	Livingston	MI	June 11,1835	NW/SW	40
Alvah BURGESS	Washtenaw	MI	June 22,1835	NE/NE	40
			Dec. 21,1835	$E\frac{1}{2}$/NW	80
Furnam G ROSE	Washtenaw	MI	Oct. 27,1835	$E\frac{1}{2}$/SE	80
James SMITH	Wayne	MI	Dec. 4,1835	$W\frac{1}{2}$/NE	80
Michael MURRAY	Wayne	MI	Dec. 5,1835	SE/NE	40
Grant T PERRY	Washtenaw	MI	Dec. 21,1835	SW/NW	40
John MURRAY	Stueben	NY	Aug. 2,1836	NW/NW	40

Section 24

Elijah WHIPPLE	Washtenaw	MI	Nov. 7,1835	$E\frac{1}{2}$/NE	80
Aaron VANCE	Washtenaw	MI	Nov. 20,1835	$W\frac{1}{2}$/NE	80
William KIRKLAND	Wayne	MI	May 11,1836	$W\frac{1}{2}$/SW	80
Kenneth DAVIDSON	Washtenaw	MI	June 1,1836	$W\frac{1}{2}$/SE & $E\frac{1}{2}$/SW	160
			June 5,1836	$E\frac{1}{2}$/SE	80
Joseph KIRKLAND	Oneida	NY	June 1,1836	$NW\frac{1}{4}$	160

127

Putnam township

Section 25

James PULLEN	Washtenaw	MI	July 22,1831	SW¼	160
Solomon PETERSON	Washtenaw	MI	Dec. 2,1831	NW¼	160
Samuel COLE	Ontario	NY	Oct. 20,1835	SE/SE	40
Elijah WHIPPLE	Washtenaw	MI	Nov. 7,1835	SW/SE	40
Alvah BURGESS	Washtenaw	MI	Dec. 21,1835	NW/NE	40
James DWYER	Wayne	MI	June 9,1836	N½/SE	80
Chester INGALS & James LOVE	Washtenaw	MI	Feb. 20,1837	E½/NE	80

Section 26

*Solomon PETERSON		MI	May 13,1828	E½/NW & W½/NE	160
Jacob COREY	Ontario	NY	May 30,1831	E½/SE	80
Simmons MALLERY	(Upper Canada)		Aug. 13,1831	W½/SE & E½/SW	160
Richard M GUGGINS	Washtenaw	MI	Mar. 27,1832	W½/NW	80
Elnathan CANFIELD	Washtenaw	MI	June 9,1834	NW/SW	40
Clarinda PARKER	Washtenaw	MI	May 8,1835	SE/NE	40
James KINGSLEY	Washtenaw	MI	June 12,1835	NE/NE	40
William KIRKLAND	Wayne	MI	May 11,1836	SW/SW	40

Section 27

Elnathan CANFIELD	Washtenaw	MI	June 9,1834	NE/SE	40
Joel BROOKS	Washtenaw	MI	July 17,1834	E½/NE	80
Daniel TOWNER	Wayne	MI	Dec. 24,1835	W½/NE	80
Mathew SAUL	Wayne	MI	Apr. 10,1835	SW/SW	40
John H PLATT	Washtenaw	MI	Apr. 4,1836	E½/SW	80
James JACOBEY	Wayne	MI	June 13,1836	SW/SE	40
Lydia JACOBEY	Washtenaw	MI	June 13,1836	NW/SE	40
Francis HOBAN	Washtenaw	MI	July 30,1836	NW/SW & W½/NW	120
Elizabeth STANSBURY	Onondaga	NY	Aug. 2,1836	SE/SE	40
James W STANSBURY & William KIRKLAND	Wayne	MI	Aug. 2,1836	E½/NW	80

Section 28

William WHITE	Livingston	MI	July 11,1835	SW/NW	40
Moses M CRANE	Seneca	NY	Oct. 19,1835	E½/SW & SW/SW	120
Thomas CAHEL	Wayne	MI	May 11,1836	E½/NW	80
James E CRANE	Washtenaw	MI	June 13,1836	SW/SE	40
Francis HOBAN	Washtenaw	MI	June 30,1836	NE¼ & SE/SE	200
Robert DUNLAP	Oswego	NY	Aug. 2,1836	N½/SE & NW/SW & NW/NW	160

*(Took up first land in Livingston County)

128

Putnam township

Section 29

Name	County	State	Date	Description	Acres
William WHITE	Livingston	MI	July 11,1835	SE/NE	40
William BARNET	Monroe	NY	Mar. 25,1836	SE¼	160
Johnson TIPLADY	Rensellaer	NY	May 18,1836	NW/SW	40
James GIBBON	Livingston	MI	May 25,1836	NW¼	160
Robert DUNLAP	Oswego	NY	Aug. 2,1836	E½/SW & SW/SW W½/NE & NE/NE	240

Section 30

Name	County	State	Date	Description	Acres
Otto S BIGNALL	Seneca	NY	May 30,1835	E½/SW	80
Solomon L BIGNALL	Seneca	NY	May 30,1835	W½/SE	80
William NOWLIN	Chautauqua	NY	Nov. 4,1835	E½/SE	80
Silas BARTON	Seneca	NY	June 6,1836	SW/NE & SE/NW	80
Patrick DILLON	Ontario	NY	July 15,1836	Wp/NWf & Wp/SWf	174
Robert DUNLAP	Oswego	NY	Aug. 2,1836	NW/NE & NE/NW & E½/NE	160

Section 31

Name	County	State	Date	Description	Acres
Otto S BIGNALL	Seneca	NY	May 30,1835	W½/NE	80
Solomon L BIGNALL	Seneca	NY	May 30,1835	E½/NE	80
Richard BIGNALL	Washtenaw	MI	Oct. 21,1835	E½/SE	80
John PATTERSON	Livingston	MI	Oct. 31,1835	Ep/NW	80
Samuel W FOSTER	Washtenaw	MI	July 1,1836	SW/SE	40
Isaac TITUS	Livingston	MI	Sept. 23,1836	NW/SE	40
Abigail BABCOCK	Livingston	MI	Dec. 22,1837	NE/SWf	40
James GAUNT	Washtenaw	MI	Oct. 3,1853	SE/SW & NW/SW	80
			Feb. 3,1866	Wp/NWf	84
Abigail BABCOCK			Nov. 17,1844	SW/SWf	40

Section 32

Name	County	State	Date	Description	Acres
Lothrup HUBBARD	Washtenaw	MI	Jan. 16,1835	SW/SW	40
Solomon L BIGNALL	Seneca	NY	May 30,1835	W½/NE & W½/SE SE/NE & NE/SE	240
Moses MARSH	Washtenaw	MI	June 19,1835	SW/NW	40
Moses M CRANE	Washtenaw	MI	June 13,1836	NE/NE	40
Samuel W FOSTER	Washtenaw	MI	July 8,1836	SE/SW	40
Robert H TITUS	Erie	NY	July 15,1836	E½/NW	80
	Livingston	NY	Sept. 23,1836	NW/SW	40
John FARMER	Wayne	MI	Jan. 17,1837	NE/SW	40
Solomon L BIGNALL & Moses BABCOCK	Washtenaw	MI	Jan. 18,1837	SE/SE	40
George B MARTIN	Wayne	MI	Mar. 2,1837	NW/NW	40

Putnam township

Section 33

Name	County	State	Date	Description	Acres
Levi RODGERS & Ebenezer BOYDEN	Washtenaw	MI	July 11,1831	E½/SE	80
John HARRIS	(Brooklyn,NY)		Sept. 24,1835	E½/NW & N½/NE	160
Burr S NORTHRUP	Wayne	MI	Nov. 7,1835	E½/SW	80
Thomas NIXON	Wayne	MI	Aug. 5,1836	E½/SW	80
Martin HARRIS	Livingston	MI	Dec. 6,1836	SW/NE	40
Hugh CLARK	Livingston	MI	Dec. 6,1836	W½/SE	80
William SAUL	Washtenaw	MI	Dec. 8,1836	SE/NE	40
James JONES	Washtenaw	MI	Jan. 27,1837	W½/SW	80

Section 34

Name	County	State	Date	Description	Acres
Flavonia WRIGHT	Wayne	NY	May 14,1828	E½/SE	80
Henry HARRIS	Somerset	NJ	Nov. 26,1834	NE¼ & E½/NW	240
Adna SHAW & Lucius S FARRAND	Washtenaw	MI	Jan. 18,1836	W½/SE	80
Isaac B TOWNER	Livingston	MI	Mar. 9,1836	E½/SW	80
Charles KINGSLEY	Washtenaw	MI	Mar. 11,1836	W½/SW	80
John HARRIS	Livingston	MI	Apr. 19,1836	W½/NW	80

Section 35

Name	County	State	Date	Description	Acres
Jacob SIGLER & Francis McGRAW	Washtenaw	MI	May 24,1833	W½/NE & E½/NW	160
Jacob SIGLER	Washtenaw	MI	July 18,1833	SW/NW	40
Selden PULLEN	Livingston	MI	Dec. 14,1835	NE/NE	40
Andrew NOWLAND	Washtenaw	MI	Mar. 7,1836	W½/SW	80
*Oscar GEIMAN	Washtenaw	MI	Apr. 30,1836	E½/SW	80
William KIRKLAND	Wayne	MI	May 11,1836	NW/NW	40
Martin DAVIS	Washtenaw	MI	May 17,1836	SE/NE & NE/SE	80
James M SOVERHILL	Ontario	NY	June 8,1836	W½/SE & SE/SE	120

Section 36

Name	County	State	Date	Description	Acres
William KIRKLAND	Wayne	MI	Aug. 6,1836	NW/NW	40
Robert DUNLAP	Otsego	NY	Aug. 6,1836	E½/NW	80
John WALLACE	Livingston	MI	July 5,1837	NW/NE	40
Pomeroy BOYDEN	Washtenaw	MI	July 23,1842	SW/NE	40
James GIBBONS	Livingston	MI	May 25,1856	W½/SW	80
Sarah M JOHNSON	Washtenaw	MI	June 30,1853	SE/SE	40
Willard F DARROW	Livingston	MI	Nov. 18,1854	NE/NE	40
			Dec. 14,1854	E½/SW	80

*(Greenman in history book)

130

TYRONE township-FIRST Land Owners

NAME	COUNTY & STATE		DATE	LAND	ACRES
Section 1					
Joseph C BLAKE	Monroe	NY	June 3,1836	W½/SE	80
Egbert HOFFMAN	Monroe	NY	June 2,1836	E½/SE	80
Charles NEAR &					
Dyer THROOP	Saratoga	NY	June 16,1836	NWf¼ & W½/NE	
				& E½/SW	317
Moses Warren SCOTT	Saratoga	NY	June 25,1836	W½/SW &	
				E½/NEf	159
Section 2					
Phineas H SMITH	Orange	NY	June 9,1836	S½/SE	80
Henry ISAACS	(Hillsborough,NY)		June 11,1836	NEf¼ & NWf¼	
				SW¼ & N½/SE	557
SEction 3					
George DIBBLE	Lapeer	MI	March 18,1834	Np/NWf	88
Daniel D RUNYAN	Oakland	MI	Feb. 19,1836	S½/SW	80
Catherine RUNYAN	Oakland	MI	Apr. 23,1836	SW/SE	40
Melvin DORR	Oakland	MI	June 16,1836	Sp/NW	80
Henry HAWKINS &					
V R HAWKINS	Genessee	NY	June 27,1836	E½/SE & NW/SE	120
Marshall J BACON	Wayne	MI	Aug. 2,1836	NEf¼	163
Isaac S TAYLOR	Oakland	MI	May 1837	N½/SW	80
Section 4					
Julian BISHOP	Genessee	MI	July 9,1835	E½/NEf	86
Vincent RUNYON	Oakland	MI	July 16,1835	E½/SE	80
Isaac AYERS	Oakland	MI	Nov. 9,1835	SE/SW	40
Robert AYERS	Oakland	MI	Nov. 9,1835	W½/SE	80
Consider WARNER	Genessee	NY	Feb. 20,1836	W½/NEf	86
*Harriet BOYAM	Genessee	NY	May 7,1836	NE/SW	40
Jirah HILLMAN	Lewis	NY	May 10,1836	Np/NWf	96
David COLWELL	Stueben	NY	June 4,1836	W½/SW	80
John THOMAS	Wayne	NY	Sept. 23,1836	Sp/NW	80

*(Harriet Bryan in history book)

131

Tyrone township

Section 5

Elisha LARNED	Aleegany	NY	Nov. 18,1835	NW/NEf	49
Elijah CRANE	Wayne	MI	Mar. 4,1836	Np/NWf	103
Jirah HILLMAN	Lewis	NY	May 10,1836	NE/NEf	49
Hiram M RHODES	Oakland	MI	June 4,1836	E½/SE	80
Anna RHODES	Oakland	MI	June 4,1836	Sp/NE	80
Delos DAVIS	Wayne	MI	Sept. 23,1836	Sp/NW	80
Jonathan IRWIN	Livingston	MI	Jan. 30,1837	W½/SE	80
Ebenezer STERNS	Yates	NY	Mar. 9,1837	NE/SW & W½/SW	120
William BEAMER	Livingston	MI	Nov. 18,1854	SE/SW	40

Section 6

Jefferson H DOWNER	Oakland	MI	Oct. 9,1835	NE/NEf	53
Elisha W POSTALL	Macomb	MI	Jan. 2,1836	NW/NEf	53
Elijah ROOT	Washtenaw	MI	Feb. 19,1836	W½/NWf	82
Ebenezer I PENNIMAN	Wayne	MI	Mar. 4,1836	NE/NEf	47
			Mar. 18,1836	SE/NWf	35
William HYATT	Oakland	MI	Aug. 2,1836	Sp/NE	80
N A LITTLEFIELD	Livingston	MI	Jan. 14,1854	E½/SE	80
William OWENS	Livingston	MI	June 13,1854	NW/SE	40
Elijah J GOODELL			Jan. 15,1889	SWf¼	142
William BEAMER				SW/SE	40

Section 7

Washington D MORTON	Washtenaw	MI	May 9,1836	SW/NWf	31
Isaac MORTON	Washtenaw	MI	May 9,1836	SWf¼ &	
				SE/NWf	184
Jonathan L WOLVERTON	Stueben	NY	June 20,1836	SE¼	160
Elijah CLOUGH Jr.	Onondaga	NY	June 28,1836	NE¼	160

Section 8

George F ROBERTS	Cayuga	NY	June 1,1836	SE¼	160
Van Renseller &					
Henry HAWKINS	Genessee	NY	June 27,1836	SW¼	160
Henry D GARRISON	Wayne	MI	Oct. 26,1836	NE¼ & NW¼	320

Tyrone township

Section 9

Elisha BEACH	Oakland	MI	Jan. 6,1836	N½/NE	80
Willard S FELLSHAM	Washtenaw	MI	June 29,1836	W½/NW & SE/NW	120
Isaac THROOP Jr.	Genessee	MI	June 30,1836	NE/NW	40
Joseph ALBRIGHT		OH	Dec. 17,1836	W½/SW	80
David MURPHY	Livingston	MI	Oct. 25,1839	NE/SW	40
William SMITH	Livingston	MI	July 6,1846	SE/SW	40
John W MAPES	Livingston	MI	May 2,1850	SE/SE	40
Daniel ODELL	Genessee	MI	Nov. 30,1852	SW/NE	40
Christopher RODGERS	Livingston	MI	Nov. 23,1853	SW/SE	40
William BEAMER	Livingston	MI	Dec. 1,1853	SE/NE	40
Nancy F BIGGS	Livingston	MI	Sept. 4,1855	NE/SE	40

Section 10

Henry ISAACS	(Hillsborough,NY)		June 1,1836	NE¼ & NW¼ & SW¼	480
Sanford BILLINGS	Oakland	MI	Mar. 5,1838	NE/SE	40
			Jan. 9,1839	NW/SE	40
Almeron SMITH	Wayne	NY	Oct. 17,1839	SE/SE	40
Mathias T TALMADGE	Livingston	MI	Nov. 15,1854	SW/SE	40

Section 11

Charles WRIGHT	Niagara	NY	May 28,1836	E½/NE	80
Phineas H SMITH	Orange	NY	June 9,1836	W½/NE	80
Charles NEAR & Dyer THROOP	Saratoga	NY	June 16,1836	E½/SE	80
Darius LAMSON	Wayne	MI	Sept. 24,1836	E½/NW	80
			Oct. 25,1836	W½/NW	80
William DUNNING	Wayne	NY	Feb. 20,1838	W½/SE	80
Seth N HOWELL	Oakland	MI	Mar. 1,1838	N½/SW	80
Leonard BROOKS	Genessee	MI	Mar. 3,1855	S½/SW	80

Section 12

Henry LARNED	Yates	NY	May 25,1836	NE/NE	40
Phillip BREWER	Niagara	NY	May 28,1836	NW¼	160
Charles NEAR & Dyer THROOP	Saratoga	NY	June 16,1836	W½/NE & SE/SE & SW¼	440

Tyrone township

Section 13

William THOMSON	Seneca	NY	Apr. 12,1836	SE$\frac{1}{4}$	160
Ezra THAYNE	Oakland	MI	May 2,1836	SW/NE	40
John BLAIR	Seneca	NY	June 13,1836	SW$\frac{1}{4}$ & W$\frac{1}{2}$/NW	
				& E$\frac{1}{2}$/NW	320
Elias B HOLMES	Monroe	NY	June 14,1836	E$\frac{1}{2}$/NE & NW/NE	120

Section 14

David N BLOOD	Monroe	NY	June 18,1836	E$\frac{1}{2}$/SE	80
Henry DRUSE	Washtenaw	MI	June 18,1836	E$\frac{1}{2}$/NE	80
Bennet D TRIPP	Wayne	NY	June 27,1836	SW$\frac{1}{4}$	160
William R MUDGE	Monroe	NY	Dec. 16,1836	W$\frac{1}{2}$/NE	80
B B KERCHIVAL	Wayne	MI	Dec. 17,1836	W$\frac{1}{2}$/SE	80
Levi STOCKWELL	Oakland	MI	May 17,1839	E$\frac{1}{2}$/NW	80
William B STOCKWELL	Oakland	MI	May 17,1839	W$\frac{1}{2}$/NW	80

Section 15

Ellery SHAW	Wayne	MI	May 17,1836	SW$\frac{1}{4}$ & SW/SE	200
Bennet D TRIPP	Wayne	NY	June 27,1836	E$\frac{1}{2}$/SE & NW/SW	120
John O'NEIL	Wayne	MI	Nov. 21,1836	E$\frac{1}{2}$/NW	80
Michael HEALEY	Wayne	MI	Nov. 21,1836	W$\frac{1}{2}$/NW	80
Abram COOK	Wayne	NY	Nov. 26,1836	W$\frac{1}{2}$/NE	80
Edward HOPPER	Livingston	MI	Oct. 11,1839	SE/NE	40
Horton L MILLER	Macomb	MI	Oct. 13,1854	NE/NE	40

Section 16 (school section)

Thomas LOVE	June 12,1847	NE/SE & SE/NE	80
A E CRASTON	June 16,1849	SE/SE	40
+BROWN & BARLEY	June 4,1850	SW/NE & NW/SE	80
J N BARNES	Nov. 13,1850	W$\frac{1}{2}$/NW	80
C B THOMAS	Nov. 15,1850	SE/NW	40
David W LOVE	July 26,1853	SW/SE & SE/SW	80
Jacob LOVE	Sept. 20,1853	NW/NE	40
D CANFIELD	Oct. 10,1853	NW/SW	40
William VAN WAGONER	Oct. 24,1853	SW/SW	40
Peter SCHAD Jr.	June 2,1854	NE/NW	40
William SCHAD	Aug. 23,1854	NE/SW	40
#Stephen W DORONER	Oct. 24,1860	NE/NE	40

+(Broont & Barley in history)
#(Downer in county history book)

Tyrone township

Section 17

Name	County	State	Date	Description	Acres
Francis MORSE	Livingston	NY	May 16,1836	W½/SW	80
John WESTFALL	Cayuga	OH	May 17,1836	SE¼	160
Henry SEABOTT & Morris M SEABOTT	Cayuga	OH	May 21,1836	W½/NW	80
James KEARNS	Oswego	NY	June 27,1836	E½/SW	80
Moses TAGGART	Genessee	NY	June 27,1836	E½/NW	80

Section 18

Name	County	State	Date	Description	Acres
John C MORSE	Oakland	MI	May 5,1836	SE¼	160
Nancy MORTON	Washtenaw	MI	May 9,1836	Ep/NW	80
Isaac MORTON	Washtenaw	MI	May 17,1836	W½/NE	80
*Edwin SOMBERGER	Monroe	NY	June 16,1836	E½/NE	80
Dillis DEXTER	Monroe	NY	July 1,1836	Ep/SW	80
John FISH	Oakland	MI	Dec. 5,1836	Wp/SWf	68
Samuel G SUTHERLAND	Washtenaw	MI	Oct. 3,1837	SW/NWf	33
Adam B BAILEY	Livingston	MI	May 25,1838	NW/NWf	33

Section 19

Name	County	State	Date	Description	Acres
David BANGS	Monroe	NY	May 5,1836	NE¼ & Wp/NWf & NE/NWf	269
	Livingston	MI	Nov. 14,1836	SE/NW	40
William N AUSTIN	Orleans	NY	May 29,1836	E½/SE	80
David L BABCOCK	Livingston	MI	Oct. 2,1836	W½/SE	80
James McKEONE	Wayne	MI	Nov. 14,1836	NE/SWf & Wp/SWf	109
James MURPHY	Wayne	MI	Nov. 26,1836	SE/SW	40

Section 20

Name	County	State	Date	Description	Acres
William N AUSTIN	Orleans	NY	May 5,1836	W½/SW	80
Francis MORSE	Livingston	NY	May 10,1836	W½/NW	80
John J DICKSON	Wayne	NY	June 6,1836	SE¼ & E½/SW	240
Phil JOYNER	Berkshire	MA	June 16,1836	E½/NE	80
David L BABCOCK	Livingston	MI	Oct. 29,1836	E½/NW	80
Hugh R HOGLE	Livingston	MI	Nov, 15,1838	SW/NE	40
Jacob CHRISPELL	Livingston	MI	Feb. 20,1839	NW/NE	40

Section 21

Name	County	State	Date	Description	Acres
Henry SEABOTT & Morris M SEABOTT	Cayuga	NY	May 21,1836	section	640

*(Soonberger in history book)

Tyrone township

Section 22

John J DICKSON	Wayne	NY	June 6,1836	W½/SW	80
Henry BALL &					
Cyrus F KNEELAND	Monroe	NY	June 13,1836	E½/NE	80
Daniel BLOOD	Monroe	NY	June 18,1836	W½/NE & E½/NW	160
Hiram BELLOWS	Franklin	NY	June 25,1836	E½/SW	80
Ira BELLOWS	Monroe	NY	June 25,1836	SE¼	160
Bennett D TRIPP	Wayne	NY	June 27,1836	W½/NW	80

Section 23

Henry BALL &					
Cyrus F KNEELAND	Monroe	NY	June 13,1836	section	640

Section 24

William THOMSON	Seneca	NY	Apr. 12,1836	NE¼	160
James BELLOWS	Monroe	NY	June 14,1836	W½/SW	80
Hiram BELLOWS	Franklin	VT	June 14,1836	W½/SE	80
Ira BELLOWS	Franklin	VT	June 14,1836	NW¼ & E½/SW	240
	Monroe	NY	June 14,1836	E½/SE	80

Section 25

Van Renseller HAWKINS					
& Henry HAWKINS	Genessee	NY	June 14,1836	section	640

Section 26

John A WELLES	Wayne	MI	Sept. 17,1835	SE¼ & SW¼	320
Henry DRUSE	Washtenaw	MI	June 18,1836	NW¼	160
William B ALVORD	Wayne	MI	Sept. 22,1836	NE¼	160

Section 27

James LOVE	Washtenaw	MI	July 1,1835	W½/SW	80
William D SNAPP	Cayuga	OH	May 30,1836	SW/SE & SE/SW	80
Peter H LINK	Oakland	MI	June 11,1836	NE/NE	40
Darius LAMSON	Wayne	MI	Aug. 3,1836	NW¼ & W½/NE & NW/SE & NE/SW	320
John A WELLES	Wayne	MI	Sept. 23,1836	E½/SE & SE/NE	120

Tyrone township

Section 28

George CORNELL	Livingston	NY	Oct. 31,1834	W½/SW	80
William H BERRY	Shiawassee	MI	Feb. 18,1835	SE/SE	40
Joseph M BECKER	Oakland	MI	Mar. 20,1835	E½/SW	80
Isaac CORNELL	Livingston	MI	Mar. 20,1835	NW/SE	40
James LOVE	Washtenaw	MI	July 1,1835	SW/SE	40
Eli CONKLIN	Washtenaw	MI	Nov. 18,1835	E½/NW & NW/NW	120
David AUSTIN	Washtenaw	MI	Nov. 18,1835	NE¼ & NE/SE	200
James WILLIS	Oakland	MI	Dec. 2,1836	SW/NW	40

Section 29

Isaac CORNELL	Livingston	MI	Mar. 20,1835	E½/SE	80
Jacob CRISPELL	Washtenaw	MI	Dec. 29,1835	S½/SW	80
Shadrach S AUSTIN	Orleans	NY	May 5,1836	W½/NW & NW/SW	120
John J DICKSON	Wayne	NY	June 6,1836	E½/NE & NW/NE	120
Mercy CHRISPELL	Washtenaw	MI	June 8,1836	NE/SW & NW/SE	80
James E CHRISPELL	Washtenaw	MI	June 8,1836	SW/SE	40
George ALLEN	Madison	NY	June 17,1836	E½/NW & SW/NE	120

Section 30

Joseph CHAMBERLIN	Livingston	NY	May 3,1836	Wp/SWf	68
Nathaniel C AUSTIN	Orleans	NY	May 5,1836	E½/NE & NE/SE	120
	Livingston	MI	Oct. 29,1836	SE/SE	40
Philo H MUNSON	Livingston	NY	June 6,1836	Wp/NWf	69
Henry A CORNELL	Livingston	MI	Sept. 23,1836	Ep/SW	80
James McKEONE	Livingston	MI	Oct. 26,1836	SE/NW	40
James AGAN	Wayne	MI	Nov. 14,1836	W½/NE & NW/SE	120
James MURPHY	Wayne	MI	Nov. 26,1836	NE/NW	40
George ABBOTT	Wayne	MI	June 21,1837	SW/SE	40

Section 31

Major CURTIS	Oakland	MI	Jan. 4,1836	NE/NE	40
Thales DEAN	Washtenaw	MI	Jan. 11,1836	SW/SWf	35
James CHRISPELL	Washtenaw	MI	Jan. 25,1836	SE/NE	40
Solomon LEWIS	Wayne	MI	Apr. 6,1836	SE¼	160
William WINTER	Genessee	NY	May 3,1836	E½/SW	80
Anson PETTIBONE	Genessee	NY	May 4,1836	NWf¼ & W½/NE	229
B B KERCHIVAL	Wayne	MI	Oct. 29,1836	NW/SW	35

Tyrone township

Section 32

Name	County	State	Date	Description	Acres
Isaac CORNELL	Livingston	MI	Mar. 20,1835	E½/NE & SW/NE	120
David CURTISS	Oakland	MI	Mar. 17,1836	NW/SW	40
George H BLUMBERG	Oakland	MI	Apr. 9,1836	E½/SE	80
Joseph TIREMAN	Wayne	MI	May 9,1836	NW¼	160
Henry HAWKINS & V R HAWKINS	Genessee	NY	June 27,1836	W½/SE & E½/SW & SW/SW	200
Henry A CORNELL	Livingston	MI	Sept. 23,1836	NW/NE	40

Section 33

Name	County	State	Date	Description	Acres
Henry A CORNELL	Livingston	MI	Mar. 20,1835	NW/NW	40
James LOVE	Washtenaw	MI	July 1,1835	NE/NE	40
Louisa WAKEMAN	Oakland	MI	Mar. 29,1836	SE¼	160
Austin WAKEMAN	Oakland	MI	Mar. 29,1836	SE/SW	40
George H BLUMBERG	Oakland	MI	Apr. 9,1836	NW/SW	40
Isaac DeGRAFF	Cayuga	NY	May 30,1836	W½/NE & E½/NW	160
Charles COLTON	Livingston	MI	May 30,1836	SE/NE	40
Chester WILSON	Orleans	NY	June 3,1836	SW/SW	40
*George BABCOX	Livingston	NY	June 6,1836	SW/NW & NE/SW	80

Section 34

Name	County	State	Date	Description	Acres
William DAWSON	Oakland	MI	Dec. 19,1834	NW/NE & NE/NW	80
James LOVE	Washtenaw	MI	July 1,1835	NW/NW	40
Robert DAWSON	Oakland	MI	Apr. 6,1836	SW/NE & SE/NW	80
Willard DANIELS	Oakland	MI	Apr. 21,1836	SW/NW	40
John J BLACKMER	Monroe	NY	Apr. 27,1836	SW¼	160
Chester WILSON	Orleans	NY	June 3,1836	SE¼ & E½/NE	120

Section 35

Name	County	State	Date	Description	Acres
John A WELLES	Wayne	MI	Sept. 17,1835	section	640

Section 36

Name	County	State	Date	Description	Acres
Hiram BELLOWS	Franklin	VT	June 14,1836	SE¼ & SW¼	320
Ira BELLOWS	Monroe	NY	June 14,1836	NE¼ & NW¼	320

*(Babcock in history book)

138

UNADILLA township-FIRST Land Owners

NAME	COUNTY & STATE		DATE	LAND	ACRES
Section 1					
Henry CASSIDY	Wayne	MI	Aug. 3,1836	SW/NW	40
Thomas SUTHERLAND	Livingston	MI	Sept. 21,1836	W½/SE & E½/SW	160
Avery BRUCE	Genessee	NY	Nov. 2,1836	NE/NEf	33
Asa P WOODARD	Washtenaw	MI	Nov. 14,1836	Sp/NE	80
Moses KEYES	Seneca	NY	Nov. 16,1836	W½/SW	80
Henry COLCLAZER	Washtenaw	MI	Nov. 19,1836	E½/SE	80
Owen MARTIN	Livingston	MI	May 2,1850	SE/NW	40
Patrick FAY	Livingston	MI	Dec. 15,1853	NW/NEf	33
Thomas FAY	Livingston	MI	Dec. 1,1855	N½/NWf	70
Section 2					
Joseph VENUS	Huron	OH	Apr. 21,1836	W½/SE & E½/SW	
				& Sp/NW	240
Bryan HART	Wayne	MI	May 28,1836	E½/SE	80
John SUTHERLAND	Washtenaw	MI	June 8,1836	NEf¼	150
George REEVES	Washtenaw	MI	June 8,1836	W½/SW &	
				Np/NWf	147
Section 3					
Caleb MUNGER	New HAVEn	CN	Apr. 29,1836	SW¼	160
Morris HOWE	Genessee	NY	June 8,1836	E½/SE	80
Solomon SUTHERLAND	Washtenaw	MI	June 8,1836	E½/NEf	72
Solomon SUTHERLAND Jr.	Livingston	MI	Sept. 21,1836	W½/NEf	72
James SUTHERLAND	Livingston	MI	Sept. 21,1836	NWf¼	139
Alfred DENIO	Livingston	MI	Dec. 16,1836	NW/SE	40
Van Renselaer T ANGEL	Livingston	MI	June 24,1851	SW/SE	40
Section 4					
Chester J TUTTLE	Cuyahaga	OH	Oct. 19,1835	NW/SW	40
Jonathan E MUNGER	New Haven	CN	Apr. 29,1836	SE¼	160
John C SHARP	Washtenaw	MI	June 7,1836	NE/SW	40
Miles A HINMAN	Genessee	MI	June 25,1836	NEf¼ &	
				Sp/NWf	214
Emery BEAL	Washtenaw	MI	Sept. 21,1836	S½/SW	80
Charles HARFORD	Livingston	MI	Nov. 3,1836	Np/NWf	49

Unadilla township

Section 5

Sameul CLEMENTS	Washtenaw	MI	Oct. 8,1835	W½/SE & E½/SW	160
Chester J TUTTLE	Cuyahoga	OH	Oct. 19,1835	E½/SE	80
John B VANDOREN	Washtenaw	MI	May 27,1836	W½/SW	80
David DUTTON	Washtenaw	MI	May 27,1836	SE/NW	40
Phillip DYER	Livingston	MI	June 7,1836	Np/NWf & SW/NWf	85
Seth EASTSON	Washtenaw	MI	Aug. 2,1836	NEf¼	125

Section 6

Sameul TOWNSEND	Niagara	NY	Apr. 22,1836	NEf¼ & NWf¼	173
John COOL	Livingston	MI	June 7,1836	SWf¼ & W½/SE	152
	Washtenaw		June 25,1836	E½/SE	80

Section 7

Levi WESTFALL & George WESTFALL	Ontario	NY	June 18,1834	SE¼	160
George WESTFALL	Ontario	NY	June 19,1835	S½/SWf	46
Myron H ROWLEY	Addison	VT	May 26,1836	NE¼	160
John COOL	Livingston	MI	June 7,1836	NWf¼	82
John HOWELL	Ingham	MI	Mar. 12,1841	N½/SWf	46
Calvin HALLOCK	Washtenaw	MI	Jan. 1,1854	SW/NWf	33

Section 8

Levi WESTFALL & George WESTFALL	Ontario	NY	June 18,1834	W½/SW	80
William H DUNN	Warren	NJ	June 4,1835	NW¼	160
Levi CLAWSON	Richland	OH	Feb. 15,1836	E½/NE	80
Sameul CASE	Livingston	MI	Mar. 25,1836	NW/NE	40
Martin DUNNING	Rensellaer	NY	June 27,1836	W½/SE	80
Lorenzo SECORD	Washtenaw	MI	July 8,1836	SE/SE	40
John T ROGERS	Genessee	NY	Sept. 24,1836	E½/SW	80
Mortimer WINDSOR	Wayne	MI	Jan. 3,1837	NE/SE	40
George W RICHMOND	Livingston	MI	Oct. 1,1844	SW/NE	40

Unadilla township

Section 9

Lemeul F CHIPMAN	Washtenaw	MI	Mar. 5,1836	SE/SE	40
Luther CHIPMAN	Washtenaw	MI	May 24,1836	W½/SE	80
Horace A SMITH	Washtenaw	MI	June 10,1836	NW/NW	40
Abram ABBOTT	Genessee	NY	June 25,1836	E½/NE	80
Sameul F VAN SICKLE	Livingston	MI	June 28,1836	W½/SW	80
Lorenzo SECORD	Washtenaw	MI	June 30,1836	SE/SW	40
Daniel S McGRANGEL	Washtenaw	MI	Aug. 1,1836	SW/NW	40
Sophronia BEAL	Livingston	MI	Jan. 11,1837	NW/NE & SE/NW	80
James WATERS	Livingston	MI	Oct. 1,1844	SW/NE	40
Van Rensellear T ANGEL	Livingston	MI	Nov. 17,1847	NE/SE	40
Hannah CHIPMAN	Livingston	MI	Jan. 16,1855	NE/SW	40
Nathaniel BRAILEY	Ingham	MI	Dec. 13,1853	NE/NW	40

Section 10

Lemeul F CHIPMAN	Washtenaw	MI	Mar. 5,1836	SE/SW	40
Abner B WOOD	Washtenaw	MI	Mar. 5,1836	W½/SW	80
Nathaniel BROWN	Genessee	NY	June 25,1836	NE/SW	40
Abram ABBOTT	Genessee	NY	June 25,1836	SW/NW	40
Sameul S CHIPMAN	Livingston	MI	June 25,1836	S½/SE	80
Solomon SUTHERLAND	Livingston	MI	Aug. 2,1836	W½/NE	80
Edward SUTHERLAND	Livingston	MI	Sept. 21,1836	NE/NW & E½/NW	120
Patrick KENAN	Livingston	MI	May 25,1837	N½/SE & E½/NE	160

Section 11

Joseph VENUS	Huron	OH	Apr. 21,1836	SW¼ & W½/SE	240
Patrick McCABE	Wayne	MI	May 28,1836	NE¼ & NW¼ & & NE/SE	360
James ELSEY	Washtenaw	MI	Oct. 26,1836	SE/SE	40

Section 12

Charles M MOSES	Washtenaw	MI	June 25,1836	NE/NE	40
Richard S SHEAR	Ontario	NY	May 12,1836	SE¼	160
Phineas PRONTY	Ontario	NY	May 12,1836	W½/NE	80
Lawrence JONES	Wayne	MI	May 28,1836	W½/NW	80
John SHEIL	Wayne	MI	May 28,1836	E½/NW	80
Patrick McCABE	Wayne	MI	May 28,1836	SW/SW	40
James ARMSTRONG	Erie	NY	July 1,1836	SE/NE	40
James ELSEY	Washtenaw	MI	Oct. 26,1836	E½/SW & SW/SW	120

Unadilla township

Section 13

Name	County	State	Date	Description	Acres
George BENNETT	Washtenaw	MI	Sept. 3,1835	E½/SE	80
Charles BULLIS	Washtenaw	MI	Oct. 26,1835	W½/SE	80
Phineas PRONTY	Ontario	NY	May 12,1836	W½/NE	80
James H WOOD	Ontario	NY	May 12,1836	E½/NE	80
George WRIGHT	Ontario	NY	May 12,1836	E½/SW	80
Robert H BULLIS	Washtenaw	MI	Jan. 11,1838	W½/SW	80
Henry STILES	Livingston	MI	July 14,1838	E½/NW	80
Charles BULLIS	Livingston	MI	Dec. 13,1853	W½/NW	80

Section 14

Name	County	State	Date	Description	Acres
Elijah D EFFNER & Ira A BLOSSOM	Erie	NY	July 2,1835	W½/SE & E½/SW	160
William S MEAD	Cayugala	OH	Oct. 19,1835	NW/NW	40
Joseph VENUS	Huron	OH	Apr. 21,1836	W½/NE & E½/NW & SW/NW	200
Julia Ann KENT	Erie	NY	June 18,1836	E½/SE	80
James ELSEY	Washtenaw	MI	Oct. 26,1836	E½/NE	80
Henry V BACON	Berkshire	MA	Oct. 26,1836	W½/SW	80

Section 15

Name	County	State	Date	Description	Acres
Sally RAY	Washtenaw	MI	Aug. 12,1834	W½/NW	80
Elijah EFFNER & Ira BLOSSOM	Erie	NY	Aug. 3,1835	E½/NE	80
Lemeul F CHIPMAN	Washtenaw	MI	Oct. 2,1835	E½/NW & W½/NE	160
Fitch CHIPMAN	Genessee	NY	Oct. 2,1835	N½/SE	80
Sameul S CHIPMAN	Genessee	NY	Oct. 2,1835	SW¼	160
William S MARTINDALE	Livingston	MI	Nov. 2,1836	SW/SE	40
William UTTER	St. Clair	MI	July 20,1846	SE/SE	40

Unadilla township

Section 16 (school section)

Dudley HILL			Sept. 16,1841	N$\frac{1}{2}$/NE/NE	20
			July 11,1844	S$\frac{1}{2}$/NE/NE	20
V R T ANGEL			Sept. 16,1841	NW/NE	40
			July 11,1844	SW/NE	40
			Feb. 26,1846	NE/NW	40
S R FITCH			Mar. 19,1846	SE/NE	40
D R HILL			Nov. 14,1846	NW/NW	40
D O DUTTON			June 31,1850	SW/NW	40
			Jan. 23,1847	NW/SE	40
John GRUNGAN			Sept. 17,1845	SE/NW	40
L BENEAN			July 11,1844	NE/SE	40
Joseph GILBERT			Sept. 28,1846	SE/SE	40
H FULFORD			July 11,1844	SW/SE	40
A L DUTTON			Mar. 18,1846	E$\frac{1}{2}$/SW	80
			June 23,1847	SW/SW	40
James BIRNEY			June 29,1847	NW/SW	40

Section 17

Cyrus JACKSON	Wayne	NY	June 23,1834	NW/NW	40
Charles TETLEY	Washtenaw	MI	July 17,1834	W$\frac{1}{2}$/SW	80
			June 17,1835	SW/NW	40
John CALLAHAN	Washtenaw	MI	Nov. 21,1834	E$\frac{1}{2}$/SW	80
James GANSON	Genessee	NY	June 29,1835	NE$\frac{1}{4}$	160
David S CURTIS	Livingston	MI	May 30,1836	SW/SE	40
Jason SWIFT	Wayne	MI	June 8,1836	E$\frac{1}{2}$/SW	80
John G SOVERHILL	Washtenaw	MI	June 10,1836	NW/SE & E$\frac{1}{2}$/SE	120

Section 18

Cyrus JACKSON	Wayne	NY	June 23,1834	SEf$\frac{1}{4}$ & SWf$\frac{1}{4}$ &	
				E$\frac{1}{2}$/NE	349
William BEATTIE	Washtenaw	MI	Nov. 21,1834	W$\frac{1}{2}$/NE	80
George FITTS	Niagara	NY	June 13,1836	NWf$\frac{1}{4}$	101

Section 19

Thomas SMITH	Wayne	MI	June 16,1834	W$\frac{1}{2}$/SWf	62
Eli RUGGLES	Fairfield	CN	July 19,1834	E$\frac{1}{2}$/SE	80
Chester S TUTTLE	Cayuga	OH	Oct. 19,1835	NE$\frac{1}{4}$	160
James D WINANS	Wayne	MI	Mar. 26,1836	W$\frac{1}{2}$/SE &	
				Ep/SWf	142
Edward BINGHAM	Wayne	MI	Apr. 12,1836	NWf$\frac{1}{4}$	117

Unadilla township

Section 20

Henry ANGELL	Washtenaw	MI	Aug. 24,1833	E½/SE & SW/SE	120
Patrick HUBBARD	Washtenaw	MI	Nov. 14,1833	SW/NW	40
Mary WINANS	Washtenaw	MI	Nov. 27,1833	W½/SW	80
Sameul HOLMES	Washtenaw	MI	Apr. 22,1834	E½/SW	80
David CURTIS	Washtenaw	MI	May 28,1835	NE/SW	40
James GANSON	Genessee	NY	June 29,1835	NE¼	160
Chester TUTTLE	Cayuga	OH	Oct. 19,1835	NW/NW	40
Jason SWIFT	Wayne	MI	June 8,1836	NW/SE	80

Section 21

Francis LINCOLN	Washtenaw	MI	Aug. 24,1833	W½ of Section	320
Philander GREGORY	Monroe	NY	May 21,1836	W½/SE	80
Edward BINGHAM	Wayne	MI	May 21,1836	NE¼ & E½/SE	240

Section 22

Cloe BUCK	Onondaga	NY	July 12,1834	SE/SW	40
John BEEDLE	Cayuga	OH	Apr. 17,1835	W½/SW	80
Charles RUDGERS	Cayuga	OH	Apr. 17,1835	W½/SE	80
Ira BLOSSOMS	Erie	NY	July 2,1835	W½/NW & NE/SW	120
Jeramiah WILCOX	Genessee	NY	May 27,1836	E½/SE	80
William MARTINDALE	Genessee	NY	June 25,1836	NE/NW	40
	Livingston	MI	Nov. 2,1836	NW/NE	40
Sarah CURTIS	Livingston	MI	Nov. 22,1836	SW/NE	40
Lorence HAYS	Washtenaw	MI	Apr. 26,1837	SE/NE & N½/NE	120

Section 23

James LIVERMORE	Tompkins	NY		SE/NE	40
George WRIGHT	Ontario	NY	June 3,1835	E½/SE	80
Noyes WILCOX	Ontario	NY	May 12,1835	W½/NE & E½/NW	160
Jeramiah WILCOX	Ontario	NY	May 27,1835	W½/SW	80
Sarah CURTISS	Livingston	MI	May 27,1835	SW/NW	40
Philip GILMAN	Livingston	MI	Nov. 22,1835	NE/SE	40
Charles RUDGERS	Livingston	MI	July 20,1838	SW/SE	40
Ebenezer PENNIMAN	Wayne	MI	July 5,1839	NE/NE	40
James LIVERMORE	Livingston	MI	Feb. 29,1840	NW/NW	40
Jeramiah B SWIFT	Livingston	MI	Nov. 27,1847	NW/SE	40
Seth B TORREY	Livingston	MI	Nov. 7,1853	SE/SW	40

Unadilla township

Section 24
George W NOBLE	Portage	OH	July 22,1834	$W\frac{1}{2}$/NW	80
H DEGRAFF &					
W H TOWNSEND	Ontario	NY	July 22,1834	$E\frac{1}{2}$/NW	80
James LIVERMORE	Tompkins	NY	June 3,1835	$W\frac{1}{2}$/SW	80
Sylvanus P GERMAIN	Albany	NY	Mar. 4,1836	$W\frac{1}{2}$/NE	80
Elnathan BOTSFORD	Washtenaw	MI	May 31,1836	$E\frac{1}{2}$/NE	80
Amos H BREED	Livingston	MI	June 13,1836	$W\frac{1}{2}$/SE	80
Phineas PRONTY	Ontario	NY	July 14,1836	$E\frac{1}{2}$/SE & $E\frac{1}{2}$/SW	160

Section 25
Robert H TITUS	Erie	NY	July 15,1836	$E\frac{1}{2}$/NE	80
Sameul PHILLIPS	(New York city)		Aug. 5,1836	$SW\frac{1}{4}$	160
Thomas J DUDLEY	Yates	NY	Jan. 31,1837	$W\frac{1}{2}$/NW	80
Alexander McPHERSON	Ontario	NY	June 19,1838	$E\frac{1}{2}$/NW	80
Gideon CHALKER	Seneca	NY	June 28,1838	$W\frac{1}{2}$/NE & NW/SE	120
Joseph HARTSUFF	Livingston	NY	Oct. 24,1853	SE/SE	40
Nelson H WING	Wayne	NY	Oct. 31,1853	SW/SE	40
William SALES	Livingston	MI	Nov. 20,1854	NE/SE	40

Section 26
William WOODBURN	Wayne	MI	Aug. 23,1834	$E\frac{1}{2}$/NE & SW/NE	120
John S PRONTY	Ontario	NY	May 12,1836	$SW\frac{1}{4}$	160
Calvin H BRYAN	Livingston	NY	June 6,1836	$E\frac{1}{2}$/NW & NW/NE	120
Mark HEALY &					
B B KERCHIVAL	(U.S.)		Aug. 4,1836	$E\frac{1}{2}$/SE	80
William S MEAD	Livingston	MI	June 24,1839	SW/NW	40
Phebe HARTSUFF	Livingston	MI	Feb. 8,1844	SW/SE	40
Thomas STANFIELD	Livingston	MI	June 28,1848	NW/SE	40
Adam SALES	Livingston	MI	July 30,1851	NW/NW	40

Section 27
Richard GUGINS	Livingston	MI	Nov. 13,1833	$W\frac{1}{2}$/SW & SW/NW	120
John LaGRANGE	Washtenaw	MI	June 2,1834	$E\frac{1}{2}$/SE	80
Cloe BUCK	Onondaga	NY	July 12,1834	$E\frac{1}{2}$/NW	80
David M HARD &					
Joseph PECK	Oswego	NY	June 20,1834	$W\frac{1}{2}$/SE & $E\frac{1}{2}$/SW	160
Stephen B SALES	Livingston	MI	Sept. 24,1834	NW/NE	40
			Jan. 15,1846	SE/NE	40
			Dec. 19,1850	NE/NE	40
Frederick HARTWIG	Washtenaw	MI	May 4,1837	NW/NW & SW/NE	80

Unadilla township

Section 28

David HOLMES	Hartford	CN	Aug. 1,1833	SE¼	160
Darwin EDSON	Washtenaw	MI	Aug. 27,1833	W½/SW	80
Stephen CORNELL	Dutchess	NY	Oct. 17,1833	E½/NW & SW/NW	120
Curtis NOBLE	Otsego	NY	Nov. 15,1833	E½/SW	80
Richard GUGGINS	Livingston	MI	Jan. 9,1834	W½/NE	80
	Washtenaw	MI	July 19,1834	SE/NE	40
Eli RUGGLES	Fairfield	CN	June 18,1835	NE/NE	40
James McCLEAR	Hartford	CN		NW/NW	40

Section 29

David HOLMES	Hartford	CN	Aug. 1833	SE¼	160
Jeramiah BULLOCK	Orleans	NY	Aug. 29,1833	NE¼	160
David M HARD	Otsego	NY	Oct. 17,1833	E½/SW	80
Abram KERN	Livingston	MI	June 14,1834	W½/NW	80
William TURNER	Washtenaw	MI	Nov. 13,1834	E½/NW	80
Stephen HAVENS	Livingston	MI	May 25,1835	NW/SW	40
Leonard BACKUS	Livingston	MI	Mar. 27,1851	SW/SW	40

Section 30

Mary WINANS	Washtenaw	MI	Nov. 27,1833	W½/NWf	62
Hatil Checkley SHARP	Livingston	NY	Mar. 19,1834	SE¼	160
David BIRD	Washtenaw	MI	June 13,1834	SWf¼	141
Elijah BIRD	Washtenaw	MI	July 4,1834	W½/NE &	
				E½/NWf	146
Robert TAYLOR	(New York)	NY	Dec. 2,1835	E½/NE	80

Section 31

John DAVIS	Washtenaw	MI	Apr. 2,1834	W½/SWf	78
James D McINTIRE	Washtenaw	MI	July 10,1834	SE¼	160
	Livingston	MI	Jan. 2,1855	SW/NE	40
Hiram PUTNAM	Washtenaw	MI	July 21,1834	SE/SWf	39
John McCONACHIE	Livingston	MI	June 8,1835	W½/NWf	74
Peter N HAND	Livingston	MI	Aug. 4,1835	SE/NE	40
Joseph SCHIDMORE	Ontario	NY	Sept. 22,1835	NE/SWf	30
	Wayne	MI	Nov. 22,1835	E½/NWf	74
James SCHOONHOVEN	Livingston	MI	Oct. 27,1835	NW/NE	40
Ann SCHOONHOVEN	Livingston	MI	Nov. 22,1835	NE/NE	40

Unadilla township

Section 32

David M HARD	Oswego	NY	Oct. 17,1833	E½/SW	80
Sally TURNER	Livingston	NY	June 6,1836	SE/SW	40
William TURNER	Livingston	NY	June 29,1836	SW/SE	40
James SCHOONHOVEN	Portage	OH	June 30,1836	N½/NE	80
Jesse McKINNEY	Tompkins	NY	June 30,1836	NE/SW & NW/SW	80
Peter N HARD	Livingston	MI	Aug. 4,1836	W½/NW	80
Marie L McKINNEY	Wayne	MI	Oct. 25,1836	SW/SE	40
Margaret WRIGHT	Livingston	MI	June 24,1851	SW/SW	40
Henry HARTSUFF	Livingston	MI	June 7,1853	SE/NE & NE/NE	80

Section 33

Eli RUGGLES	Fairfield	CN	June 20,1833	N½/SW	80
David HOLMES	Harford	CN	Aug. 1,1833	NE¼	160
Mary WINANS	Washtenaw	MI	Nov. 7,1833	SE¼	160
Amos WILLIAMS	Washtenaw	MI	July 19,1834	SE/NW	40
Warren SPALDING	Washtenaw	MI	July 23,1834	SW/SW & E½/SW	120
Garry BRIGGS	Livingston	MI	June 27,1837	SW/NW	40
Anson DENTON	Livingston	MI	July 21,1849	NW/SW	40

Section 34

James CRAIG	Harford	CN	Aug. 1,1833	W½/SW	80
Archibald MARSHALL	Harford	CN	Aug. 1,1833	E½/SW	80
Curtis NOBLE	Washtenaw	MI	Dec. 20,1833	W½/SW	80
David M HARD	Oswego	NY	May 27,1836	E½/SW & W½/NE	160
John GUTEKUNST	Washtenaw	MI	June 6,1836	NE/NE	40
Phineas PRONTY	Ontario	NY	June 21,1836	SE¼	160
Joseph L HARTSUFF	Livingston	MI	Aug. 25,1847	SE/NE	40

Section 35

Robert GLENN	Seneca	NY	May 25,1837	W½/SW	80
	Washtenaw	MI	Dec. 2,1835	SE/SW	40
Robert L GLENN	Washtenaw	MI	Dec. 7,1836	E½/SE	80
*Robert MINNIS	Washtenaw	MI	June 11,1835	NE/NW	40
John GUTEKUNST	Washtenaw	MI	Oct. 22,1835	W½/NW	80
Sally M GLENN	Washtenaw	MI	Dec. 2,1835	SW/SE	40
Luke MONTAGUE	Cayuga	NY	May 19,1836	W½/NE & SE/NW	120
	Livingston	MI	May 15,1837	SW/SE	40
John DRAKE	Livingston	MI	Oct. 29,1836	NE/SW	40
George DAVIS	Livingston	MI	June 2,1837	SE/NE	40
Justice L FIELD	Livingston	MI	Aug. 21,1841	NE/NE	40

*(listed as Robert WINANS in history book)

Unadilla township

Section 36

Luke MONTAGUE	Cayuga	NY	Aug. 4,1836	SW/SE	40
Junius FIELD	Berkshire	MA	Sept. 23,1836	W½/SW	80
	Livingston	MI	Aug. 26,1841	NW/NW	40
			Nov. 8,1843	NE/NW	40
Alex MONTAGUE	Livingston	MI	May 15,1837	NE/SW	40
William FAULK	Livingston	MI	June 2,1837	SE/SW	40
Charles GLENN	Washtenaw	MI	June 21,1839	SW/NW	40
Nelson WING	Washtenaw	MI	June 21,1839	SE/NW	40
Daniel GLENN	Livingston	MI	Feb. 25,1853	SE/SE	40
*Joseph HARTSTUFF	Livingston	MI	Oct. 24,1853	NE/NE	40
			Nov. 22,1854	W½/NE	80
			Dec. 26,1856	SE/NE	40
Nelson GLENN	Washtenaw	MI	Jan. 8,1855	SW/SE	40
James GAUNT	Washtenaw	MI	Jan. 8,1855	NE/SE	40

*(Hartsuff in history book)

148

INDEX

DWYER
James, Put. 25
DYER
Elizabeth, Ios. 31
John, Ios. 31
Joseph, Ios. 31
Phillip, Ios. 32, Un. 5

EAGER
William, Oc. 6,7
EAMAN
Benjamin, Put. 3,18
John, How. 36
EARL
Benjamin, Gen. 3,4, Oc. 33
Henry, Gen. 26
Riley, Oc. 33
EASTERBROOK
Jonathan, Mar. 2
EASTON
Pomeroy, Oc. 21
EASTSON
Seth, Un. 5
ECKLER
Phillip, Con. 23
EDDY
Jefferson, De. 1
Jonathan, Bri. 31
EDGAR
Robert, Bri. 26
EDMINISTER
William, Ham. 30,31,32
EDMONDS
John, Coh. 6, Hdy. 5,7
Thomas, GO. 4
EDSON
Darwin, Un. 28
EDWARDS
Robert, Oc. 8,9
EFFNER
Elijah, Mar. 1,2, Un. 14,15
EGGLESTON
Chauncey, Ios. 22
ELA
Isaac, GO. 32
ELDRED
Benjamin, Oc. 10,14,15
ELDREDGE
Charles, Mar. 11
ELLIOT (Eliott)
Charles, Con. 9
Orson, Gen. 5, Oc. 32
ELLIS
John, Gen. 4,5,8
ELSWORTH
Henry, Con. 34,35
ELSEY
James, Un. 11,12,14

ELWELL
Pierce, Mar. 16
EMERSON
Charles, Gen. 24
Thomas, Ht. 2
EMERY
Lucius, Ios. 4
EMONS
George, GO. 20
ENOS
Joseph, Ht. 11
ESTES
Edward, Mar. 10,14
ESTEYS
Edward, Mar. 10,14
ETSON
Caleb, GO. 5
EULER
Joseph, Gen. 11
John, Gen. 12
Lawrence, Gen. 12,22
Peter, Gen. 12
EVANS
Eli, De. 26
EWERS
Alvah, Coh. 19,20
EZEL
John, Mar. 18

FAGAN
James, Ham. 30
FAIRBANKS
George, De. 5
FAIRCHILD
Abram, De. 22,23
Ezra, Mar. 22,28
FARGO
Eli, Bri. 30
FARLEY
Byran, Ham. 30
Owen, Ham. 30
Patrick, Ios. 34
William, Con. 26
FARMER
John, Put. 32
FARNSWORTH
Elen, GO. 8
John, GO. 6
FARR
Wells, Ht. 35
FARRAND
John, Coh. 26, Mar. 32
Put. 4
Lucius, Put. 34
FARRELL
Henry, Ham. 7,8

INDEX

PULLEN
    James, Put. 25
    Selden, Put. 35
PULTZ
    Marcus, Bri. 13
PURDY
    Edgar, Con. 12
    Lyman, De. 11
PURVIS
    William, Ham. 2
PUTNAM
    Hiram, Un. 31

QUINN
    Joseph, Ham. 17,18,19,20

RADE
    Erastus, GO. 2
RAMER
    Henry, Con. 16
    John, Coh. 16
RANDALL
    Henry, How. 3
    Robert, Mar. 3
RANNEY
    Samuel, Ios. 8
    William, Ios. 8
RANSOM
    Rastus, Bri. 19
RASDALE
    Martin, Con. 27
RASH
    George, Mar. 18,22
    Lincy, Mar. 18
RATHBURN
    Dean, Coh. 5
RAUSHER
    George, Gen. 23
RAY
    Sally, Un. 15
RAYMOND
    Silas, Mar. 29
REDDING
    William, Oc. 13
REDFIELD
    William, Ios. 3,4
REDWAY
    Joel, GO. 1,2
REED
    Charles, How. 16
    Olive, Con. 34
REEVES
    George, Ios. 35, Un. 2
REUN
    William, Hdy. 31

RHOADES
    Daniel, De. 14
    Oren, Gen. 11
RHODES
    Anna, Ty. 5
    Rueben, Ios. 22
RICE
    Caleb, Mar. 31
    John, Ht. 5
    Thomas, Ham. 36
RICH
    George, Hdy. 18
RICHARD
    William, Con. 3
RICHARDSON
    David, Ios. 19,32
    Emory, Ham. 14
RICHMOND
    Alex, Ios. 5
    George, Un. 8
RICKER
    William, Coh. 23
RIDDLE (Riddel)
    Andrew, Oc. 21
    John, Mar. 4,11
    Samuel Jr. How. 24
RIDER
    Joseph, Gen. 17
RIKER
    Abraham, Coh. 28
    William, Coh. 23
RINGE (Ring)
    Fred, Bri. 4,5,10, Coh. 19,20
RISE
    John, De. 2
ROBB
    Henry, De. 17
ROBBINS
    Isaiah, Gen. 14,15
    Lavina, Gen. 11
ROBERTS
    Abner, Ht. 6
    George, Ty. 8
    Guy, GO. 1, Oc. 1,13
    Henry, Ht. 6
ROBIE
    Rueben, Con. 6,7, Put. 8,9
ROBINSON
    Charles, Bri. 5, Ht. 32
    Ezra, GO. 27
    John, Gen. 27
    Joseph, GO. 32, Ht. 32
    Ransom, Ham. 19
    Robert, Ios. 24
ROCHE
    Michael, GO. 10
ROCKWELL
    David, De. 32
    Dennis, DE. 32

176

INDEX

WAIT
    Timothy, Con. 13
    William, Put. 11
WAITE
    Benjamin, Ht. 19
WAKEMAN
    Austin, Ht. 4, Ty. 33
    Louise, Ty. 33
WALDOE
    Samuel, Bri. 8
WALDEN
    Samuel, De. 26
WALDRON
    James, Coh. 3,9,10
WALKER
    Abel, Ios. 12
    George, Ham. 1, Oc. 20
    Ira, Coh. 22
    John, Oc. 32,33
    Joseph, Mar. 19,20
WALLACE
    John, Ham. 19, Put. 36
WALLEN
    George, Coh. 2
WALSH
    Franklin, Ht. 33
    Michael, Ht. 33
WARBURTON
    John, Con. 14
WARD
    Alfred, Bri. 25
    Eli, De. 16
    Henry, Gen. 27
    Hiram, Ios. 13,36
    John, Bri. 16,25
    Josiah, Gen. 18
    Lucius, Bri. 25
    Olive, Ios. 36
    William, Bri. 25
WARDEN
    Robert, Bri. 30, GO. 13,15
    Robert Jr. GO. 14
WARNER
    Consider, Ty. 4
    Hiram, Bri. 10,11,14, Ht. 33
    Ira, Bri. 16
    Levi, De. 5
    Myron, De. 19,29,31
WARREN
    Ebenezer, How. 3
WATERBURY
    Shellick, Con. 8
WATERS
    James, Un. 9
WATKINS
    Joseph, Bri. 35
WATROUS
    Erastus, Gen. 3
WATSON
    John, Put. 1

WEBB
    F. Jr. Put. 16
    Freeman, Put. 8,9,17
    Gideon, Put. 19
    Thomas, Put. 20
    William, GO. 24
WEBBER
    James, Ht. 4,9
    John, Ham. 10
WEBSTER
    Enoch, Gen. 19, 30
             Ios. 26, Mar. 12
    William, Mar. 13
WEEDEN
    Joseph, Ht. 19
WEISS
    Joseph, De. 1,2
WELCH
    Benjamin, GO. 36
    James, Gen. 20
    Joseph, De. 12,23,24,25,
             26, 35
WELLER
    Antha, Put. 8
    Benjamin, Put. 23
    Charles, Gen. 27
    Henry, Ham. 8
    Hiram, Put. 5,9
    Thomas, Put. 4
WELLES
    John, Ty. 26,35
WELLS
    David, Gen. 32
WELTZ
    Fred, Con. 16
WEMMELL
    Peter, Bri. 21
WEST
    Itha, How. 26,27
    Samuel, Gen. 4,9, Oc. 20
    Sylvanus, Coh. 30
    Thomas, How. 26
WESTERVELT
    Jacob, Ht. 3,4
WESTFALL
    John, Ty. 17
    John Jr. Con. 27
    George, Un. 7,8
    Louis, Hdy. 29,30,31
    Levi, Un. 7,8
    Simon, Coh. 32
WETMORE
    David, Mar. 2
WHALEN
    Dennis, Ht. 8,10,13,14
    James, Ht. 13
    John, Ht. 6,11,12
    Josiah, Ht. 3,11
WHARNER (Warner)
    Hiram, Ht. 33

183

WOOD
   Abner, Un. 10
   Agnes, How. 23
   Benjamin, Ht. 35,36
   Caleb, De. 3
   David, Mar. 21
   Henry, Ios. 10,11,17
   Jane, Gen. 11
   James, Ios. 12, Put. 18
        Un. 13
   John, Ht. 36, Ios. 10
   Joseph, Bri. 36
   Lavina, Gen. 11
   Martha, Ios. 11
   Pamelia, Gen. 11
   Rueben, Con. 30
WOODARD
   Asa, Un. 1
WOODBURN
   William, Un. 26
WOODEN
   Henry, Ios. 5
WOODRUFF
   Ebert, Bri. 34
WOODWORTH
   Whitley, How. 17
WOOL (Woll)
   Conrad, Con. 30, Mar. 9,10
WORDEN
   Maria, De. 19
   Trumen, Bri. 31, Gen. 25
WRIGHT
   Andrew, Con. 28
   Charles, De. 17,24, Ty. 11
   Flavonia, Put. 34
   George, Un. 13,23
   James, Ios. 29,30
   John, Ios. 16
   J. S., Ios. 16
   Margaret, Un. 32
   Orestus, Hdy. 32,33
   Walter, Ios. 16
   William, De. 30,32

YANGER
   William, Gen. 21
YAUGER
   William, Gen. 21
YOUNG
   Joseph, Ht. 34
   R. T., De. 16
YOUNGLOVE
   Aaron, Mar. 33,34, Put. 3,4

ZULAUF
   George, Gen. 12